The Fundamentals of Organizational Behavior

WHAT MANAGERS NEED TO KNOW

T0355539

To my brothers, Don and Louis, two branches that have made the third one strong.
. . .

Henry Tosi
University of Florida

To my daughter Samantha and son Brent who serve as a constant inspiration to their father. Through their faith and devotion, they have both chosen to dedicate their lives to helping others achieve their potential. They not only "talk the talk" but they "walk the walk" and for that, I am extremely proud.

Neal P. Mero
University of Mississippi

The Fundamentals of Organizational Behavior

WHAT MANAGERS NEED TO KNOW

HENRY L. TOSI AND NEAL P. MERO

Blackwell
Publishing

350 Main Street, Malden, MA 02148-5018, USA
108 Cowley Road, Oxford OX4 1JF, UK
550 Swanston Street, Carlton South, Melbourne, Victoria 3053, Australia
Kurfürstendamm 57, 10707 Berlin, Germany

First published 2003 by Blackwell Publishing Ltd

Library of Congress Cataloging-in-Publication Data

Tosi, Henry L.
    The fundamentals of organizational behavior : what managers need to know /
Henry L. Tosi and Neal P. Mero.
        p.   cm.
Includes bibliographical references and index.
    ISBN 1–40510–074–5 (pbk)
    1. Organizational behavior—Handbooks, manuals, etc.   2. Management—Handbooks,
manuals, etc.   I. Mero, Neal P.   II. Title.
    HD58.7 .T653 2003
    658′.001′9—dc21

                                                                        2002008435

A catalogue record for this title is available from the British Library.

Set in 10/12½ Galliard
by SNP Best-set Typesetter Ltd., Hong Kong

For further information on
Blackwell Publishing, visit our website:
http://www.blackwellpublishing.com

Contents

Acknowledgments   ix

Block I   Introduction

1   Managing Organizational Behavior   2

    Basic Model of Behavior   4

    The Context of Twenty-First-Century Organizational Behavior   5

    The Field of Organizational Behavior   9

    Managing Organizational Performance   14

    What Do Managers Really Do?   15

Block II   A Focus on the Individual

2   Personality and Individual Differences   20

    Fundamentals of Personality   22

    Personality in Organizational Settings   30

    Ability   32

3   Attitudes and Accommodation to Work   37

    Fundamentals of Work Attitudes   38

    A Model of Attitudes   40

    Attitudinal Consistency and Cognitive Dissonance   42

    Socialization: Developing Work-Related Attitudes and Behaviors   44

    Organizational Commitment and Accommodation   48

4 Individual Perception, Judgment, and Attribution   54

Fundamentals of Perception   55

Judgment Biases and Errors   58

Attribution Theory: Finding Causes of Behavior   60

Some Organizational Implications of Perceptual and
Attributional Biases   64

5 Motivation and Performance   68

Motivation and Performance   69

The Fundamentals of Motivation and Performance   70

Motivation: The Content Theories   73

Motivation: The Process Theories   80

Block III The Context of Organizational Behavior

6 Group and Team Performance   94

The Fundamentals of Groups and Teams   96

Group Development   99

Team Effectiveness Issues   101

Group Processes   103

Group Dynamics   106

Social Influences on Behavior   109

Virtual Teams   110

7 Culture: National and Organizational   114

The Hofstede Model of National Culture   115

Organizational Consequences of National Cultural Differences   119

Organizational Culture   123

The Modal Personality of Top Management and
Types of Organizational Cultures   131

Organizational Subcultures   133

Organizational Culture: Some Special Cases   134

8   Organizational Structure and Design   139

    The Fundamentals of Organizational Structure   140

    Organizations: The Effects of Technology and Markets   142

    Formal Organizations: Design and Structure   149

    Organizational Design Alternatives   150

Block IV   Integrating Behavioral Theory into Effective Management and Leadership

9   Managing Performance: The Influence of Technology and Knowledge   162

    The Context of Performance Management   164

    Task Specialists: Managing their Performance   168

    Managing Knowledge Workers   175

10 Conflict   183

    The Nature of Conflict   185

    Diagnosing Conflict   191

    Individual Responses to Conflict   194

    Improving Organizational Response to Conflict   198

11 Decision-Making   204

    Characteristics of the Decision-Making Process   206

    Models of Decision-Making   207

    Improving Individual Decision-Making   210

    Improving Group Decision-Making   213

    Social Influences on Group Decision-Making   217

12 Power and Politics in Organizations   222

    A Model of Influence Processes in Organizations   223

    Acquiring and Maintaining Organizationally Based Influence   230

    Acquiring and Maintaining Personal-Based Influence   235

    Organizational Politics   238

13 Leadership   247

    Trait Approaches to Leadership   249

    Behavioral Approaches to Leadership   250

    Contingency Theories of Leadership   253

    Process Theories of Leadership   259

    Substitutes for Leadership   262

14 Organizational Change   268

    How our Work Life is Changing   269

    Stages of Successful Change   271

    Resistance to Change   273

    Helping Individuals Cope with Change   278

    Organizational Development   281

Name Index   286

Subject Index   291

Acknowledgments

There are several people who helped us in many ways with this book in many ways. Of special note are the contributions of Christine Jackson, Simone Francis, Jo Ann Brown, Amy Brownlee, and Cheryl Mero. We would also like to express our gratitude to the staff at Blackwell, especially Rosemary Nixon and Linda Auld who have provided patient support and encouragement on this project.

Professor Mero would also like to thank his colleagues at Ole Miss, Bekki Guidice, Bob Robinson, Dwight Frink, Greg Rose, and Mike Harvey for their constant support and encouragement.

Block I: Introduction

BLOCK I
INTRODUCTION

Chapter 1   Managing Organizational Behavior

BLOCK II
A FOCUS ON THE INDIVIDUAL

BLOCK III
THE CONTEXT OF ORGANIZATIONAL BEHAVIOR

BLOCK IV
INTEGRATING BEHAVIORAL THEORY INTO EFFECTIVE
MANAGEMENT AND LEADERSHIP

Managing Organizational Behavior

BASIC MODEL OF BEHAVIOR

THE CONTEXT OF TWENTY-FIRST-CENTURY ORGANIZATIONAL BEHAVIOR

THE FIELD OF ORGANIZATIONAL BEHAVIOR

MANAGING ORGANIZATIONAL PERFORMANCE

WHAT DO MANAGERS REALLY DO?

Opening Fig

Allen Bence sat at his desk reflecting on the day's events. Allen had started with Techtronics ten years earlier after graduating at the top of his class. Despite the offers and opportunities available to him, Allen liked working at Techtronics, a small company that developed memory storage devices for many different technology applications. His instincts had been correct, as Techtronics had grown rapidly from a business employing eight people with $1 million in annual sales to a business that would this year grow to sales of $500 million. In the same time, employee numbers grew to 300 people. Allen had enjoyed the success and had seen his career grow just as quickly. He quickly went from an entry-level engineering position to become a project engineer, to head of the engineering division, and was just this year named president. As he thought about this rapid growth, Allen felt ill-prepared to manage an organization the size of Techtronics. Allen knew the industry well and was a skilled and creative engineer, but when it came to managing people, that was another story.

Allen had just met with his key staff to discuss the unexpectedly high turnover rate of Techtronics employees. Across the organization, the average time an employee stayed with the company was 18 months. For Techtronic engineers, the retention rate was worse, with entry-level engineers leaving on average after only 11 months on the job. Allen had asked each member of his staff to develop ideas of how to increase employee retention. Unfortunately, there was no consensus on what needed to be done. One person thought the answer was to increase compensation and benefits. "Pay them enough so they won't even think about looking elsewhere for a job" said Julie Turner, Techtronic's vice-president for engineering. "We need to change the culture" was the response of the director of human resources Peter Sanchez. "The average employee works 50+ hours per week and people are just getting burned out. People just don't like working here because while the rewards are great, people are looking for more than just money in their work organizations." Director of marketing Alyson Martin thought the answer lay in changing the organizational structure. "We have grown so fast that we don't have procedures and policies in place that work. Every time a new problem arises we develop a new rule and as a result, we have become so bureaucratic that our people feel like they no longer have a direct involvement in the organization. We want to continue to be organized like a small company, but we are not a small company any more!"

Allen knew that Techtronics was already paying well above the industry average to all employee groups. He also knew that his employees were being heavily recruited by other high-tech firms who needed employees with similar skills. He also acknowledged that Techtronic's structure, including its policies and procedures, were appropriate when there were eight employees but had become insufficient now that there were 300. Allen wished there was a simple answer to the problem. "We provide great pay and challenging work, but still have the highest turnover rate in the industry" Allen thought. "People problems

> ...they take up to 90 percent of my time and my answers never seem to be the right ones. The day had started with such promise, and now I find myself yearning for a complex engineering problem to work on because at least I am confident that I can find the optimum answer."

This book is for managers and leaders like Allen Bence, individuals who often reach positions in organizations that require less reliance on their technical skills and more reliance on their ability to manage people. It is also for leaders who want to update their skills at managing in today's new economy with its highly demanding and stressful environment that includes global competition, pressure to improve product quality, significant change in workforce demographics and almost daily changes due to the increased reliance on technology. As Allen found out, "people problems" are among the most difficult issues that they face. Like Allen, some think that these people skills are just "common sense," or something that we can learn from our own experiences with others. The problem is that common sense is not so common and, at the same time, human behavior often contradicts conventional wisdom.

BASIC MODEL OF BEHAVIOR

If you believe that people can "make or break" an organization, then it is critical to know something about human behavior. Such knowledge will be useful to you when selecting and training employees, increasing motivation, improving decision-making, reducing stress, and enhancing teamwork. Managers cannot be professional psychologists, but they need to know enough to manage from sound principles rather than from myths and guesswork. One useful way to think about this is to understand the classic psychological model that states that behavior (B) is a function of the Person (P) and the environment (E), or $B = f(P \times E)$. This is shown in figure 1.1. This model is the basis of this book. If you keep it in mind as you read later chapters, you can put these concepts into a useful perspective about managing people in organizations.

The **environment** contains the many elements that exist in the world outside the person that may trigger behavior. For managers, one important aspect of the environment is the organization in which they manage. Another is the culture of the organization, concepts that we discuss in later chapters. The environment interacts with the attributes of the **person**, which also explain and govern behavior. In the next chapters we talk about personality, ability, attitudes, and perceptions.

Of course, we are interested in what people do in organizations, how they act. **Actual behavior** refers to an overt act of the person that can be observed and measured, but it tells us little about why it occurred. Observable behavior can never give

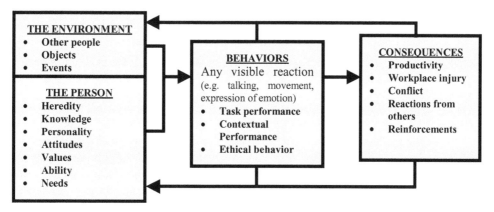

Figure 1.1   Basic model of human behavior

a complete picture of what goes on inside people, but such behavior does serve as a window to it. Behavior at work can be thought of in terms of task, contextual, and ethical performance. These categories of workplace behaviors and performance each are important for organizational success and will be discussed later in this chapter. In addition to focusing on the behavior of employees in organizations, sometimes the behavior we are interested in is how someone acts as a leader and decision-maker.

From a manager's perspective, behavior is important because of its **consequences**, both intended and unintended. Behavior influences productivity, workplace injury and can lead to conflict or trigger positive or negative reactions from others. Each of these consequences is of direct interest to managers and leaders. Those consequences also serve to reinforce certain behaviors and as a result affect the probability of a behavior's recurrence. This is an important implication, as you will see in our discussion of motivation in a later chapter.

Finally, the feedback arrows in figure 1.1 show how a person can learn from their behavior and its effects. As a child growing up we quickly learned that there were consequences to our behavior and we learned to adjust our behavior to achieve certain desired consequences. Also, behavior can change the environment, such as when we turn down the volume on a loud stereo to make it less annoying to others.

THE CONTEXT OF TWENTY-FIRST-CENTURY ORGANIZATIONAL BEHAVIOR

There are many reasons why managing people is viewed by many managers as the most complex aspect of their job. The significant social and cultural forces occurring across the globe have changed not only the way we conduct business but the very nature of our organizations and the characteristics of the people who operate those businesses. In the following pages, we focus on some of the challenges that managers will face in the future from the new economy, the changing workforce, and some of the important changes in the way that organizations are structured and managed.

The changing economy

In the USA, one of the most important changes has been the *changes in the manufacturing sector*. After World War II, basic manufacturing, such as steel, basic metals, and the auto industry formed the economic backbone of a strong economy. However, the 1960s and 1970s saw a serious decline in productivity and American manufacturers found it increasingly difficult to match the efficiency of foreign competitors with relatively new plants. US firms lagged in modernizing their plant and equipment, partly because they failed to recognize the threat of foreign competition.

The decline in the competitiveness of the manufacturing sector of the US economy led to a change in managerial strategy as managers became increasingly aggressive in dealing with labor issues by emphasizing the need for increased productivity and by supporting the development of less labor-intensive operating facilities. These changes in managerial approach also led to an overall managerial strategy focusing on **increased quality** while reducing costs. As a result, companies began asking for, and winning, concessions from unions with respect to work rules and wages – a trend that continues today. This shifted the balance of power in the direction of management. These factors, coupled with the significant advantage foreign competitors often have because of significantly lower labor costs, have led to a reduction in the number of manufacturing jobs and, as a result, a **decrease in the power and the role of unions**. The decline in manufacturing, however, was offset by the **growth of the service sector**. The service economy accounts for over half of the gross domestic product. Hotel and food service organizations, insurance, transportation, and retail are all part of the service sector of the economy. One implication of the increase in the service sector is that this sector employs a greater number of entry-level workers and also includes many lower-wage positions and a great number of part-time employees. While these factors may reduce direct wage and fringe-benefit costs to employers, they could give rise to more government programs to provide health care and retirement programs for workers who, in the past, had these benefits as part of their compensation packages in larger manufacturing firms.

In addition to a shift from a manufacturing-based economy to a significantly service-based economy, we have seen the **globalization of business**. Companies now compete in worldwide markets in different ways, and the nature of the competition itself is changing. In the past, each country was a separate producer and a separate market. Historically, products and product components would be manufactured in the home country and then exported to foreign markets. For many years, for example, Honda automobiles were built only in Japan and then shipped to the US. Similarly,

US products and parts were built in the USA and exported. Firms are now locating manufacturing facilities in foreign countries. Now Daimler-Chrysler produces the Mercedes in the US, General Electric builds small appliances in the Far East, and Sony has manufacturing facilities in the US. The challenge for the multinational firm is to integrate diverse, and often culturally different, units into an effective organization.

Finally, the new economy is increasingly technology-driven. Technology has changed how we manage information, communicate with our customers, market our products, and manage our employees. The e-business revolution has led to the virtual organization and introduced a host of managerial issues. We will discuss this issue in more depth in the next section and throughout the book.

The changing workforce

In the 1960s, the workforce in the United States was relatively homogenous. White Anglo-Saxon men dominated the managerial workforce and the better-paying manufacturing jobs. This is nothing like the workforce of the future; there have already been major changes in its gender, ethnic, and racial composition and there are more changes to come. **Workforce diversity** has changed the face of our organizations and the workforce will become even more diverse over the next 20 years. The proportion of white males will decline as more women, Black Americans, Asians, Latinos, Native Americans, and other minorities enter the workforce. According to the Census Bureau, between 1990 and 1999 the Asian and Pacific Islander population grew 43 percent and the Hispanic population grew 38.8 percent. The cultures of organizations, which have been dominated by the values of white males, will slowly change as these others move into positions of power and influence. The resulting conflict that is inevitable with these significant organizational changes will continue to be a major managerial challenge.

There will also be a significant increase in the average **age of the workforce**. As baby boomers age and life expectancies increase, it is anticipated that they will remain in the workforce longer. According to the Bureau of Labor Statistics, workers in the civilian labor force over the age of 55 will increase by 48 percent between 1998 and 2008. In the long term, this will lead to a decrease in the working-age population and this may result in **potential labor shortages**. This poses some interesting challenges for managers, including pressure to increase wages to attract and retain highly qualified employees. If this predicted labor shortage occurs, then there will be economic incentives for companies to retain older employees. However, belief and value differences between older and younger generations of workers may lead to a greater diversity of attitudes in the workplace, further complicating a manager's job.

Finally, in the last 40 years, there have been substantial **changes in work values**. Prior to 1960, the **work ethic** was a dominant value in US culture. Most people believed that hard work was good, that it was necessary to provide for one's family, that it would lead to success, and that one could be successful by finding a position in a good company and doing the job well. By 1965, there began a shift away from this perspective toward one that the US value system was too materialistic, that the structure of social relationships was too rigid, and that there were more important things in life than work. The move was away from conservatism and more toward liberalism. By 1975, however, a more conservative attitude re-emerged. People again valued work and success in much the same way as they had in the past. As we enter the twenty-first-century, work values are again likely to change as values of the "Baby Boom" and "Baby Bust" generations conflict with those of "Generation X" and "Generation Next."

Changes in organizations and the way they are managed

One of the most important forces that managers must deal with is the **technological revolution** driven by advances in computer technology. Desktop computers, cellular and satellite communication technologies, and other information technologies facilitate communications within and between individuals and organizations all over the world. These networks have made possible the almost instant transfer of data, e-mail, chat, and teleconferencing applications that led to the creation of **virtual organizations** comprised of workers who may live and work in different parts of a country or in different countries. This has also led to **telecommuting**, the process whereby employees can complete many if not all work tasks from their home. While these advances can improve employee morale and productivity and improve the overall quality of work life, they also provide significant challenges for managers. In this text you will see several discussions of the implications of technology for twenty-first-century managers.

One result of the increased use of technology to complete work is **leaner organizational structures**. Information technology and the downsizing of firms driven by competitive forces have resulted in the need for fewer people to produce the same or more output. Many firms have flattened the organizational structure, eliminating at least one layer of management in the hierarchy, and reducing the number of managers at other levels. Designing these lean structures takes more managerial skill than just reducing the number of workers and often leads to a different managerial challenge, which is **increased delegation** of responsibility and authority. More people, both managers and workers, at lower organizational levels have increased authority. Many of the newer management approaches – such as high-involvement strategies, self-directed work teams, and employee empowerment programs – require extensive delegation of control. To accomplish this, managers must trust the workers and take a hands-off approach. At the same time, workers must believe that managers will not violate the integrity of those areas that have been delegated to them. This kind of relationship only develops when the workforce is well informed about the operations of the firm and they feel secure that management is not hiding anything.

THE FIELD OF ORGANIZATIONAL BEHAVIOR

The field of study that focuses on the "human skills" which managers need to be effective is called **organizational behavior**. Organizational behavior is the systematic and scientific analysis of individuals, groups, and organizations; its purpose is to understand, predict, and improve the performance of individuals and, ultimately, the organizations in which they work. It applies theory and research from psychology, sociology, and managerial theory that help us to understand how to use this knowledge to improve the effectiveness of organizations.

Why study organizational behavior?

To some, the idea of applying theory and research in human behavior to solve work problems is too "academic," something that is for professors to worry about, but not for managers; managers are pragmatic and have to solve real, not hypothetical, problems. Nothing could be further from the truth. The fact is that everyone has personal theories about how to manage or affect others, and these theories guide their actions. Unfortunately, many of these personal theories are based on misinformation, stereotypes, or limited experience. For example, many managers develop theories about motivating others that are based on factors that motivate themselves. If such a manager is achievement-oriented, he or she may try to motivate all employees by offering measures of achievement such as advancement and promotion as incentives. Unfortunately, they may find their theory of motivation is less useful if they are trying to motivate an employee who doesn't value achievement but instead values time with his or her family. The important point is that while we all use theories – not all theories are equally valid. Effective managers are those that have a significant knowledge of the fundamental aspects of human behavior and who rely on theories developed over significant experience.

The ultimate test of the value of theory and research in organizational behavior is if it leads to improved performance levels. We describe many instances of useful and important applications of theory-supported research throughout this book.

A brief historical view of contemporary organizational behavior

The concern about how to organize people and manage them is not new; it has been with us since the dawn of civilization. The difference between then and now is that there was less attention to the management of commercial activities in ancient times, while more attention was focused on the large-scale endeavors of military, political, and religious organizations. The development of economic sciences and management practices began around the start of the seventeenth century. The Industrial Revolution and Adam Smith's writing on political economy are key marker events, particularly

9

for most Western management thinkers. While there may be some debate about when serious consideration of management problems began, it is very clear that it became more important when the economic sectors of societies throughout the world became larger and more complicated.

Antecedents of contemporary organizational behavior

Though contemporary organizational behavior began to emerge as a distinct area of research and academic specialization in the late 1950s and early 1960s, it can trace its roots to the beginning of the late nineteenth and early twentieth centuries and four approaches to management that started then:

- Scientific management
- Administrative theory
- Industrial psychology
- The human relations perspective.

The first major impetus to the field of organizational behavior was the **scientific management approach**. Scientific management focused on the lowest level of organization – the worker and the boss. The basic question it addressed was, "How can the job be designed most efficiently?" Many people were associated with the beginnings of scientific management, but the most prominent was Frederick W. Taylor – who is known as the "father of scientific management." His ideas, when applied, resulted in significant productivity increases. In the well-known shoveling experiment, Taylor found that the optimum-size shovel for handling material carried about 21 pounds of material. He was able to increase productivity from 16 to 59 tons of material shoveled per day while the number of shovelers needed per day was decreased from 500 to 140. Such results were typical when scientific management was applied, and they led to a strong advocacy of scientific management methods.

By the late 1920s, another perspective had emerged. A number of writers began to analyze the work of managers. Their ideas concerned understanding the basic functions of management and developing guidelines, or principles, about how to manage effectively, and came to be called **administrative theory**. Management functions are those activities that all managers perform in whole or in part. The administrative theorists defined these and did the most extensive early analysis of the managerial functions of planning, organizing, and controlling. They developed **principles of management** which are general guides that tell a manager what to do when faced with problems of designing an organization, making decisions, or dealing with people. Principles of management were developed for nearly every phase of the managerial task: leadership, objectives, single accountability, unity of command, equity, and authority. Drawn from real-world experiences, they were meant to facilitate high performance. These principles can, of course, be useful guides to action. While they are typically narrowly focused, they do give managers a place to start when faced with a problem.

Around 1900, at about the same time that the scientific management movement began to gain impetus, the **industrial psychology** movement began to grow. An early success of industrial psychology was personnel selection for the US army in World War I. Faced with the problem of drafting, inducting, and placing millions of men, the army sought the assistance of the American Psychological Association. These early attempts by psychologists at personnel selection and classification developed into a series of refined techniques to improve these processes by the beginning of World War II. For instance, screening instruments were used to predict the probability of success at completing different types of military training. Because of the large-scale production effort to produce defense materials during World War II, under conditions where workers had been lost to the armed services, new techniques for training employees had to be developed.

A quite different behavioral perspective emerged after the Hawthorne experiments at Western Electric in the late 1920s: the **human relations perspective** [1]. This was the first widely recognized approach to attempt to utilize the broader range of human potential and to suggest ways to do this. The Hawthorne experiments were carried out in the Hawthorne plant of Western Electric, an AT&T subsidiary in Cicero, Illinois. In perhaps the most famous of the studies, two groups of workers were observed to determine the effects of different levels of illumination on worker performance. In one group, the level of illumination was changed; in the other, it was not. They found that when illumination was increased, the level of performance increased. However, productivity also increased when the level of illumination decreased, even down to the level of moonlight. Moreover, productivity also increased in the control group. These results seemed contrary to reason, and so the engineers examined other factors that might have affected the results. The workers were responding in a way that they thought the experimenters wanted and because they liked being the center of attention. Obviously, the subjects were responding not to the level of light, but to the experiment itself and to their involvement in it. The researchers concluded that how people were treated made an important difference in performance. Since that time, this effect in research has been known as the **Hawthorne effect**.

Other studies followed and continued to demonstrate the importance of leadership practices and work-group pressures on employee satisfaction and performance. They showed that the importance of economic incentives in worker motivation was overrated, and they stressed the importance of recognizing that employees react to a wide set of complex forces, rather than to one factor alone.

Contemporary organizational behavior

Contemporary organizational behavior took roots in the late 1950s and early 1960s. In addition to those writers already discussed, other psychologists, sociologists, anthropologists, and social scientists had studied worker and management problems from a behavioral perspective before 1960, and managers were always concerned with human problems. However, since 1960, a somewhat unified body of knowledge and thinking has developed that falls under the general label of contemporary organizational behavior.

Flowing logically from the prior works, two distinct but related approaches to the study of human behavior in organizations emerged around this time. **Organizational theory** is a focus on organizations as the unit of analysis. Individuals and groups are not prominent in the analysis. **Organizational behavior** is more concerned with the individual and the group as the main object of study, and less so with the organization. Our view of contemporary organizational behavior contains both these perspectives.

Organizational theory

This approach is concerned with how organizations are structured and how they can be designed to operate more effectively to achieve objectives in a "rational" way. The organizational theorists look at organizational problems rather than at individual problems. This broad view was reflected in the work of Max Weber [2], a German sociologist who was an important influence on writing and theory about the study of organization. Weber developed a theory of **bureaucracy**, and his analysis considered organizations as part of a broader society. Weber felt that bureaucracy emphasized predictability of behavior and results and showed greater stability over time. He suggested that organizations naturally evolved toward this rational form.

Chester Barnard [3] had a significant effect on organization theory. Barnard developed the concept of the **informal organization** more fully and added much to the thinking about organizations with such concepts as the **zone of indifference**, the **acceptance theory of authority**, and the organization as a social system. Using concepts from Barnard in their book *Organizations*, James March and Herbert Simon [4] integrated psychology, sociology, and economic theory. They extended the Barnard view of the organization as a social system. Following Barnard, they presented a more elaborate motivational theory than the scientific management writers and the administrative theory writers. This approach emphasized individual decision-making.

Another very important development in the study of organizations is **contingency theory**, a concept based upon the idea that the organization structure and the management approach must be tailored to the situation. Critics of the administrative and scientific management theorists claimed that the early management writers advocated that there is one best way to manage. These critics correctly argued that "it all depended," but they never really told anyone how to proceed to develop a proper managerial strategy. It did all depend – but on what? One theory described how the structure of an organization is affected by outside restraints, so that the organization develops both formal and informal systems that help it to adapt to the outside environment and, thus, to survive [5]. Other researchers found that the differences in the organizational structures of these firms could be traced to the nature of the technology used and to the markets served by the firms [6, 7] and by the rate of technological change for the products produced [8]. Lawrence and Lorsch [8] concluded that organizations in a stable environment are more effective if they have more detailed procedures and a more centralized decision-making process while organizations in an unstable environment should have decentralization, participation, and less emphasis on rules and standard procedures to be effective.

Organizational behavior

Some of the early contributors to contemporary organizational behavior are Douglas McGregor, Chris Argyris, and Rensis Likert. Although others helped to forge the discipline of organizational behavior as we know it today, the work of these scholars deserves special mention. Douglas McGregor [9], in *The Human Side of Enterprise*, said that most managers make incorrect assumptions about those who work for them. He called these assumptions, collectively, **Theory X**. Theory X assumed that people were lazy, with personal goals which ran counter to the organization's, and that because of this, people had to be controlled externally. In a work context, this meant close supervision and guidance so that management could ensure high performance. **Theory Y** assumptions were based on greater trust in others. Human beings were more mature, self-motivated, and self-controlled than Theory X assumed. McGregor suggested that there was little need for rigid organization or interpersonal controls.

Chris Argyris [10, 11] also made a strong case for reducing the amount of organizational control. He believed that many constraints placed by organizational structure on human beings were self-defeating to organizational goals of effectiveness and efficiency. The thrust of his argument, along with McGregor's, is that the bureaucratic form of organization is incongruent with the basic needs of the healthy individual and that it treats lower organizational members like children. This fosters dependence and leads to the frustration of the highest-order human needs. This frustration expresses itself in lack of work involvement and anti-organizational activities, such as sabotage.

In 1961, Rensis Likert, a psychologist, published *New Patterns of Management*, a book that was to have a powerful impact on thinking about human problems of management. Likert [12] believed that "managers with the best record of performance in American business and government were in the process of pointing the way to an appreciably more effective system of management than now exists." He proposed that leaders (or managers) would be most effective using a supportive approach. This means that they must create a work environment in which the individual sees his "experiences (in terms of his values, goals, expectations and aspirations) as contributing to and maintaining his sense of personal worth and importance." Likert went on to give details of the characteristics of these managers and organizations.

The work of these writers – and others whom we have not mentioned, as well as others we do discuss in this book – is important because they broadened the scope of traditional behavioral approaches and introduced some of the critical factors that the scientific management writers and the administrative theorists had not addressed.

MANAGING ORGANIZATIONAL PERFORMANCE

A person contributes more to the organization than simply performing assigned tasks. Rather than taking a narrow view of performance, in this book, we take a managerial view of performance. That means we define performance in terms of the results that managers must obtain to keep the firm viable as an economic entity. This view of performance includes three dimensions: the task performance dimension, the contextual performance dimension, and the ethical performance dimension.

The **task performance dimension** is what most of us focus on: the set of activities and their results that you must do to accomplish the work. For example, if you are manager of a manufacturing plant, you must manage production and quality levels, prepare work schedules, order supplies, deal with subordinates, and run staff meetings. If you are a systems analyst, you must be able to analyze the flow of work through an organization, be able to specify the modification of existing technology so that it can be adapted to the work flow, and then instruct the users about how to use the system in the future.

The **contextual performance dimension** considers how you might contribute to the effectiveness of the organization or co-workers in ways other than "just doing your job." This performance dimension reflects the extent to which you are willing to go beyond the norms of performance and involvement of your work role. These sorts of actions might be seen by some as trivial and irrelevant, but they contribute in an important way to the effectiveness of the organization [13]. Helping a co-worker with a task, lending encouragement to a co-worker, and volunteering for an unpleasant task are all examples of important workplace behaviors considered as contextual. Such behavior, which goes beyond task performance, is essential if organizations are to excel, because success depends on employees going beyond formal role requirements [13, 14].

The **ethical performance dimension** focuses on doing the right thing. This sounds simple, but the fact is that nearly everyone faces ethical dilemmas at work. One survey of workers [15] reported that almost 50 percent of the respondents admitted to some kind of unethical or illegal actions at work. The most frequent acts were cutting corners on quality control, covering up some incident, abusing or lying about sick days, deceiving customers, and putting inappropriate pressure on others at work. Here are some of the reasons given for the unethical actions:

- Pressure to meet budgets and quotas
- Weak leadership
- No management support
- Internal politics
- Poor internal communications
- Work hours and workload

- Lack of recognition by the company
- Insufficient resources
- Balancing work and family
- Personal financial problems.

These results suggest that sometimes, when doing what you think is required for your job, you may feel pressure to act in unethical ways. In other words, managing ethical behavior requires organizations to look at policies, procedures, incentive structures and other areas to fully consider the causes of unethical behavior.

As we will discuss throughout this text, managing ethical behavior is often more complex than it first appears. Behaving ethically or "doing the right thing" is a standard that may have different meanings to different people. The fact is that what is the right, or ethical, thing to do is not easy to define, because different standards and values exist in a society. So, an organization must develop a common set of values that are expressed in some way as a guide to deciding about how to act. The most basic guide, but certainly not one that is sufficient, is that our actions must be legal. Usually, however, society demands that we apply a higher standard of what is right.

WHAT DO MANAGERS REALLY DO?

We conclude this chapter with a broader discussion of the nature of managerial work. It is likely that some of you will have experience in managing organizations while others will have little or no experience. As a result, it is important that prior to beginning a study of managing behavior we all have some understanding of the nature of managerial work. Traditional stereotypes of managers often include a belief that managers are systematic and rational planners who engage in strategic activities rather than involve themselves in the day-to-day operations of the organization. While managerial jobs vary, there are some characteristics that all managers have in common and which challenge the traditional notions of what managers really do [16].

1   **Managers work at a pace that is unrelenting and managerial activities are varied, fragmented, and brief.** Rather than being rational systematic planners, managers work very hard at a frantic pace. They are constantly exposed to one problem after another, and most of these need an immediate solution. Seldom does a manager have the luxury of starting a project and finishing it, without interruption. The work is discontinuous. For instance, a manager may begin a project at 7.30 a.m. and make some progress, but then be interrupted with a question from her boss which needs an answer. She sets aside the project, and finds an answer to her boss's problem. Before she can return to the project, something else interrupts her day. It may be hours before she returns to the work she started in the morning. Also, much of what a manager does takes only a short time. Half of a manager's tasks are finished in less than ten minutes and only 10 percent take more than an hour.

2 **Managers prefer live action**. Managers tend to do the more active, current, and interesting parts of their work first and set aside the routine parts for later. They are more interested in current issues and problems rather than focusing on longer-term issues.

3 **Managers prefer verbal communication**. Managers prefer to use verbal communications from nontraditional sources rather than traditional information channels. Managers find that this information is often more timely and accurate. Traditional views that managers prefer the aggregated information found in formal management information systems are questionable.

4 **Much managerial work is controlled by others**. An interesting aspect of managerial work is how much of it is controlled by others, meaning that the manager is often reacting. As noted earlier, managers are interrupted by their subordinates, called by their bosses or customers, and often must deal with problems that arise unexpectedly.

The overall effect of these studies of managerial work is that they help us understand that managers work in an environment that is complex and dynamic. As a result of this, effective managers are those that learn to adapt quickly to changing contexts and who can learn from the experiences and ideas of others. In other words, effective managers have a broad understanding of the fundamental theories of human behavior and can apply those theories where appropriate in a constantly changing environment. We believe this book will contribute significantly to the knowledge base required by you to be one of those effective managers.

Guide for Managers:
UNDERSTANDING WHY PEOPLE BEHAVE AS THEY DO

Trying to make judgments about people is one of the most frustrating aspects of managerial work. Too often, as amateur psychologists, we make mistakes about others as we try to judge whether they will work out well. Many times, this is because of attribution errors of the type that we will discuss in chapter 4. This text will provide many useful theories that will help improve your ability to understand behavior. The models of personality, judgment, and motivation are among the many topics we believe effective managers use, improving their ability to understand behavior. Regardless of which model you are considering though, here are some basic ideas that will help you make better judgments about the factors that influence the behaviors of others.

DON'T TRUST EXPLANATIONS. People cannot always fully explain their own behavior. The employee who refused an assignment might say, "I don't feel very well today." But this does

---

not explain the cause of the resistance. Because of the difficulties in interpreting what people say we need to seek other information to help understand the behavior.

LOOK FOR CAUSES. When interpreting employee behavior, look for causes in both the employee's characteristics and in the environment or situation that might have triggered the behavior. The model presented at the beginning of this chapter shows that how a person behaves is determined by the person's characteristics interacting with the elements in his or her environment. You must understand this interaction between the person and the environment, and avoid overemphasizing one in favor of the other when interpreting human behavior. You might decide that an unproductive worker is lazy or inattentive (personal attributes) when actually the worker was behaving in response to pressure from peers or faulty equipment (environmental forces).

LOOK FOR SEVERAL CAUSES. Behavior may result from one or more causes. Suppose an employee gets very upset over a request to perform an assignment. If you believe that your request is the only cause of the employee's reaction, you might conclude that this is just another case of uncooperativeness. Suppose, however, that you think about other possible causes that might explain the employee's refusal. You might discover that the employee is not only worried about falling behind in his work, but also feels unfairly treated because co-workers are not carrying their share of the load.

USE PAST BEHAVIOR AS A PREDICTOR OF FUTURE BEHAVIOR. Keep in mind that past behavior is a pretty good predictor of future behavior. In many ways people are stable and predictable. There is some truth to the statement that past behavior is the best predictor of a person's future behavior. It is fairly safe for a manager to assume that what a worker has done in the past is quite likely to be repeated unless something significant changes. Stability of behavior, however, does not mean that people do not change. Given the right circumstances, even deeply held values and beliefs may be changed.

SUMMARY

The context of twenty-first-century organizational behavior is dynamic as a result of the changes in the economy, in the diversity of the workforce, and in the way our organizations are structured and managed. These changes have led to an increased need for managers to improve their ability at managing people. This book is a primer designed to introduce the present state of knowledge in this field. While we are limited in terms of space and time constraints, we feel we have outlined the essential elements of organizational behavior necessary for anyone who wants to improve his or her "people skills."

REFERENCES

1 Roethlisberger, F. J. and W. J. Dickson. 1939. *Management and the Worker*. Cambridge, MA: Harvard University Press.

2 Weber, M. 1947. *The Theory of Social and Economic Organization*. New York: Free Press.

3 Barnard, C. 1938. *The Functions of the Executive*. Cambridge, MA: Harvard University Press.

4 March, J. G. and H. A. Simon. 1958. *Organizations*. New York: John Wiley.

5 Selznick, P. 1949. *TVA and the Grass Roots*. Berkeley: University of California Press.

6 Burns, T. G. and G. M. Stalker. 1961. *The Management of Innovation*. London: Tavistock Institute.

7 Perrow, C. 1970. *Organizational Analysis: A Sociological View*. Belmont, CA: Wadsworth.

8 Lawrence, P. R. and J. W. Lorsch. 1969. *Organization and Environment: Managing Differentiation and Integration*. Homewood, IL: Richard D. Irwin.

9 McGregor, D. 1960. *The Human Side of Enterprise*. New York: McGraw-Hill.

10 Argyris, C. 1957. *Personality and Organization: The Conflict Between the System and the Individual*. New York: Harper & Row.

11 Argyris, C. 1964. *Integrating the Individual and the Organization*. New York: John Wiley.

12 Likert, R. 1961. *New Patterns of Management*. New York: McGraw-Hill.

13 Organ, D. W. 1988. *Organizational Citizenship Behavior: The Good Soldier Syndrome*. Lexington, MA: Lexington Books.

14 Borman, W. C. and S. J. Motowidlo. 1993. Expanding the Criterion Domain to Include Elements of Contextual Performance. In N. Schmitt and W. C. Borman, eds., *Personnel Selection in Organizations*, 71–98. San Francisco: Jossey Bass.

15 Jones, D. 1997. 48% of Workers Admit to Unethical or Illegal Acts. In *USA Today*, p. 1-A.

16 Mintzberg, H. 1973. *The Nature of Managerial Work*. New York: Harper & Row.

Block II: A Focus on the Individual

BLOCK I
INTRODUCTION

BLOCK II
A FOCUS ON THE INDIVIDUAL
Chapter 2   Personality and Individual Differences
Chapter 3   Attitudes and Accommodation to Work
Chapter 4   Individual Perception, Judgment, and Attribution
Chapter 5   Motivation and Performance

BLOCK III
THE CONTEXT OF ORGANIZATIONAL BEHAVIOR

BLOCK IV
INTEGRATING BEHAVIORAL THEORY INTO EFFECTIVE
MANAGEMENT AND LEADERSHIP

CHAPTER 2
Personality and Individual Differences

FUNDAMENTALS OF PERSONALITY

PERSONALITY IN ORGANIZATIONAL SETTINGS

ABILITY

Three months ago Jean Moore hired a new writer for the sports section of the *Times Leader*, the most important newspaper in town. She was happy when she hired Dale Felton because she had been reading his articles for several years and he had exactly the investigative and reporting style that Jean thought would significantly increase the readership of the *Times*.

In his first couple of months, everyone liked Dale. He was bright, literate, funny, and always uplifted the humor of any group he was in. But recently, Jean was hearing rumors about Dale – and also rumors about other people from Dale himself. For example, Dale told Jean, he said in confidence, that Pete O'Doul, who had been writing a sports column for ten years, was thinking about leaving for a rival paper. Dale assured Jean that all of this was secret, but he had a close friend who told him how unhappy Pete was with the *Times* since Jean had hired Dale. This led Pete to start negotiating with another paper. Dale thought that if Pete left, it wouldn't be a problem. He told Jean how Pete was undercutting her reputation with everyone at the *Times*.

Jean's next surprise came from Pete. Pete asked for a meeting with her. They talked and Pete told her how much respect he had for Dale – and surprisingly – that Dale had for him. Pete wanted to tell Jean, further, that both he and Dale were disappointed with the work of Luis Mendez, a Hispanic reporter whose work was always good, who had a wonderful reputation in the local sports community.

As time passed, Jean began to notice a pattern. Dale was at the center of these rumors, either coming directly to her or passing them to her through someone else. She noticed something else. Almost everyone with whom she talked seem to be having the same experience with Dale. He was complimentary when he talked with them about themselves but negative, even mean-spirited, when he spoke about others. It seems that was his *modus operandi*. He was spreading gossip and rumor and, Jean concluded, he was benefiting from it more than anyone else. Morale at the *Times* was suddenly very low. People were upset, they were talking of leaving. And all of this began to happen after Dale arrived. Jean wondered to herself, "What is the matter with Dale? He is competent and conscientious, but insecure. He seems very agreeable, but only when you're with him. Otherwise, he's political, malicious, and neurotic. I don't understand him at all."

The example of Dale Felton can help you understand something important about people at work. It isn't all about performance. Dale, after all, was a great writer. A lot of it is about the kind of person that Dale is, his personality. And in this case, it is a personality that is destructive for the *Times Leader*. When you finish this chapter, you will understand this sort of problem much better.

Personality is a useful concept for interpreting and managing in many organizational situations like the one the Jean Moore is facing. The **attraction-selection-attrition cycle** in organizations explains how personality and organizations affect each other [1]. People are attracted to and select the situations they prefer to enter. Once they are in the organization, they make the situation what it is. As similar people become attracted, and as dissimilar people leave, the organization becomes more homogeneous because the personalities are more alike. The people who make up the organization define it by establishing norms and maintaining the culture. So, while the situation may affect behavior, it is the people that define the situation. Homogeneity of personalities may become a threat to the organization's survival. If one wants to change such a situation, it is necessary to change the mix of people and to select new people so as to add variability. Throughout this book, reference is made to personality in explaining a variety of topics.

- The personalities of managers in the dominant power coalition determine an organization's culture.
- Personality is a key factor in understanding adjustment to work and career, coping with stress, and problem-solving and decision-making behavior.
- Personality is central to the dynamics of motivation, and interpersonal conflict and politics.

There are a few things to keep in mind as you read about these different ways to characterize personality.

1   There are different ways to view people and you will see that some of the approaches are similar in some ways with others, while some are very distinct.
2   Each perspective represents a motivational force that is likely related to some important organizational behavior, attitude, or perception.
3   Most of the characteristics we are describing represent just one way to describe behavior, and that each of us can be described in terms of any one of the theories, and some may seem to be more accurate than others.

We have selected only some of the more important personality approaches to highlight in this chapter. As you read other parts of the book, we say again, you will find other ways to characterize personality, but these are more strongly associated with a specific subject area in organizational behavior (such as Type A/B personality and stress or Achievement/Power Theory and motivation) and they are better discussed in that section.

FUNDAMENTALS OF PERSONALITY

The term personality is used in many different ways. Sometimes we say that a person has a good personality or a bad personality, meaning that he or she is pleasant or unpleasant. Sometimes it is used to mean an important or famous person, like saying that the President of the United States is an important personality. In this book, we use the term **personality** to mean the relatively stable organization of all a person's characteristics, an enduring pattern of attributes that define the uniqueness of a person. Because attitudes and values are part of the pattern, personality includes attitudinal predispositions as well as patterns of actual behaviors.

In this chapter, we present several different perspectives on personality because there is no single theory that integrates all we know about personality; each theory and approach has its own way of characterizing it. For example, some approaches emphasize predispositions, and the traits, attitudes, and needs that drive behavior [2, 3, 4, 5]. There are learning theories of personality, such as social learning theory. Other approaches stress personality in terms of the perceptions, thoughts, and judgments people engage in as they cope and mature in the world around them [6]. Finally, some theories look at the tensions that exist inside a person, and see personality as the consequence of internal conflicts and how they are resolved. You are probably familiar with the work of Freud, who dramatized the struggle between our inner impulses and our moral conscience [7].

How and when personality operates

In chapter 1 we discussed the psychological model that shows that behavior is a function of the person and the environment ($B = f(P \times E)$). Even though the environment affects behavior, personality-driven behavior can show a good deal of consistency across different environments, or situations [8]. This is especially true for a broad disposition, such as one's need for social approval. Those with a high need for social approval seek it in almost all situations in which they find themselves. On the other hand, a specific trait such as honesty may vary more with the situation, but even specific traits will affect behavior when conditions are appropriate [9]. For instance, a person who wouldn't steal in general might be perfectly willing to copy a piece of software without paying the license fee. It is also likely that personality will help to determine the kinds of

Guide for Managers: USING INDIVIDUAL DIFFERENCES

Managers often fail to understand the value of having clear models of individual differences. It might be easier to prefer to rely on generalized models of behavior that can be applied to groups. Unfortunately, while these models may explain a group's average reaction to an organizational situation, they may be useless in understanding why a subordinate behaved in particular way. Here are two keys to using models of personality as part of your management strategy:

Account for individual differences
Try to account for individual

23

situations that people may seek to be in. Shy persons will avoid social situations. When in these situations, the trait may still emerge, such as when a shy person experiences tension at a party. In some settings, however, personality attributes may be squelched. For example, sociability may be impossible to express in a hostile or threatening environment.

When is personality more or less likely to operate, and to be the main cause of behavior? Personality is less powerful in **strong situations**. These are structured situations where constraints such as clear and precise cues, rules, and task demands act to limit behavior [10, 11]. Rewards, tight standards, and expectations can add to the limits, making personality differences between individuals less evident. Think, for example, about watching a military unit in a parade – this is the epitome of a strong situation and personality will not influence behavior. The constraints on behavior are very tight: all wear the same uniform, march at the same pace, move on command, and salute when ordered. It is impossible to know anything about the personality differences of the soldiers from watching them march.

There are some cases of strong situations in organizations. For example, working on an assembly line, in an operating room, or being an astronaut on a space shuttle mission are examples. In all of these cases, you want the person to perform the tasks as they are specified, otherwise the product will have flaws, the patient might suffer, or the mission won't be successfully completed.

The role of personality is much stronger in **weak situations**. These are differences and don't overgeneralize about them when you deal with people. People are alike in many ways. Similarities allow us to generalize about people. Some generalizations are relatively safe (for example, people dislike being embarrassed). Others are more questionable or even dangerous (for example, punishment will eliminate behaviors that cause work accidents). On the other hand, knowing that people are different can complicate things because we might try to treat every person as unique. When dealing with others, it is probably best to err on the side of appreciating individual differences. This, at least, can help prevent poor generalizations.

Recognize personality differences are critical to many organizational decisions

SELECTING AND ASSIGNING PEOPLE TO JOBS. Consider important personality differences to make sure that an individual's personality is related to what the job requires for success. How effective would an introvert be as a salesperson? Consider that people differ in their dedication to the organization. This requires knowing the difference between organizationalists, professionals, and indifferents.

ORGANIZATION DESIGN. Consider the reactions of different personalities to the structure of the organization. An overemphasis on hierarchy may lead to the emergence of authoritarian and Machiavellian personality types. This may lead to an increase in ambiguous situations that are loosely structured, so personality characteristics become a stronger explanation and cause of behavior. You would therefore expect personality characteristics to be more evident in loosely structured organizations with few rules and policies, as compared to bureaucratic settings [12]. This is why you often see prima donna singers or musicians act very individualistically in rehearsals, expecting to be treated as special because of their unique skills. However, when it comes time to go on stage, a more controlled situation, usually they play the part and sing on key. Therefore, if you want to understand behavior in personality terms, it is best to observe people when structure is loose or has broken down. Also, if you want personality to operate more fully in a situation so that you might capitalize on personality differences, you may have to loosen controls and expectations, and otherwise permit more situational freedom. This may be helpful when creativity or adaptation to a novel problem is needed.

influence tactics and other political behavior and create an environment that interferes with task accomplishment.

JOB DESIGN AND DEVELOPMENT OF INCENTIVE PROGRAMS. Expect some of your employees to be much more internally motivated, self-controlling, and independent. As a result, they will expect more freedom and responsibility in job design. Developing motivation programs that are heavily based on external incentives may undermine their internal motivation.

The bases of personality

It is now generally agreed that personality has a genetic component (i.e., it is in part inherited from our parents) and that it also has a learning component, that it develops as a result of our upbringing. While the nature-nurture argument about the bases of personality is an old one, recent evidence shows that both sides are right: a significant portion of personality is a result of heredity, but a large part is due to the life experiences we have, particularly in our early life. We know, for example, from studies of twins who have been raised in different families, often in very different national cultures, that about 30 percent of the variance in job satisfaction and 40 percent of the variance in work values can be explained by heredity [13, 14].

While these effects of heredity are quite strong, this still leaves a large part of the personality that develops as a result of how we actually learn in our early experiences to adapt to the world around us. Even though we all start with the genetic makeup that we inherit from our parents as the base for our personality, as we grow we are exposed to socialization processes that also have a significant effect on our personality. **Socialization** is the process through which a person learns and acquires the values, attitudes, beliefs, and accepted behaviors of a culture, society, organization, or group. We learn that some behaviors are more rewarding to us while others lead to negative consequences; we learn group norms and values from our parents, as well as observing the behaviors of others. Over a period of time, these experiences shape the way we adapt to the world in which we live. The result is our personality, the unique set of values, attitudes, and behaviors in our adult lives that have been shaped around our genetic character.

Some approaches to understanding personality

In this section, we describe some of the more common ways that personality has been the focus of theory, research, and practice in management situations. We discuss some of the more important approaches to highlight in this chapter. These are (1) the "Big Five" Personality Dimensions, (2) Positive and Negative Affectivity, (3) Machiavellianism, (4) Locus of Control, (5) the Myers-Briggs Dimensions, and (6) Organizational Personality Orientations. In other chapters, you will come across other personality concepts that show how it is related to leadership, stress, and power (such as Type A/B personality and stress or Achievement/Power Theory and motivation).

The "Big Five" personality dimensions

A **trait** is some particular relatively stable and enduring individual tendency to react emotionally or behaviorally in a specific way. For example, we might characterize a person as being agreeable, responsible, or considerate. Over the years, hundreds of studies have been done which have used specific traits to define personality, but they were not very successful. Recently, however, these many trait studies have been analyzed and these traits have been grouped into higher-level classifications that have resulted in the identification of the "Big Five" dimensions of personality [15]. These are general personality dimensions that reflect similar specific traits and characteristics that fall within each dimension repeatedly in research and theory. They are:

1 Extroversion
2 Emotional stability
3 Agreeableness
4 Conscientiousness
5 Openness to experience.

Some of the more specific traits of persons high in **extroversion** are that they tend to be sociable, like to be with others, and are energetic. Of course, **introverts** are the reverse. They tend to be less sociable, like to be alone, and do not interact much with others. Extroversion is related to job success for managers and salespeople and success in training [16].

Emotional stability, viewed from the negative side, is also called **neuroticism**. Among the traits of someone low in emotional stability (or highly neurotic), are that they tend to be emotional, tense, insecure, have high anxiety levels, are depressed, easily upset, suspicious, and low in self-confidence. There is some evidence that shows that greater emotional stability of employees is related to better supervisory ratings of performance [17]. Both extroversion and emotional stability are also related to an expatriate's willingness to continue in an overseas assignment [18].

Agreeableness is a trait of people who are simply easier to get along with than others. They are likely to be more tolerant, trusting, generous, warm, kind, and good-natured. They are less likely to be aggressive, rude, and thoughtless.

Conscientiousness denotes persons who are responsible, dependable, persistent, punctual, hard-working, and oriented toward work. Conscientiousness is related to success on the job and in training for managers, professionals, salespeople, police, and skilled/semi-skilled workers [16, 19] and higher performance ratings for expatriate managers [18].

Openness to experience refers to people who are imaginative, curious, cultured, broad-minded, have broad interests, and tend to be self-sufficient. Those who are more open to experiences appear to react very positively to different kinds of training [17].

Positive and negative affectivity: being in a good or bad mood

Two general traits that have been related to how people are oriented toward their work are positive affectivity and negative affectivity [20]. **Positive affectivity**, similar to extroversion, means that you have a strong, positive sense of your personal well-being, that you think of yourself as active and involved in activities that you like and that you are, overall, a pleasant person in most situations. If you are high in positive affectivity, you are active, elated, enthusiastic, peppy, and strong. If you are low in positive affectivity, you are drowsy, dull, sleepy, and sluggish. The term that comes to mind for a person high in positive affectivity is "an overall happy, nice human being."

Negative affectivity, similar to neuroticism, means that you are not very happy, you feel under stress and strain, you tend to focus on failure and you tend to view yourself and others in negative ways, even when the conditions in which you are operating do not warrant these perceptions. The high negativity person is distressed, fearful, hostile, jittery, nervous, and scornful. The low negativity person is at rest, calm, placid, and relaxed. The term that comes to mind for a person high in negative affectivity is "sourpuss."

The research to date suggests that these two traits – positive affectivity and negative affectivity – are independent; they do not exist as separate ends of the same continuum. If they were on the same continuum, it would mean that if you are high on positive affectivity, you must be low on negative affectivity. Instead, being independent means that a person might be high on both positive affectivity and negative affectivity, low on both, high on one and low on the other [20, 21]. For example that the person with high positive affectivity is more active and enthusiastic while the low positive affectivity person is more dull, slow, and sleepy. On the other hand, the person high in negative affectivity is more likely to be nervous and hostile, while the low negative affectivity person is more relaxed and laid back.

Having a strong positive or a strong negative disposition can affect your work life. If you are high on positive affectivity, you are less likely to have accidents at work than if you are high on negative affectivity [22]. Or, if you are positive at work, you are more likely to be rewarded by your boss for good performance [23]. Also, effective managers tend to be highly positive [24]. Highly positive people are seen as better leaders, having higher management potential, and are more satisfied with their work and their life.

Machiavellianism

The personality characteristic Machiavellianism has interpersonal and leadership implications for the workplace [25]. High Machiavellians (high Machs) have high self-esteem and self-confidence and behave in their own self-interest. They are seen as cool and calculating, attempt to take advantage of others, and seek to form alliances with people in power to serve their own goals. High Machs might lie, deceive, or compromise morality, believing that ends justify means. Truly high-Mach people experience no guilt; they somehow detach themselves from the consequences of their actions. They also use false or exaggerated praise to manipulate others. They take care not to be swayed by considerations of loyalty, friendship, and trust. A high Mach might give lip-service to such things, but when the chips are down, he or she will not let them stand in the way of personal gain. This gives them a big advantage over those who value friendship and act on trust.

High Machs are able to select situations where their tactics will work: face-to-face, emotional, unstructured, and ambiguous conditions. Not distracted by emotions, they are able to calmly exert control in power vacuums or novel situations. Machiavellianism is not rare in today's society. Studies show that there are many people with moderate to high Mach orientations.

Locus of control

People can be characterized according to their **locus of control**, i.e., whether they believe what happens to them is externally controlled or whether it is controlled internally by their own efforts [26]. A person who believes that others control important outcomes has an **external locus of control**. An **internal locus of control**, however, reflects self-control over one's outcomes. A person with an internal locus of control has needs for independence and a desire to participate in decisions that affect them. Internal control is also correlated with better adjustment to work in terms of satisfaction, coping with stress, and job involvement [27].

Rules, policies, and other management controls can interact with the locus of control to affect motivation. A variety of responses are possible when one's orientation toward control is inconsistent with the environment. Internal locus of control employees might experience frustration and respond with hostility or leave the organization. Those with an external locus of control might react negatively to tasks or jobs that call for independent action. Thus, they might resist efforts such as job enrichment and improving quality of work life that add autonomy and decision-making responsibility to jobs.

Myers–Briggs personality dimensions

The Myers–Briggs approach to personality classifies people according to the kinds of jobs and interactions they prefer, and the ways in which they approach problems [28, 29]. Four **Myers–Briggs dimensions** are used to describe the personality underlying these preferences:

1 Sensing-intuition
2 Thinking-feeling
3 Introversion-extroversion
4 Perceptive-judgment.

Each dimension forms a continuum that people fall along.

Sensing-oriented people like structured situations, an established routine, realism, and precise and uncomplicated details. They enjoy using skills already learned. **Intuitive people** prefer new problems; they dislike repetition, and are impatient with routine. They enjoy learning new skills; they follow their inspirations, and jump to conclusions.

Thinking individuals are unemotional, and often, unknowingly, they hurt people's feelings. They like to analyze and put things in a logical order. They seem impersonal and hard-hearted. **Feeling types** are more aware of other people, and enjoy pleasing them. They like harmony and are influenced by other people's needs; they relate well to most people.

Introverts prefer quiet concentration and think a lot before acting. They work well alone and can stay with one project for a long time. Much thought precedes action, sometimes without action. Introverts dislike interruptions; they forget names, and can have problems communicating. **Extroverts** show impatience with long, slow jobs and like to work fast, uncomplicated by procedures. They prefer variety and action to contemplation. They are good with people and like them around; usually they communicate quite well.

Perceptive people adapt to change and welcome new ideas. They can leave things unsolved and delay decisions without grave concern. They may start too many new projects, postpone unpleasant ones, and leave things unfinished. **Judgment types** prefer to plan work and follow the plan. They settle things on just the essentials and are satisfied with conclusions. They decide too quickly and dislike switching off a project in progress.

29

These four Myers–Briggs concepts can be used in a variety of ways, such as making employees appreciate the different styles of their co-workers or in selecting people for different types of assignments. They can also be used to improve decision-making. People can be taught when it is best to exert their sensing, intuition, thinking, or feeling modes. They can also learn when it is best to pair with each other to improve decision-making. This is referred to as the **mutual usefulness of opposites** and it works as follows:

1 The sensing type needs an intuitive to generate possibilities, to supply ingenuity, to deal with complexity, and to furnish new ideas. Intuitives add a long-range perspective and spark things that seem impossible.
2 The intuitive needs a sensing type to bring up facts to inspect, to attend to detail, to inject patience, and to notice what needs attention.
3 The thinker needs a feeling type to persuade and conciliate feelings, to arouse enthusiasm, to sell or advertise, and to teach and forecast.
4 The feeling type needs a thinker to analyze and organize, to predict flaws in advance, to introduce fact and logic, to hold to a policy, and to stand firm against opposition.

PERSONALITY IN ORGANIZATIONAL SETTINGS

Most theories of personality focus on the person's adaptation to life in general. One, however, is more directed at how people accommodate to work situations [30]. We call these different types of accommodation the **organizational personality orientation**. You can think of it this way, some people are more oriented toward the place they work (we call this type and **organizationalist**). Others are more focused on the work they do, not where they do it (this type is called the **professional**). Finally, some people aren't strongly focused on the organization or the work, but on things outside the work context (this type is called the **indifferent**).

The **organizationalist** is a person with a strong commitment to the place of work. These are the tendencies of a person with an organizationalist orientation:

1 A strong identification with the organization; they seek organization rewards and advancement which are important measures of success and organizational status.
2 High morale and job satisfaction.
3 A low tolerance for ambiguity about work goals and assignments.
4 Identification with superiors, showing deference toward them, conforming and complying out of a desire to advance; maintains the chain of command and compliance, and views respect for authority as the way to succeed.
5 Emphasis on organizational goals of efficiency and effectiveness, avoiding controversy and showing concern for threats to organizational success.

Professionals are job-centered – not organization-centered – and see organization demands as a nuisance that they prefer to avoid. However, they can't: the professionals must work in some organization, so they have to deal with them. For example, a software programmer who has a greater interest in developing complex information networks might prefer to work alone and at strange hours, but he or she probably has to work in an organizational setting that might be very uncomfortable. Professionals tend to:

1   Have experienced occupational socialization that instills high standards of performance in the chosen field; highly ideological about work values.
2   See organizational authority as nonrational when there is pressure to act in ways that are not professionally acceptable.
3   Feel that their skills are not fully utilized in organizations and their self-esteem may be threatened when they do not have the opportunity to do those things for which they have been trained.
4   Seek recognition from other professionals outside the organization, and refuse to play the organizational status game except as it reflects their worth relative to others in the organization. Professionals are very concerned with personal achievement and doing well in their chosen field. Organizational rewards are not without value, however, since they may reflect the professional's importance relative to others in the system. The recognition may be extremely fulfilling, especially when he or she is accorded higher status and pay than others.

Indifferents are people who work for pay. For them, work is not a critical part of their life structure. They may do their work well, but they are not highly committed to their job or the organization. These are some of the characteristics of indifferents:

1   More oriented toward leisure, not the work ethic; separates work from more meaningful aspects of life, and seeks higher-order need satisfaction outside the work organization.
2   Tends to be alienated from work and not committed to the organization; more alienated than either organizationalists or professionals [31].
3   Rejects status symbols in organizations.
4   Withdraws psychologically from work and organizations when possible.

Do not assume, however, that only lower-level organization personnel are indifferents. Some may be organizationalists and others might have a distinctively professional orientation to their work. Also, it could be that higher-level employees who once had an organizational orientation and were highly loyal may no longer follow orders without question. For example, early in a working career, a manager may be extremely committed to the organization. He or she may seek its rewards and want to advance. However, in later career life, after having been passed over several times for promotion, the person seeks reinforcement elsewhere. Thus, it is possible that

through their promotion practices, organizations may turn highly committed organizationalists into indifferents.

The mature personality in organizations

Some who write about organizations believe that there is often a fundamental
conflict between the mature personality and the demands that many organizations
place on employees [32]. As people mature, they go from being passive to active,
develop from a state of dependence to independence, and go from a simple behavioral repertoire to a complex one. Maturity also moves people toward deeper and
varied interests, from a short to a longer time perspective, from subordinacy to equal
or superordinate roles, and to higher states of self-awareness and self-control.

Many managerial practices are inconsistent with the mature personality. Jobs
are frequently highly specialized, consisting only of a few simple tasks. Managers,
not workers, make most of the decisions and do most of the things that involve
judgment and maturity. This makes employees feel dependent, externally controlled,
and pressured to be passive rather than active at work. In short, they feel frustrated
because they cannot act as mature human beings at work. A sense of failure develops
because they cannot pursue meaningful goals. They experience inner conflict, and
this will be strongest among those with the most mature personalities. The conflict
is also more severe at lower organizational levels, where more directive controls are
likely.

If you find yourself in one of these frustrating organizational situations, a way to
escape it is by quitting or by getting promoted, but these are not always possible. If
you can't, it is more likely that you might find yourself responding to your work situation by daydreaming, aggression, regression, or becoming apathetic and disinter-
ested in work. Employees might also form cliques or unions to protect themselves,
and develop norms to withhold productivity, hide errors, and demand increased pay
and benefits. At home, frustrated employees might teach their children to become
indifferent toward work or their employers.

Frustrating conditions at work often get worse, not better. As employees react
defensively, managers might become more directive, tighten controls even further,
or try programs that fail because they are not based on the needs of a mature personality. Thus the situation feeds on itself.

ABILITY

Like personality, people differ in abilities. And, like personality, there is a nature-
nurture basis for ability; that is, there is a genetic component and a learned component to ability. An example of the genetic effects of ability is the case of the 1997
Nobel prize-winner in economics, Robert Merton. His father, also Robert Merton,
is a renowned scholar who made important contributions to sociology. The learned

effects on ability can be observed in the case of a person, especially an adult, who learns to speak a second language.

Ability is the capacity to carry out a set of interrelated behavioral or mental sequences to produce a result. For example, to play the piano requires that one be able to read music, understand chord structures, and have the manual dexterity to finger the keyboard. Both the definition and the example say that there is more than one dimension, or type, of ability. We discuss four different classes of ability in this book [33, 34].

1 Cognitive ability
2 Emotional intelligence
3 Perceptual ability
4 Psychomotor ability.

Cognitive ability

Cognitive ability, or cognitive intelligence, is the capacity to understand complicated ideas, to reason, to learn, to think, and to process information. However, psychologists who study intelligence have discovered that there are different aspects to it. For example, verbal ability is the capacity to comprehend meaning from language and use language to convey meanings. One with high mathematical ability can solve arithmetic problems and understand numbers. Other types of specific cognitive abilities are reasoning skill, deductive skill, and the capacity to remember.

Emotional intelligence

A recent idea that proposes a different type of intelligence and that has received much attention is emotional intelligence [34, 35, 36]. Unlike cognitive intelligence (which more or less means "how smart you are"), emotional intelligence refers to the skills to manage your own feelings as well as the feelings of others. It is composed of four components [34]:

1 The ability to perceive emotions. This is the person's ability to understand his or her emotional state, as well as those of others. Understanding verbal and non-verbal signals is one aspect of this. You will see later, in the chapter on power, that this is one of the skills of a charismatic leader.
2 The ability to access and generate emotions to assist thought. A person with high emotional intelligence knows how to use emotions and feelings in problem-solving.
3 The ability to understand emotions and emotional meanings. Knowing what emotions are and what they mean are part of emotional intelligence. This simply means that you have to be aware of how different emotions and feelings (e.g., frustration, anger, or joy) might affect your relationship with others.

4   The ability to regulate emotions to promote better emotion and thought. Knowing how to manage your emotions and the emotions of others is an important skill. For example, in conflict situations, one might precipitate anger in an opponent to try to gain a negotiation advantage. Similarly, knowing how to control your own feelings and what to do to reduce feelings of anxiety or anger in others may facilitate reaching a sound solution.

Perceptual ability

As we discuss in more detail in chapter 4, perception is the way that we organize information about people and things, the attribution of properties to them on the basis of the information and the way we make cause/effect attributions about them. A person high in perceptual ability has the capacity to comprehend complex visual patterns and is high in cognitive complexity, the ability to find patterns and relationships that exist in a situation, even though the patterns and relationships are embedded in noise and confusion. Interestingly, cognitive complexity skills are an attribute of people with a political orientation, as we discuss in the chapter on power and politics.

Psychomotor ability

Psychomotor abilities are physical skills. They include manual dexterity, physical coordination, and strength.

SUMMARY

Managers need to learn all they can about human behavior because people are critical to an organization's success. One important area to know about is how and why people are different and how these differences affect performance. Specifically our focus is on personality and ability. In this chapter, we have set out some of the basic concepts about these issues that will be important as you read later chapters.

Personality is a way to characterize people. Many theories and concepts of personality exist. It is a useful way to understand and predict success at work and accommodations to organizational life. Personality is central to understanding many aspects of work, ranging from culture to motivation. For example, the authoritarian, bureaucratic, and Machiavellian personality types are of interest in interpreting interpersonal and hierarchical relationships. Internal or external locus of control may be related to a person's leadership ability and promotability.

Abilities refer to the competencies of a person and, like personality differences, there are important differences between people with respect to the types of competencies and the level of each one.

REFERENCES

1 Schneider, B., H. W. Goldstein, and D. B. Smith. 1995. The ASA Framework: An Update. *Personnel Psychology*, **48**(4): 747–73.

2 Cattell, R. B. 1950. *Personality: A Systematic, Theoretical and Factual Study.* New York: McGraw-Hill.

3 Allport, G. W. 1961. *Pattern and Growth in Personality.* New York: Holt, Rinehart & Winston.

4 Murray, H. A. 1962. *Explorations in Personality.* New York: Science Editions.

5 Maslow, A. H. 1970. *Motivation and Personality.* New York: Harper & Row.

6 Rogers, C. R. 1942. *Counseling and Psychotherapy.* Boston: Houghton Mifflin.

7 Freud, S. 1933. *New Introductory Lectures on Psychoanalysis.* New York: Norton.

8 Epstein, S. and E. J. O'Brien. 1985. The Person–Situation Debate in Historical and Current Perspective. *Psychological Bulletin*, **98**(3): 513–37.

9 Funder, D. C. 1991. Global Traits: A Neo-Allportean Approach to Personality. *Psychological Science*, **2**(1): 31–9.

10 Mischel, W. 1977. The Interaction of Person and Situation. In D. Magnusson and N. S. Enders, eds., *Personality at the Crossroads: Current Issues in Interactional Psychology*, 166–207. Hillsdale, NJ: Erlbaum.

11 Weiss, H. M. and S. Adler, 1984. Personality and Organizational Behavior. In B. M. Staw and L. L. Cummings, eds., *Research in Organizational Behavior*, 1–50. Greenwich, CT: JAI Press.

12 Tosi, H. L. 1992. *The Environment/Organization/Person Contingency Model: A Meso Approach to the Study of Organizations.* Greenwich, CT: JAI Press.

13 Arvey, R. D., et al. 1989. Job Satisfaction: Environmental and Genetic Components. *Journal of Applied Psychology*, **74**(2): 187–93.

14 Keller, L. M., et al. 1992. Work Values: Genetic and Environmental Influences. *Journal of Applied Psychology*, **77**(1): 79–89.

15 Costa, P. T. and R. R. McCrae. 1992. *Revised NEO Personality Inventory (NEO-PI-R) and NEO Five Factor Inventory (NEO FFI).* Odessa, FL: Psychological Assessment Resources.

16 Barrick, M. R. and M. K. Mount. 1996. Effects of Impression Management and Self-Deception on the Predictive Validity of Personality Constructs. *Journal of Applied Psychology*, **81**(3): 261–73.

17 Barrick, M. R. and M. K. Mount. 1991. The Big Five Personality Dimensions and Job Performance: A Meta-Analysis. *Personnel Psychology*, **44**: 1–26.

18 Caligiuri, P. M. 2000. The Big Five Personality Characteristics as Predictors of Expatriates' Desire to Terminate the Assignment and Supervisor-Rated Performance. *Personnel Psychology*, **53**: 67–88.

19 Dunn, W. S., et al. 1995. Relative Importance of Personality and General Mental Ability in Managers' Judgements of Applicant Qualifications. *Journal of Applied Psychology*, **80**(4): 500–10.

20 Watson, D. and L. A. Clark. 1984. Negative Affectivity: The Disposition to Experience Aversive Emotional States. *Psychological Bulletin*, **96**(3): 465–90.

21 George, J. M. 1992. The Role of Personality in Organizational Life: Issues and Evidence. *Journal of Management*, **18**(2): 185–213.

22 Iverson, R. and P. Erwin. 1997. Predicting Occupational Injury: The Role of Affectivity. *Journal of Occupational and Organizational Psychology*, **70**(2): 113–29.

23 George, J. M. 1995. Leader Positive Mood and Group Performance: The Case of Customer Service. *Journal of Applied Psychology*, **25**(9): 778–95.

24 Staw, B. M. and S. G. Barsade. 1993. Affect and Managerial Performance: A Test of the Sadder-but-Wiser vs. the Happier-and-Smarter Hypothesis. *Administrative Science Quarterly*, **38**(2): 304–28.

25 Christie, R. and F. Geis, eds. 1970. *Studies in Machiavellianism*. New York: Academic Press.

26 Rotter, J. 1966. Generalized Expectancies for Internal vs. External Control of Reinforcement. *Psychological Monographs*, **80**(609).

27 Spector, P. E. 1994. The Contribution of Personality Traits, Negative Affectivity, Locus of Control and Type A to the Subsequent Reports of Job Stressors and Job Strains. *Journal of Occupational and Organizational Psychology*, **67**(1): 1–12.

28 Jung, C. G. 1939. *The Integration of the Personality*. New York: Farrow & Rinehart.

29 Myers, I. B. and K. C. Briggs. 1962. *Myers–Briggs Type Indicator*. Princeton, NJ: Educational Testing Service.

30 Presthus, R. 1978. *The Organizational Society*. New York: St. Martin's Press.

31 Greene, C. N. 1978. Identification Modes of Professionals: Relationship with Formalization, Role Strain and Alienation. *Academy of Management Journal*, **21**: 486–92.

32 Argyris, C. 1964. *Integrating the Individual and the Organization*. New York: John Wiley.

33 Lubinski, D. and R. Dawis. 1992. Aptitudes, Skills and Proficiencies. In M. D. Dunnette and L. M. Hough, eds., *Handbook of Industrial and Organizational Psychology*, 1–60. Palo Alto, CA: Consulting Psychologist Press.

34 Mayer, J. D. and P. Salovey 1997. What Is Emotional Intelligence? In P. Salovey and D. J. Sluyter, eds., *Emotional Development and Emotional Intelligence: Educational Implications*, 3–34. New York: Basic Books.

35 Goleman, D. 1995. *Emotional Intelligence*. New York: Bantam Books.

36 George, J. 2000. Emotions and Leadership: The Role of Emotional Intelligence. *Human Relations*, **53**(8): 1027–35.

CHAPTER 3

Attitudes and Accommodation To Work

FUNDAMENTALS OF WORK ATTITUDES

A MODEL OF ATTITUDES

ATTITUDINAL CONSISTENCY AND COGNITIVE DISSONANCE

SOCIALIZATION: DEVELOPING WORK-RELATED ATTITUDES AND BEHAVIORS

ORGANIZATIONAL COMMITMENT AND ACCOMMODATION

Opening Fig

The CEO's challenge to the HR manager was clear, "Go find out what our sales people think about working for Lindley Pharmaceuticals. I want to know how they feel about every aspect of working here. I'm tired of guess work about why our people are leaving; rather than telling me what you think, tell me what they think and why they think that!"

Attitudes can have a significant effect on the behavior of a person at work. In the world of work we are concerned with attitudes toward supervision, pay, benefits, promotion or anything that might trigger positive or negative reactions. Employee satisfaction and attitudes represent one of the key areas of measuring organizational effectiveness. This chapter considers the role of workplace attitudes in influencing important organizational outcomes and the methods organizations use to develop these attitudes in their workers.

FUNDAMENTALS OF WORK ATTITUDES

Attitudes are propensities, or tendencies, to react in a favorable or unfavorable way toward an object. The object could be almost anything in the world around us. Attitudes reflect a person's likes and dislikes toward other persons, objects, events, and activities in their environment. It makes sense to study and know about attitudes because strong attitudes will very likely affect a person's behavior. Attitudes toward supervision, pay, benefits, promotion, or anything that might trigger positive or negative reactions. As a result, employee satisfaction and attitudes represent one of the key areas for measuring organizational effectiveness.

Because of the importance of the links of task, contextual, and ethical performance with important measures of organizational effectiveness, one of the key goals of managers should be to create linkages between employee performance and their satisfaction. However, it is not always easy to change a person's attitudes about their work. The reason is that, as you will see, attitudes toward work may be only one important aspect of the person's structure of attitudes. They might be linked strongly to other important ones, making them deeply embedded, and thereby limiting how much managers can succeed in altering the way employees feel and act. However, particular attitudes and satisfactions at work can and do change, sometimes quickly, as events change. Employees who are happy and productive one day can become dissatisfied and resentful overnight as a consequence of some managerial action. This is one of the reasons why many organizations pay close attention to attitudes by conducting periodic **attitude surveys** of employees, and by seeking feedback in other ways. The hope of managers such as the one in the case that opened this chapter is that assessing employee attitudes can provide important information about the effectiveness of different management strategies.

Psychological functions attitudes perform for people

Attitudes perform some useful psychological functions for people. For example, suppose someone on your work team that you admire and look up to comes under attack in a staff meeting by a team from another department. Your positive attitudes toward her and the things she stands for will help you to come to her (and your own) defense. In doing so, you protect your self-image, and have a motive to express the values that you and your friend espouse. Your attitude toward the attackers could shift toward the negative, providing you an even stronger justification about how to deal with them in the future. Here are some things that attitudes do for you [1].

1 They provide a **frame of reference**. Attitudes help us to make sense of the world by giving us a frame of reference from which to interpret our world. We selectively perceive only a part of the total world around us. We are likely to select those facts that are consistent with our attitudes and ignore or discount those that are not.

2 People **express values** through their attitudes. Words and actions demonstrate our values and allow us to share them with others and to affect the world in which we live. Strong democratic values might emerge at work in staff meetings where employees are given a chance to participate in solving a problem or making a decision.

3 Attitudes help us **protect our ego**. Attitudes help us to maintain our self-image and self-respect. For example, a supervisor might have feelings of superiority regarding subordinates. An attitude that subordinates are lazy and not trustworthy, or that they are not trained well enough to assume much responsibility, probably tends to enhance the supervisor's feelings of superiority.

4 Attitudes can facilitate **reconciling contradictions**. Most of us have some contradictory attitudes or beliefs, yet, in many instances, these inconsistencies do not cause us to feel uneasy or have a sense of dissonance. This happens when the contradictions between inconsistent beliefs, behaviors, or attitudes are reconciled by **compartmentalization**. We are able to place the contradictions in separate compartments and not connect them, thereby reconciling them [2].

5 Attitudes aid in **personal adjustment**. We tend to develop attitudes consistent with those parts of our life we find satisfying or dissatisfying. For example, blue-collar workers may be more favorable to political parties which support higher wages, more protectionist trade policies, and better health benefits in general since these might be viewed by workers as being more valuable to them. Similarly, you would expect executives in oil companies to have more favorable attitudes toward politicians who favor more offshore drilling or increased exploration in national parks.

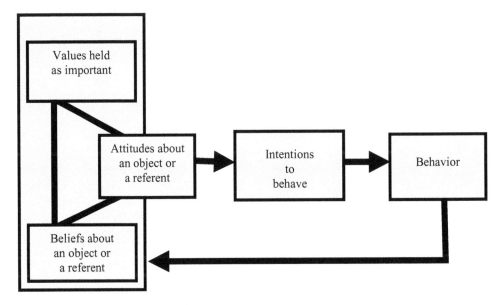

Figure 3.1   A model of attitudes

A MODEL OF ATTITUDES

Attitudes can be understood more easily if they are viewed in terms of their components and their dynamics. Figure 3.1 shows that attitudes are tied to values and beliefs, and they precede intentions to behave and actual behavior.

The affective component

The basic way that we refer to attitudes is to say that they are "positive" or "negative." The **affective component** is the emotional tone generated by or toward the object of the attitude. It simply means that we have some preference – like or dislike – toward the object. Strong and important attitudes are more likely to lead to a behavioral or a psychological response than weak attitudes.

The object of attitudes

Attitudes always apply to some identifiable **object**. People have attitudes about something or someone, for example, toward the federal government, their supervisor, their job, or the use of seat belts. It is not technically accurate to say someone has a good attitude or a bad attitude without specifying the object of the attitude.

The cognitive component

The affective component of the attitude develops as a result of things that we observe in the world around us that we associate, positively or negatively, with the object of the attitude. These are called the **cognitive dimensions of attitude**. If we take the example of attitudes toward the job, or job satisfaction, some of the cognitive components that you might associate with it could be your pay, the actual working conditions, the parking facilities, the hours that you work, and so on. What is important is that your specific attitude toward your job will be a function of perceptions and evaluations about these factors. Another person might have a different set of cognitions associated with work, he or she might even be in a job very similar to yours and even in the same firm. For example, if they are not highly committed to the work, they might focus on the amount of time available for vacation, the hours worked, the level of strict versus loose supervision. The key point is that these relevant cognitions about work can vary from person to person, in large part depending upon their personality and how they view the world.

Values and beliefs

Values reflect a sense of right and wrong. Values are more general than attitudes, and they need not have an identifiable object. They define the good life, and identify goals worthy of our aspiration. Values are expressed in statements such as "equal rights for all," and "hard work is the road to success."

Attitudes form as your cognitions (perceptions) of your environment are evaluated in terms of your relevant values. For example, if you value economic well-being, then the amount of your pay is assessed to determine if it is consistent with the value that you put on "economic well-being." If it is, then a belief is formed that pay is a positive factor and it will contribute to the positiveness of the attitude. If it is seen as a negative factor, then cognitions about pay will contribute to the negativeness of the attitude. We know, for instance, that employees who have high positive affectivity and whose basic values are not met at work are more likely to leave, while those who find their values are met will remain [3].

Beliefs are the thinking component of attitudes. They do not refer to favorable or unfavorable reactions; they only convey a sense of "what is" to the person [4]. However, beliefs may not necessarily be factual even though they represent the truth for a particular person. Beliefs also can vary in how absolute they are. One might believe that nuclear power plants are all unsafe, or believe that this is only sometimes true.

Values underlie attitudes and are usually consistent with them. Cognitions are evaluated against values, and beliefs are formed about whether they are positive or negative. When there are strong positive beliefs about those cognitions that we associate with our work, then these beliefs and values should lead to a positive feeling about work. If they are negative, our attitudes about work may be negative. If they are mixed, then we might have an indifferent attitude about work.

Attitudes and intentions

Managers are concerned about our attitudes toward our job because they might lead us to take some action. Suppose our attitudes toward work are negative and we are frustrated because of what we judge to be low pay and poor working conditions. This could foster intentions, or motivate us, to seek promotion to a job where pay is higher and conditions are better, or maybe even to seek a job elsewhere. Our choice will depend on which alternative we feel has the greatest likelihood of success.

Attitudes and overt behavior

Attitudes often lead to overt behaviors, but not always. Except for behavior, all other aspects of attitudes are internal to the person; they are not observable. The behavioral component of attitudes is important because people draw inferences about attitudes, beliefs, values, and intentions by observing what you say and what you do. For example, if you have a co-worker who has been spending a great deal of time working late at the office, you might infer that he or she has a very positive attitude toward work and the company. However, it could be something else, such as an overdue credit-card bill that your co-worker is trying to pay off.

ATTITUDINAL CONSISTENCY AND COGNITIVE DISSONANCE

An attitude does not usually exist in isolation. You do not, for example, have an attitude toward your work that exists independently of other attitudes that might also be linked to work. It is likely, for example, that your attitude toward where you work is linked with your attitudes toward the work itself that you do, your co-workers, the location of the workplace, and so forth. These different, related attitudes form an **attitude cluster** and more than likely, though not always, they will be consistent with each other as well as the specific values, cognitions, and beliefs for each specific attitude in a specific attitude cluster. However, they also will be consistent with other attitude clusters to which they are strongly linked. For example, we can say that you have a work attitude cluster, a family attitude cluster, and a political attitude cluster. Each of these will include specific attitudes that make up the cluster. One attitude cluster might or might not be linked to another. For example, the work attitude cluster might be very tightly linked to the family attitude cluster but not to the political attitude cluster.

The theory of **cognitive dissonance** is based on the idea that people need to have consistency between their behavior and attitudes, beliefs, or thoughts (cognitions) [5].

When there is inconsistency (dissonance), we are motivated to reduce it because we experience discomfort. Another basic idea of this theory is that we are motivated to explain or justify our behavior, thoughts, or feelings. In short, feelings, thoughts, and behaviors must be consistent with each other. Suppose you are quite happy with your work and have been for a long time because the specific attitudes that make up the work attitude cluster (how you feel about the job, the supervisor, and the location) are all positive. Then, along comes a new manager and you find that his actions toward the work group are demeaning, demanding, and distant, resulting in your attitude toward your boss becoming negative. Now you have a dissonant attitude in the work attitude cluster. One way to deal with this is to modify your overall attitude toward work by reducing your level of job satisfaction. You might recall examples of times when you had problems with him, how he deals in negative ways with other workers, or tell others that he is not important to your success. If your work attitude cluster does become negative and, if at the same time, there are cognitive elements that are common with your family attitude cluster, this could produce dissonance.

We know, for example, that there is strong positive relationship between work satisfaction and life satisfaction [2]. This means that some cognitive dimensions will be common in both the work and the life attitude cluster. For example, one cognitive dimension of your work attitude cluster and your family attitude cluster could be "location." You like your job because it is located near other members of your family and, at the same time, you are contented because your spouse and family are happy there. This overlap will lead to some discomfort when things at home are going well, but you are dissatisfied at work. However, suppose that there is no overlap of cognitive elements with your political attitude cluster, this would pose no adjustment problems.

Dissonance can also arise when there is **insufficient justification** for what you do. This is called **decisional dissonance**. Dissonance can be reduced before you take action. Suppose your new boss tells you to reprimand a subordinate, a behavior that you find unpleasant and harsh. If you were ordered to do so, you may have little or no dissonance because your boss has given you **sufficient justification** (a direct and clear-cut order) to do it. However, in the absence of such an order, the justification may be insufficient. Following the act, the dissonance may remain strong and the motivation to reduce it persists. You would therefore have to rationalize your action. You might justify the reprimand by convincing yourself that your boss wanted you to do what you did but just did not say so. If the employee has a hostile reaction to the reprimand, it can serve to confirm that he deserved it, reducing your dissonance even further.

Dissonance also arises when there are **disconfirmed expectations**. If a customer complains about one of your products, dissonance arises because it is inconsistent with your image of the company's reputation. Here again, developing a belief that rationalizes, or explains, the condition can reduce dissonance. You might think that the complaint was triggered by the customer's failure to follow directions in using the product.

Not surprisingly, dissonance is more severe when we are personally involved, such as when our own decisions lead to an unexpected problem. People often refuse to admit they have made a mistake. Dissonance theory predicts that people will persist in the original decision. They will even repeat it as a way of justifying it, thus compounding the bad decision rather than face the dissonant admission that they were wrong in the first place [6, 7]. In one study [8], students played a business game in which they allocated funds to different projects. Those students who allocated funds to unsuccessful projects made subsequent further investments in the same unsuccessful project, especially when they felt responsible for the bad decision.

SOCIALIZATION: DEVELOPING WORK-RELATED ATTITUDES AND BEHAVIORS

Socialization is one way to understand how people develop the values and beliefs that lead to a whole range of general and specific attitudes about work. It can also have significant influences on our behaviors. Through socialization, we are exposed to countless personal experiences that have lasting effects. The human mind has the capacity to link common events and to generalize across them. These associations may also result from very remote experiences. For example, if you had a bad experience with a sales clerk years ago, that experience could affect your attitude toward a whole company or toward the sales profession in general. Socialization is a process that begins when you are born and continues throughout your life. In this section we will review socialization experiences that occur early in your life, those that directly prepare for your professional life, and the continued socialization that occurs within work organizations.

Early socialization experiences

In your very early years, you begin learning how to respond to authority and authority figures, such as parents and teachers. These authority figures have power, can give rewards or withhold them, and can administer punishment or refrain from its use. Responses to parents learned at home become further developed and reinforced in churches, schools, and other organizations. These experiences set the stage for the development of work attitudes and values, all affected by parental influence, socio-economic background, sociocultural factors, and personality.

During this socialization period, you have experiences that affect later feelings about work [9, 10]. Toward the end of this period, around 18 to 20 years of age, you begin to separate from family and early friends, and take steps toward independence and into the adult world. Preliminary organizational and career choices are made, and usually some commitment to training of some kind. Those who attend college pick a major, some join the military, others go into vocational training, or take entry-level work positions.

Parental influence

One way that parental influence has an effect on what career you choose is whether the child-rearing practices of the parents lead to an orientation "toward people" or "not toward people" [11, 12]. A person who has developed an orientation toward people is likely to have a career in the service industry, business, or in the arts and entertainment; they are likely to have come from a home in which there was a loving, over-protective environment [13]. Those whose early home atmosphere was one in which there was avoidance by the parents and, perhaps, rejection, are likely to be oriented "not toward others," and seek careers in science, technology, or in some form of work in the outdoors.

Socioeconomic factors

Your social class (upper, middle, or lower), family income, occupational status, and education levels also affect work orientations. First, parents from higher social classes tend to earn more and have better connections that they can use to help their children [14]. Second, children from higher social classes usually aspire to careers in business or in the professions, while children from lower-class families tend to believe that they will work in service trades. Third, children initially aspire to a career similar to that of the father and other family members (mothers and grandparents) and are likely to choose one that resembles it [13]. This, of course, is determined to some extent by the educational opportunities available, which are most often dependent on family income.

Higher social classes also pass different work values on to their children from those in lower social classes. For example, fathers from the upper classes place a higher value on self-direction and less value on conformity, while the opposite is true for fathers from the lower classes [15]. One way that this is reflected is in the ways that young managers from a higher socioeconomic status react to career mentoring at work. Those from higher socioeconomic backgrounds who had good career mentoring had higher promotion rates and pay than those from lower socioeconomic backgrounds who had similarly good mentoring [16]. More than likely, they are able to capitalize at work on what they learned in early years from their family experience.

Preliminary work socialization

You begin to develop more specific orientations toward a certain career – or orientations relevant to a particular type of organization – during **preliminary work socialization** before beginning a career in a work organization. This occurs in three ways:

1 You begin to develop some specific competence.
2 You experience some degree of occupational socialization.
3 You make choices about your first place of work.

The early phase of this aspect of work socialization occurs from age 17 to about 33 [17]. During this period, the center of your life will probably shift from your family to your own world. You become immersed in a career and in an organization, but as an apprentice, a novice, a beginner, learning the relevant skills, attitudes, and culture of a specific organization and a specific job.

Occupational competence is developed as you make early choices about what knowledge and skills to acquire. Becoming competent in an occupation and learning the ropes takes several years. For instance, even great artists and chess players do not achieve prominence until they have worked at their craft for at least ten years [18]. You can expect the same thing for your work career. By the end of this stage, however, if you have worked at it, you can achieve a level of competence so that you can be a full contributor to an organization.

For some careers, **occupational socialization** begins in professional school, where the would-be professional is first exposed to the perspectives, values, and ways of thinking characteristic to the chosen field. Students in clinical psychology or architecture, for example, not only learn technical aspects of their field but also learn how to act like psychologists and architects, as they work on projects or as psychology or architectural interns.

Sometimes occupational socialization can be a very controlled process, such as happens in medical schools, seminaries, convents, and military academies. If you were to choose these careers, you would find yourself, in the early years, separated from other parts of society and becoming submerged in the organizational culture as well as learning the skills of the profession. Professional values are fostered by participation in student groups, by taking courses, and through interaction with teachers. After successfully completing this training, the person is admitted to the field and is commissioned, ordained, or passes through some other acceptance ritual. By this time, important organizational and occupational values have become deeply embedded.

On the other hand, most preliminary work socialization is less formal, such as your experience in secondary schools, universities, and colleges and sometimes what you learn in a part-time job during your early years. These less formal and less controlled forms of occupational socialization do not have as strong effects, but they still shape later work experiences.

Organizational socialization

After you have joined a work organization, organizational socialization begins: adapting to the unique culture of the organization. Among the important things learned as a result of organizational socialization are lessons about the norms and expectations of organizational members. These norms and expectations are reflected specifically in the **psychological contract**, the mutual expectations between an organization and its members. "These expectations not only cover how much work is to be performed for how much pay but also involve the whole pattern of rights, privileges, and obligation between the worker and organization" [19]. The psychological contract is informally and continuously negotiated throughout the organization socialization process and during your career in the organization. It is an important and useful concept that you will see in later chapters.

There are two types of organizational norms learned through the socialization process. The most important are called **pivotal norms**, those that must be accepted by everyone in the organization. Failure to comply with pivotal norms results in pressures to leave from others in the organization [19]. For example, an important and large retailing organization has a "customer is right" norm for returning purchases. A salesperson who questions and angers a customer is very likely to be fired. **Peripheral norms** are less important. They are desired, but it is not essential that the person accept them. An example of a peripheral norm is the recent custom of "dress down Friday," a day on which employees in professional offices may, if they wish, wear more casual clothes instead of coats and ties for the men, or skirts and jackets for the women.

The first significant exposure to the organization's norms and expectations in the psychological contract comes during the phase of organizational entry, the time after you join the organization and experience it for the first time as one of its members. It is a period when you become aware of what differences exist, if any, between your personal values and the requirements of the organization. This can be a disrupting experience as you face changes, contrasts and a few surprises, and have to make some sense of all this [20].

Organization entry is affected by a number of factors. One is the **person–organization fit**, the congruence between patterns of organizational values and your own individual values. When this fit is good, you are likely to be more satisfied and have stronger intentions to stay in the firm [21]. A second factor is the expectations that you bring to the job. Before starting the job, most people have positive but often inaccurate expectations about the company, working conditions, co-workers, and opportunities for advancement. When these expectations are not met, the results are lower job satisfaction, lower organization commitment, higher intentions to leave, lower organization tenure, and lower performance [22].

The form of the organization socialization process itself is a third factor. For example, persons may be brought in with a group and experience group socialization, while in other instances they come in singly, one at a time [23]. Group socialization is often used when large numbers of recruits are brought into an organization at one time. Indeed, many firms have extensive management training programs to socialize college graduates who all join the firm following spring graduation. One study found that those who entered in group socialization were more satisfied with their job and had less conflict between their job and family roles as compared to those who were brought in individually [24].

ORGANIZATIONAL COMMITMENT AND ACCOMMODATION

After being in an organization for a while, you eventually reach some level of psychological and behavioral commitment and accommodation to it. This is not to say that you will have high job satisfaction and be highly committed to the organization itself. It only means that a balance has been achieved between the way that you relate to the organization and the way that it relates with you.

Accommodating to an organization is usually expressed in two ways:

1 One is how willing you are to meet the norms of task, contextual, and ethical performance requirements. This is a very basic and key aspect because it means that you can perform your job at least well enough that the organization sees your performance contribution as good enough.

2 The second aspect of accommodation is that you achieve some level of organizational commitment. **Organizational commitment** is the degree to which you identify with the organization, relative to other factors that affect you at work, such as the work itself or factors outside the organization that compete with it for your commitment and identification.

Organizational commitment is a multidimensional concept. This means that there are at least three facets that pull on you from the work perspective and that you will have some level of identification, or orientation, toward each. As we have pointed out earlier, this results from your socialization experiences both before and after you enter a work organization. These three facets of commitment can be easily understood if you refer to the three organizational personality orientations that were introduced in the previous chapter: the **organizationalist**, the **professional**, and the **indifferent**.

It is useful to think of these three orientations as a commitment profile. It is unlikely that a person would be oriented toward only one of the facets and not toward any of the others [24]. Instead, it is probably safer to say:

1 At any one time, you may have a dominant focus of commitment. For example, a person could have a strong organizational commitment, but have a weak professional commitment and indifferent foci.

2 The dominant orientation at the time of job choice will affect the kind of position you seek. If you have a strong organizationist focus, you are likely to seek a position in an organization that offers you opportunity for career advancement *within* the firm. If you have a strong professional orientation, you will be looking for work that will give you plenty of freedom to work in your chosen work area.

3 The focus of commitment may change over time. There are many circumstances that may lead you to change. For example, if you start with a strong

organizational focus but find that you are passed over several times for promotion, that orientation may diminish and an indifferent orientation might become stronger as your positive reinforcement from the organization is reduced.

There are different motivations for sustaining the identification you have with an organization, regardless of your organizational personality. Those who have studied organizational commitment have identified three different reasons for, or bases of, commitment [25]:

1 Continuance commitment
2 Affective commitment
3 Normative commitment.

Continuance commitment means that you stay with an organization because you feel you cannot afford to leave. You might not be able to find a higher-paying job; you might believe that to leave you will be working in a company with lower status or reputation; or you might not want to lose the long-term investment that you have made that will be paid off in terms of a good set of retirement benefits.

Affective commitment means that you identify strongly with the organization because it stands for what you stand for; you believe strongly in its goals and objectives. For example, many whose work careers are with political parties make that choice because their own political beliefs and those espoused by the party are the same.

Normative commitment means that you stay with an organization because of pressures from others in your life who think you should be there. For example, you might work in the same company that your mother or father worked in for many years, simply because they made it clear to you that they believe this is the best place for you to work.

Table 3.1 shows how these different types of commitment and the organizational personality orientations may be related. For example, you can see that a person with a professional orientation may have continuance commitment, affective commitment, or normative commitment. Obviously, when the basis of commitment is not consistent with the organizational personality orientation, you can expect some uneasiness and stress to occur.

As you might expect, a high level of organizational commitment is something that most firms would like to see in their employees have because it reduces some managerial problems. For example, strong organizational commitment is related to lower turnover and absenteeism [26] and to the level of contextual behaviors, or organizational citizenship activities, that a person is willing to engage in at work [27].

Table 3.1 Organizational personality orientations and different bases of commitment

Bases of commitment	Organizational personality orientation		
	Organizationist	Professional	Indifferent
Affective	you have been positively reinforced over your work career by pay increases and promotion for your performance and loyalty	you are a specialist working in an organization whose major product is what you do occupationally, e.g. pharmacologist in a pharmaceutical firm	you are not likely to have high affective commitment
Continuance	you are well paid and in a high-level position but it is unlikely that you would be able to better yourself by changing firms	you are a research scientist in a prestigious university who would like to move to a warmer climate but all of your opportunities are at lesser schools or places with inferior research facilities	you have a job that permits you to spend more time at your real love (fly fishing), so even though the pay is less than you want, you won't leave
Normative	you have a promotion opportunity to another firm located elsewhere but do not accept it because your spouse and family are happy in your present city	you have an opportunity to move to another position with a better research facility but do not move because it would mean leaving your project team and good colleagues	you wouldn't think of moving to another company because the pay is good and most of your family has worked in the same place for the past 30 years

Guide for Managers:
Making Better Judgments

There are a number of things that we can do to make better judgments about attitudes of others in evaluating their suitability for almost everything that goes on in organizations. For example, in interviews, prospective employees are often asked, "How do you feel about working here?" or "How satisfied were you with the type of work that you did in your previous job?" Attitudes are also important when evaluating someone for promotion. We hear comments like, "He doesn't have a good attitude toward affirmative action" or, "He just doesn't believe enough in quality to do the job right." This means that we should be very careful about judging attitudes of others (as well as our own, we might add).

FOCUS ON SPECIFIC, RATHER THAN GENERAL ATTITUDES. Rather than generalizing, such as saying that an employee has a good or a bad attitude, it is better to try to focus on employee attitudes in terms of their more specific objects, such as attitudes toward pay, toward supervision, and so on. This helps you decide what you have to change in the organization, such as modifying the pay system or training supervisors. There is often very little that you can do about these general attitudes, since they may reflect the positive or negative affectivity of the person.

NOTICE DEPTH OF FEELING AND BEHAVIOR. Do not dismiss or underestimate the depth of feeling and the behavior associated with attitudes, values, and beliefs. Don't trivialize the attitudes of others by thinking or telling them that their feelings aren't important. Attitudes are very important to the psychological well-being of people and some are strongly held, especially those linked to the person's self-image. More importantly, they may be related to attitudes, values, and beliefs that are not directly related to work itself.

UNDERSTAND HOW ATTITUDES WORK AT WORK. Negative attitudes toward the job or the organization may lead an employee to want to avoid work or quit, and they may do so because job satisfaction is negatively related to turnover and to commitment. However, never assume that a satisfied employee is always a productive employee or that a productive employee is satisfied. There is a weak relationship between attitudes and task performance, though it is statistically significant.

PERIODICALLY ASSESS EMPLOYEE ATTITUDES AND SATISFACTION. It is a good idea for organizations to evaluate attitudes and satisfaction with employee surveys. It is also useful to involve the employees in the design, collection, and interpretation of the study. However, never conduct surveys unless you are fully committed to act on the findings and report the actions you have taken.

ACCEPT PEOPLE'S TENDENCY TO JUSTIFY, RATIONALIZE, AND EXPLAIN THEIR BELIEFS. It helps them reduce cognitive dissonance, and appear consistent to themselves and others. However, you should strive to ensure that they understand as clearly as possible what is expected in terms of work performance and that you can accept their attitudes so long as they do not have negative effects on others or on their own performance.

SUMMARY

Attitudes refer to what people like and dislike; they predispose them to act favorably or unfavorably toward an object or event. They function in several ways to help people to adapt to their world. Attitudes are related to beliefs and values, all of which are acquired from infancy through our experiences and associations with people, events, and the media. Specific attitudes can be learned at any time and applied to any experience. Employee attitudes about various aspects of their job are often studied by employers, because it is known that attitudes affect attendance, retention, work commitments, interpersonal relationships. They affect satisfaction, performance, and constructive voluntary contributions to organizational success. They can make a huge difference in the effectiveness of an organization.

There are a number of different factors that contribute to our attitudes about our work life. Child-rearing practices that affect the individual's personality and self-concept can be important early influences. Work socialization is how individuals must learn about the characteristics and culture of their chosen occupational field. Organizational socialization is the process of learning about the norms of our work organization. These may be directly taught by others, may be learned through the process of observing others, or may be learned through the process of conditioning – by behaving in certain ways and having such behaviors responded to in different ways by others.

If we don't adjust well to our job or the organization in which we work, it can negatively affect an individual's performance, morale, and health as well as those of others associated with them, both at work as well as family members and friends.

REFERENCES

1 Katz, D. 1960. The Functional Approach to the Study of Attitude Change. *Public Opinion Quarterly*, **24**: 163–204.

2 Judge, T. A., J. W. Boudreau, and R. D. Bretz. 1994. Job and Life Attitudes of Executives. *Journal of Applied Psychology*, **79**(5): 767–82.

3 George, J. M. and G. R. Jones. 1996. The Experience of Work and Turnover Intentions: Interactive Effects of Value Attainment, Job Satisfaction and Positive Mood. *Journal of Applied Psychology*, **81**(3): 318–26.

4 Fishbein, M. and I. Ajzen. 1975. *Belief, Attitude, Intention and Behavior. An Introduction to Theory and Research*. Reading, MA: Addison-Wesley.

5 Festinger, L. 1957. *A Theory of Cognitive Dissonance*. Evanston, IL: Row, Peterson.

6 Staw, B. M. and J. Ross. 1987. Knowing when to Pull the Plug. *Harvard Business Review*, 68–74.

7 Staw, B. M. and J. Ross. 1987. Behavior in Escalation Situations: Antecedents, Prototypes, and Solutions. In L. L. Cummings and B. M. Staw, eds., *Research in Organizational Behavior*, 39–78. Greenwich, CT: JAI Press.

8 Staw, B. M. 1976. Knee-Deep in the Big Muddy: A Study of Escalating Commitment to a Chosen Course of Action. *Organizational Behavior and Human Performance*, **16**: 27–44.

9 Pulakos, E. D. and N. Schmitt. 1983. A Longitudinal Study of a Valence Model for the Prediction of Job Satisfaction of New Employees. *Journal of Applied Psychology*, **68**: 307–12.

10 Staw, B. M., B.N.E., and J. A. Clausen. 1986. The Dispositional Approach to Job Attitudes: A Lifetime Longitudinal Test. *Administrative Science Quarterly*, **31**(1): 56–77.

11 Roe, A. 1957. Early Determinants of Occupational Choice. *Journal of Counseling Psychology*, **4**: 212–17.

12 Roe, A. and M. Seigelman. 1964. *The Origin of Interests*. The SPGS Inquiry Series. Vol. 1. Washington, DC: American Personnel and Guidance Association.

13 Osipow, S. H. 1973. *Theories of Career Development*. 2nd edn. New York: Appleton-Century-Crofts.

14 Tinto, V. 1984. Patterns of Educational Sponsorship to Work. *Work and Occupations*, **11**(3): 309–30.

15 Kohn, M. L. and C. Schooler. 1969. Class, Occupation, and Orientation. *American Sociological Review*, **34**: 659–78.

16 Whitely, W., T. W. Daughterty, and G. F. Dreher. 1991. Relationship of Career Mentoring and Socioeconomic Origin to Managers' and Professionals' Early Career Progress. *Academy of Management Journal*, **34**(2): 331–50.

17 Levinson, D., et al. 1978. *Seasons of a Man's Life*. New York: Ballantine Books.

18 Simon, H. A. 1982. *Solving Problems and Expertise. in Symposium*. University of Florida.

19 Schein, E. A. 1970. *Organizational Psychology*. New York: Prentice-Hall.

20 Louis, M. R. 1980. Surprise and Sense Making: What Newcomers Experience in Entering Unfamiliar Organization Settings. *Administrative Science Quarterly*, **25**: 226–51.

21 Chatman, J. 1991. Matching People and Organizations: Selections and Socialization in Public Accounting Firms. *Administrative Science Quarterly*, **36**: 469–84.

22 Wanous, J. P. et al. 1992. The Effects of Met Expectations on Newcomer Attitudes and Behaviors: A Review and Meta-Analysis. *Journal of Applied Psychology*, **77**(3): 288–97.

23 Van Maanen, J. 1978. People Processing: Strategies of Organizational Socialization. *Organizational Dynamics*, 64–82.

24 Zahrly, J., and H. Tosi 1989. The Differential Effects of Organizational Induction Strategies on Early Work Role Adjustment. *Journal of Organization Behavior*, **10**, 59–74.

25 Dunham, R., J. E. Grube, and M. B. Castaneda. 1994. Organizational Commitment: The Utility of an Integrative Definition. *Journal of Applied Psychology*, **79**(3): 370–81.

26 Lee, T. W., et al. 1996. Commitment Propensity, Organizational Commitment and Voluntary Turnover: A Longitudinal Study of Organizational Entry Processes. *Journal of Management*, **18**(1): 15–33.

27 Organ, D. W. 1997. Organizational Citizenship Behavior: It's Construct Clean Up Time. *Human Performance*, **10**(2): 85–97.

CHAPTER 4

Individual Perception, Judgment, and Attribution

FUNDAMENTALS OF PERCEPTION

JUDGMENT BIASES AND ERRORS

ATTRIBUTION THEORY: FINDING CAUSES OF BEHAVIOR

SOME ORGANIZATIONAL IMPLICATIONS OF PERCEPTUAL AND ATTRIBUTIONAL BIASES

Opening Fig.

In the Old Testament book of Kings, Solomon was known for the great wisdom he demonstrated when making judgments. The most common story exemplifying his wisdom and judgment concerns the case of two women who appeared before him arguing over a child who both mothers claimed was theirs. Solomon ordered that the child be cut in half so that each mother could have a part of the child. One mother objected and agreed to give the child to the other mother. Solomon knew quickly that this was the actual mother.

A deeper look at Solomon's judgment in this case suggests that at the core of this wisdom was an exceptional knowledge of human behavior. Solomon probably never intended to actually kill the child, instead he wanted to watch the reaction of the mothers, believing that from their behavior he could draw conclusions about which was the true mother. While their decisions do not typically involve life or death, managers make myriad judgments each day and certainly wish for the "Wisdom of Solomon." In this chapter we will consider the underlying individual processes of perception, judgment, and attribution that are critical elements of making wise managerial decisions.

FUNDAMENTALS OF PERCEPTION

Perception is the psychological process of creating an internal picture of the external world. It is the way that we organize information about people and things, the attribution of properties to them on the basis of the information and the way we make cause/effect attributions about them. It is a process of interpreting what information our senses provide to us so as to give meaning to the environment we are in. The resulting interpretation is the perceiver's reality, and even though several people may observe the same environment the perception of it can vary widely from person to person. Perception is a dynamic process, a search for the best interpretation of available data, though that does not necessarily mean that the interpretation is an accurate one. For example, optical illusions are a good example of how what things seem to be is not the same as what they are.

In this next section, we focus on the feeling and thinking aspects of perception and then we examine how our perceptions affect behavior. We discuss the perceiver, the event or object being perceived, and the situational context in which the perception occurs. Figure 4.1 illustrates these elements and shows that they interact to determine both the interpretation and the action that takes place.

The way we perceive is learned, and what we learn affects our perception. **Selection** is at the heart of the perceptual process, and it is driven by our personal

55

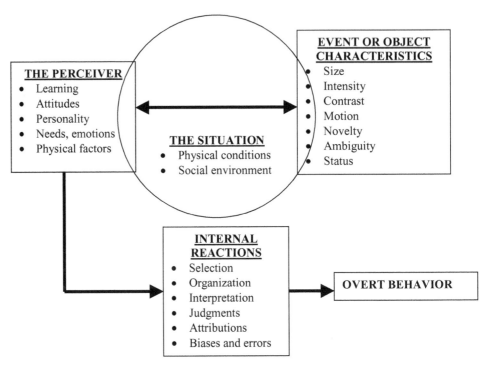

Figure 4.1   A model of the perceptual process

characteristics, attributes of the object itself, and the situation in which perception takes place. For example, Inuits have no concept that corresponds to what most people call snow. They actually perceive different kinds of snow depending on its particular characteristics and its potential uses, and have several concepts for it. There is good reason for this: their survival depends upon snow. This means that out of the many stimuli that bombard people, only a few actually penetrate and become part of their experience and are used in making judgments. The remaining stimuli are excluded.

Another powerful mechanism is **perceptual organization**. Information has an expected pattern that we have learned from our past experiences: a pattern that might be very general and abstract or very specific and detailed. These patterns are called categories, or **schemas**. As you are exposed to information in the environment, you tend to group certain stimuli into patterns so that they become meaningful wholes rather than fragmented parts. The way that they are grouped depends upon your schemas. An example is the words that you are now reading. The separate letters are ignored in favor of the whole word. Another example is the inclination to see physical patterns. It takes only three dots for us to see a triangle and four to see a rectangle or square.

Suppose one of your subordinates is late for work and is working slowly, producing below par. You are going to organize these facts in a way that makes sense to you, perhaps that slow work and lateness go together. Perhaps your schema about this set of information is that it reflects lack of caring and indifference. You may explain the behavior, then, in terms of laziness and irresponsibility. You would also seek consistency in surrounding events. Irresponsibility explanations would be reinforced if there was union trouble in the plant and you believed the worker was slowing down under union pressure. However, if there were no union problems and you believed the worker was a loyal employee, it would be more consistent to believe his or her behavior was due to a temporary condition, such as an illness.

Physical and emotional states can also shape and determine our reality. When a person is hungry, sights and sounds that point to food tend to become salient. Emotional states can distort perception, as in the example of the level of excitability of eyewitnesses to a crime. Eyewitness perceptions may be so inaccurate that one must wonder why they are relied on so often [1]. Some eyewitnesses report things that never happened, and overlook both small details and glaring stimuli. For example, some may fail to see a bright red shirt or hear an important statement made by a person committing a crime.

Characteristics of the event or object

Certain attributes of events and objects affect whether they are perceived and how they are perceived. Some are:

1 **Size** has an effect: larger objects are more likely to be seen than smaller ones.
2 **Intensity** of stimuli is another factor: particularly loud noises are likely to be heard, and bright or shining objects will likely be seen.
3 **Contrast effects** also affect perception, so anything that stands out against its background is more likely to be attended to. Motion and novelty also facilitate perception: a moving object or unusual things draw attention. Experts in advertising creatively manipulate such characteristics of objects and apply them to magazine and newspaper ads, to billboards, and to radio and television commercials.
4 **Ambiguity** also has an impact on perceptions. Ambiguous or incomplete events are actually more subject to personal interpretation. Ambiguity is discomforting, and can be reduced by adding meaning to the stimuli or attributing motives to a person associated with the stimuli. For example, after interviewers talk to an applicant for a job, they often draw conclusions that are not justified by the applicant's behavior. They often fill in gaps about the applicant's past experience, and do it in a way that confirms their good feelings or negative suspicions about a candidate with no good reason.
5 **Characteristics of other people** affect perception. One example of this is how the status of a person affects perception. Higher-status people are more likely to be noticed, and they usually are perceived to be more knowledgeable, accurate, and believable.

Situational effects

Under **different conditions**, the same cues can easily result in different perceptions. Imagine seeing a person holding a knife in a kitchen in which food is being prepared for a meal. Now imagine the same person holding a knife the same way in the middle of a public demonstration. The knife is often unnoticed in the kitchen setting but would be prominent in the demonstration. Furthermore, your predictions about what might happen would probably be different for each situation.

Perceptions can also be affected by the **presence of another person**. Suppose your boss criticizes you in the presence of a higher-level manager. You might conclude that your boss is seeking favor from the higher manager. If the higher manager is absent, you are less likely to draw such a conclusion. In short, perceptions occur in a context, which predisposes us to expect certain events and lends an additional ingredient to how we interpret, judge, and react.

JUDGMENT BIASES AND ERRORS

Perception plays a huge role in how accurate we are in the conclusions and judgments we make about others. Of particular interest are judgments that distort or misrepresent the facts, or that disagree with the perceptions of others. Distortions and disagreement are at the root of a host of problems in managing people. There are several human tendencies that lead to inaccurate or unreliable judgments.

For managers, the most important **perceptual biases** are those that arise in relationships with other people. There are many such situations at work: performance appraisals, selection interviewing, group meetings, customer relations, and so on [2]. Perceptual biases create distortions that are particularly crucial to understand. Once understood, it is easier to overcome judgment errors [3].

First impressions

Strong and lasting impressions of others tend to be formed very early in a relationship. Since early interactions are usually of a short duration, these early impressions may be based on very limited information. This tendency is a critical problem because first impressions are often lasting ones. In other words, we use only a few cues when judging others, and then continue to maintain the judgment.

There are two reasons why first impressions are so strong: the principles of closure and consistency. The **principle of closure** is that humans need a relatively complete conception, or idea, about things. The **principle of consistency** is that the conception should be congruent with other attitudes, perceptions, and beliefs. Suppose you meet someone for the first time. It is very difficult to know most of the things that you should know to form an accurate impression. What happens is that you focus on those cues that strike you as important at the time and then use these as a basis for "completing" your picture of the person. When this happens, you no longer have limited information, but a fairly full model of the other person, made up of the relatively few cues gathered in your first impression and those that you added to it, which will be consistent with the first information. Later information obtained about the person should be evaluated against this more complete image that you have created, but because you have created this more complete concept now, it becomes difficult to change it when you receive new information.

Halo: one characteristic tells all

The use of one or a few characteristics of a person to affect the evaluation of other characteristics is called the **halo effect**. Many people find a particular attribute that they like or dislike strongly in others. For example, if how one dresses is an important concern for a person, it can become a dominant basis to make biased judgments about others – positive or negative – if the halo effect is operating. How another person dresses would determine their overall evaluation. We see this often in the case of employment interviews when the interviewer makes a judgment that a job candidate is dressed in a way that seems consistent with the dress norms of the company. The interviewer assumes because the candidate is dressed well she will fit well in the firm and, during the interview, has his or her other judgments are colored by this factor.

Halo is likely to be related to our own self-image. We tend to have very positive evaluations of those who possess characteristics we believe we have. A manager who is always on time for work is more favorably disposed toward subordinates who are punctual; they may be negatively disposed toward those who arrive late.

Projection

Projection is a psychological mechanism by which people attribute their own traits to others. Sometimes the trait is one that we like in ourselves. For example, we might attribute potential success to an interview applicant because we discover that she, like us, pays particular attention to spelling and neatness on her résumé and other application materials. Sometimes the trait is one we dislike in ourselves. For example, we might blame a co-worker's mistake on sloppiness when sloppiness is one of our own faults. If others do not possess what we project onto them, our behavior is governed by the false impression, and further misperceptions will likely follow.

Implicit personality theory

Statements such as "honest people are also hard-working," "late sleepers are lazy," or "quiet people are devious" all link together two characteristics of a person. When

59

we make such linkages, we are creating our own **implicit personality theory**. Any of the linkages could be wrong. Hard work and honesty need not go together. The late sleeper might have a medical problem. The quiet person might simply be shy. Engaging in implicit personality theory is amateur psychology at its worst. It is much safer to link two characteristics together only if we witness both characteristics on repeated occasions.

Stereotyping

In **stereotyping**, we link characteristics of people to characteristics of a group with which we associate them. Surely not all members of a given group possess the characteristic they are said to have, yet stereotyping is common and widespread. It persists because it is useful, and helps us to organize the world around us. Often, however, stereotyping is nothing more than a perpetuation of old myths and prejudices. It is fed by prejudices and ambiguity, and sometimes by fear or threat, and reinforced in many ways. For example, if we know that someone is Italian, we might conclude he is emotional and likes pasta and good wine; if he is Irish, we might conclude he drinks whiskey and is prone to be quick-tempered. Countless other examples exist, often very negative. Ethnic groups, older people, men, women, lawyers, used-car sales person, or just about any other group can be stereotyped.

Stereotypes also appear in our language, in words such as "chairman" or "cleaning woman." They are often so embedded in society that they are difficult to change. Think of how women are portrayed in many television commercials and movies. Women's rights organizations spend much time and energy fighting to try to change stereotypes. It is a fact, however, that members of groups do share certain values and beliefs, and will exhibit similar traits or behaviors. In some cases, therefore, it is quite safe to draw conclusions about people based on their group membership. We are usually correct in concluding that professional athletes are healthy, or that the average woman cannot lift as much weight as the average man can lift. However, even these generalizations require qualification and have to be carefully stated. For example, there are women who can out-perform men in lifting weights.

ATTRIBUTION THEORY: FINDING CAUSES OF BEHAVIOR

It is human nature to want to explain the causes of our own and others' behavior. An unexplainable event can leave us in a state of dissonance and that motivates us to try to explain the situation to reduce the dissonance. If we know why something happened, it helps us decide how to react to an event. Suppose our supervisor gives us an unpleasant assignment. If we see the assignment as caused by unfairness, we are tempted to fight it. If we attribute the cause to a higher manager's wishes, we might have a different reaction to the whole situation.

Attribution theory explains why and how we determine these causes. It focuses on key errors people make in attributing causes. The attributions are judgments that subsequently affect our feelings, our behavior, and the conclusions we draw about our experiences. Wrong inferences about causation will create problems similar to those created by perceptual errors.

Judging other people's behavior

Earlier we pointed out that behavior is determined by the person and the environment, but when we judge others, we have a strong tendency to attribute causes of behavior to the internal characteristics of the person. This is called the **fundamental attribution error** [4], overestimating the role of the person relative to the environment as a cause of behavior. Thus if we see people steal, we are more likely to characterize them as dishonest than to conclude that their family is starving.

We have a tendency to underestimate the situation as a cause of behavior even when we know the person was forced or instructed to behave as he or she did. For instance, if we observe a debate in which participants are assigned to defend a defined position, we will most likely attribute their arguments to their beliefs rather than to the debating rules they are following. Somehow, what people say or do, even under instructions or other situational pressures, leads us to conclude more about them than about the situation. Perhaps this is because we see the situational influences as operating through people and not independent of them.

Guide for Managers:
USING THEORIES OF PERCEPTION AND OF THE ATTRIBUTION OF CAUSES AND EFFECTS

Theories of perception and of the attribution of causes and effects are also useful to managers. Think about problem-solving, for example. We can solve only those problems of which we are aware, or perceive. But beyond simply recognizing that a problem exists we are faced with the question, "What is the cause?" The same is true for evaluating the performance of another. We need to know why performance is high or low. Here are some ways to sharpen your perceptions and attributions.

DON'T ASSUME YOUR REALITY IS ANOTHER PERSON'S REALITY. Perceptions of events (selecting, interpreting, organizing) will vary from person to person, and become each person's individual reality. Many things affect the accuracy of a perception. It pays to seek confirmation of events. If you are part of a group trying to solve a problem, try to find a consensus definition of the situation. Be careful, however, not to be stampeded into an agreed upon, but wrong, set of perceptions.

KEEP THE COMMON JUDGMENT TENDENCIES IN MIND. You can

There are several reasons for the fundamental attribution error. First, if you believe that the other person has free choice in the situation, you are more likely to attribute causality to him or her personally. This makes sense, because you can conclude that the person was free to do otherwise, but chose to act as he or she did. Second, you are more likely to attribute internal motives to people when they take action you view as important, and especially when those actions affect you personally. Suppose someone dents your car in a parking lot but leaves the scene before you appear. You would characterize them unfavorably for failing to leave a note or call a police officer. If, however, you seek a situational cause, you might speculate that he or she had to rush home to take care of a dire emergency.

There are several other factors that affect our attributions about others [5]:

reduce the common errors that lead to inaccurate assessments by not rushing to judgments based on stereotyping, halo, and so on. These can be reduced through training and other techniques that seek factual data from several sources. Also remember that the self-serving bias is widespread and impossible to eliminate; it must be accepted as a factor in interpreting what other people say and do. Also don't forget that it applies to you yourself.

FIGHT THE FUNDAMENTAL ATTRIBUTION ERROR. Seek environmental or situational causes to explain someone's behavior instead of blaming their personality. This is particularly important wherever judgment tendencies and errors are causing problems, such as when women, minorities or any employee is unfairly treated as a consequence. Examples may be found in how performance appraisals, task assignments or promotion decisions are made.

1   **Consistency**. If a person behaves the same way in similar situations, we are more likely to see the behavior as internally motivated, such as when a friend is almost always late.

2   **Distinctiveness**. Distinctive behaviors are those that are relatively unique to a situation. If a behavior is more distinctive, we are less likely to make internal attributions. If our friend was always on time, we are apt to evaluate a lateness as due to some unforeseen difficulty thrust on them.

3   **Consensus**. When the person we are judging acts differently than others act in the situation, we are more likely to think of that person's behavior as internally motivated.

4   **Privacy of the act**. Actions that are taken in the absence of other people are more likely to be judged as internally motivated. When others are present, we might attribute the action to social pressure. When people are alone, we attribute the action to them.

5   **Status**. In general, higher-status people are seen to be more personally responsible for their actions. They are thought to have more control over their own

actions and decisions and do things because they choose to, not because they have to.

One important reason for making the fundamental attribution error – as well as the use of first impressions, halo, projection, stereotyping, and the use of implicit personality theory – has to do with the way that we process information. Recall that we said earlier that perception has to do with how we organize information. We often make these errors because we use **automatic information-processing**. This means that when we recognize some key information, or stimulus, we recall schemas or categories into which that particular information fits and our judgment is then biased toward the general characteristics of that category. Take the use of stereotypes as an example. Suppose we have a negative stereotype of lawyers, and then we learn that a dinner guest is a lawyer. If we automatically use our occupational stereotype, then we are likely to attribute all of the negative aspects of the stereotype to him, without ever having taken the time to learn anything more about him. Automatic processing obviously occurs in performance evaluation, and is more likely to occur when a rater observes positive performance. Then they are more likely to attribute other positive characteristics to the person that have not been observed and to make relatively quick judgments [6].

To avoid the fundamental attribution error and the other perceptual problems, it is necessary to use a "controlled" approach to information-processing. In the **controlled information-processing** approach, we pause and reflect on the situation as well as the person and try to identify both the situational forces and the personal causes of behavior before making our judgment. This approach requires searching for more information. While this can complicate and delay matters, it may lead to a more accurate and less biased judgment. This is what raters will do when they observe negative performance of a person being rated [6]: they tend to take more time and have more accurate recall of the negative aspects of the person's performance.

Judging our own behavior

Self-judgments are affected by a **self-serving bias** – a tendency to perceive oneself favorably. People credit themselves when they succeed but blame external factors when they fail [7]. Success is usually attributed to hard work, ability, and good judgment. Failure, on the other hand, is attributed to bad luck, unfair conditions, or impossible odds. If you play golf, for example, think what happens when you are playing a close match. When your opponent makes a long putt, you tell her, "You're lucky." When you make a long putt, it is because of your skill.

Self-serving attributions and self-congratulatory comparisons operate in many ways. We tend to overrate ourselves on nearly any factor that is subjective and socially desirable [8], seeing ourselves as better than average in intelligence, leadership ability, health, life expectancy, interpersonal skill, and so on. We believe flattery more readily than we believe criticism. We overestimate how well we would act in a given situation and overestimate the accuracy of our judgments. For example, a psychologist who is well known for his work in the development of selection tests and who advocates their widespread use was asked what he thought about a candidate for a position at his department. He had only talked in a very general way for about thirty minutes with the candidate, who was not selected through the use of any test. When asked what he thought of the candidate, he replied without hesitation, "We shouldn't hire him. He will never work out here. I could tell it in the first five minutes of our discussion." This is a good example of how he trusted his own selection judgment without the test, but it is likely that he would not trust the judgment of others unless selection tests had been used.

When we deal with others, we often see our own actions as externally justified, but attribute others' actions to their internal disposition. You are angered by your boss because you were provoked by a "stupid" order that he or she gave. However, when your boss is angry with you, it is attributed to his or her "neurotic personality." The objective truth hardly matters, and the self-serving attributions persist even in the face of contrary evidence.

Interestingly, the self-serving bias seems to be strongest among people with high self-esteem. People with low self-esteem are more self-deprecating and engage in self-blame rather than blaming external events for failure. They are less likely to exhibit the self-serving bias. On the other hand, when low-self-esteem people have a strong need for respect, they could be more likely than the average person to exhibit the self-serving bias. This is why some people constantly talk about their own activities, exploits, and successes. The self-serving bias acts as a boastful cover for their feelings of low self-esteem and is an attempt to gain recognition and thus to enhance self-esteem.

SOME ORGANIZATIONAL IMPLICATIONS OF PERCEPTUAL AND ATTRIBUTIONAL BIASES

We have already given several examples of how perceptual distortions and attribution biases can affect people at work. We now discuss three specific areas that should be specially noted:

1 Problem-solving and decision-making
2 Performance appraisal
3 Managing workplace diversity.

Problem-solving and decision-making

Effective management requires making good decisions when solving problems, and effective problem-solving requires identifying the most likely cause of the problem. The importance of correct problem identification is obvious: trying to solve the wrong problem will not correct the situation and biased attributions can occur in identifying problems. For example, a committee will blame other groups or departments when problems occur. Here, the self-serving bias can damage cooperation between groups and fail to uncover the true causes of the problem. Another difficulty in problem identification occurs because we tend, when looking at difficult situations, to interpret them in terms of our own experiences and capacity to solve problems. For example, when faced with identifying problems to be solved in a complex business situation, managers have a tendency to define the problem in ways that reflect their own functional competence than other functional areas [9, 10]. This means, for example, a human resource manager is more likely to perceive a problem to be based on personnel deficiencies while a production manager is likely to see the problem as having more technical issues that must be solved. There are a couple of reasons for this. First, our experiences provide the framework which we use in analyzing problems. Second, if the problem is defined in terms of our own expertise, then we are more likely to be involved in solving it – and this might result in a more positive impression of ourselves by others.

Performance appraisal

Attribution biases operate very strongly in performance appraisal. The attribution errors can create serious disagreements between raters and ratees about performance. We tend to look at both effort and ability in evaluating performance – but give more weight to effort [11]. Effort is weighted higher for both good and poor performance: good performance is rated higher and poor performance lower when effort, rather than ability, is seen as the cause. Thus we are evaluated more on how hard someone who is judging us thinks we are trying. If our boss feels we put in a lot of effort, we will be appraised higher when we succeed. If we are seen as not trying very hard, we will be rated more poorly when we fail.

Managing workplace diversity

Perceptual errors are even more critical problems when ethnic or sex differences are added to the situation. The workforce in the USA is now far more multicultural than ever, but still the number of women and minorities in management jobs is underrepresented. One reason for this situation lies in how these groups are evaluated. One evaluation of the research on selection procedures and performance evaluation shows that minorities are rated lower by supervisors [12]. Hiring biases are also affected by other factors such as gender (Latino women suffer less hiring discrimination than Latino men), the source of recruitment (private employment agencies are more discriminatory), the type of job (there is more discrimination for jobs not requiring college degrees), and location of the job (there is greater bias when selecting for inner-city jobs) [13]. However, the bias issue does not exist only in the dominant white male group. For example, a survey of males, females, African Americans, Asian Americans, Native Americans, and Hispanic Americans reveals that there is bias and stereotyping of other groups by these groups. In addition, there is bias and stereotyping within their own groups as, for example, the view of women by men within each group [14].

Other studies uncovered a tendency to attribute female successes to hard work or luck rather than to ability [15]. Men, on the other hand, are more protected from adverse evaluations. Interestingly, both women and men make these biased attributions. Their successes usually are attributed to competence, and their failures to bad luck. Such gender-biased attributions insult women and place them at a disadvantage because they are given less credit than men for their skills. From a woman's perspective, it is better if her successes are attributed to ability, rather than to effort or situational conditions.

SUMMARY

The study of perception is central to understanding how people react. We each have certain perceptual tendencies that define the world from our own personal point of view. Values, emotional states, needs, attitudes, and personality all come into play. Both what we observe and the situation in which we observe it also affect what we select, how we organize what we perceive, and how we make interpretations. Most critical are the errors in judgment we make about the world around us. An important tendency is how we make causal inferences about what we perceive. We tend to attribute other people's behavior to their personality rather than to situational forces. When judging ourselves, however, we are more likely to have a self-serving bias. We also attribute our successes not to external forces, but to our own skills and abilities.

REFERENCES

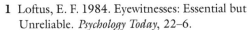

1 Loftus, E. F. 1984. Eyewitnesses: Essential but Unreliable. *Psychology Today*, 22–6.

2 Parsons, C. K. and R. C. Liden. 1984. Interviewer Perceptions of Applicant Qualifications: A Multivariate Study of Demographic Characteristics and Nonverbal Cues. *Journal of Applied Psychology*, **69**: 557–68.

3 Cardy, R. L. and J. F. Kehoe. 1984. Rater Selective Attention, Ability, and Appraisal Effectiveness: The Effect of a Cognitive Style on the Accuracy of Differentiation Among Ratees. *Journal of Applied Psychology*, **69**: 589–94.

4 Ross, L. D. 1977. The Intuitive Psychologist and his Shortcomings: Distortions in the Attribution Process. In L. Berkowitz, ed., *Advances in Experimental Social Psychology*, 174–220. New York: Academic Press.

5 Kelly, H. H. 1973. The Process of Causal Attribution. *American Psychologist*, **28**: 107–28.

6 Kulik, C. T. and M. L. Ambrose. 1993. Category Based and Feature Based Processes in Performance Appraisal: Integrating Visual and Computerized Sources of Performance Data. *Journal of Applied Psychology*, **78**(5): 821–30.

7 Zuckerman, M. 1979. Attribution of Success and Failure Revisited, or the Motivational Bias is Alive and Well in Attribution Theory. *Journal of Personality*, **47**: 247–87.

8 Felson, R. B. 1981. Ambiguity and Bias in the Self-Concept. *Social Psychology Quarterly*, **44**: 64–9.

9 Dearborn, D. C. and H. A. Simon. 1958. Selective Perception: A Note on the Departmental Identifications of Executives. *Sociometry*, **21**: 140–4.

10 Walsh, J. P. 1988. Selectivity and Selective Perception: An Investigation of Managers' Belief Structures and Information Processes. *Academy of Management Journal*, **31**(4): 873–96.

11 Knowlton, W. A., Jr. and T. R. Mitchell. 1980. Effects of Causal Attributions on a Supervisor's Evaluation of Subordinate Performance. *Journal of Applied Psychology*, **65**: 459–66.

12 Martocchio, J. J. and E. M. Whitener. 1992. Fairness in Personnel Selection: A Meta-Analysis and Policy Implications. *Human Relations*, **45**(5): 489–506.

13 Bendick, M. et al. 1991. Discrimination and Latino Job Applicants: A Controlled Experiment. *Human Resource Management*, **30**(4): 469–84.

14 Fernandez, P. 1991. *Managing a Diverse Work Force*. Lexington, MA: Lexington Books.

15 Feldman-Summers, S. and S. B. Kiesler. 1974. Those who are Number Two Try Harder: The Effect of Sex on the Attribution of Causality. *Journal of Personality and Social Psychology*, **30**: 846–55.

CHAPTER 5

Motivation and Performance

MOTIVATION AND PERFORMANCE

THE FUNDAMENTALS OF MOTIVATION AND PERFORMANCE

MOTIVATION: THE CONTENT THEORIES

MOTIVATION: THE PROCESS THEORIES

Suppose that you are the chief education official in your state and you decide that you want to improve the academic performance of students. You believe that the best way to do this is to create financial incentives for teachers. You set about, with experts, to develop a plan to provide cash incentives to teachers when their school's scores on a test to evaluate student performance increase. The idea is simple and straightforward: reward teachers for improved student performance. If it is discovered that student performance drops, a plan is in place to provide the school with administrative and managerial assistance to move it in the right direction.

The idea seems to be going well. For the first several years, you pay out substantial financial bonuses to teachers and schools for very significant test score improvements. However, when the program is critically evaluated, you discover several things. First, you find in evaluating written essays that over 75 percent of the grades are much too generous because exams have been graded by teachers in the school, the very teachers who would receive bonuses if students improve. It is often a case of improvement by reducing grading standards. For the portions of the exam that have been graded by an outside consulting firm, it is discovered that in some schools teachers have done a number of things to help students do better that are outside the realm of normal classroom teaching. For example, some reviewed the questions that were on the test before the test was given. Others permitted the students to ask questions to clarify parts of the exam while they were taking it. Can you analyze what failed in your program?

The above situation is a fairly common result when an organization tries to implement a plan to motivate its members to perform better. You will discover that sometimes, even though you find improvements in results, the reason is that it is the results themselves (like the test scores) that are artificially improved, or maybe it is better to say manipulated. That is, you don't get what you expected. As you read this chapter, you will find some of the answers to the question you have in your mind about this program, in other words, "Why didn't it work?"

MOTIVATION AND PERFORMANCE

One of the first things that you must understand about motivation is that it is not the only important factor that affects performance. Consider this example. Lance Roberts has a burning desire to be a good tennis player. He spends hours practicing, reads all the instructional magazines, regularly takes lessons, and plays

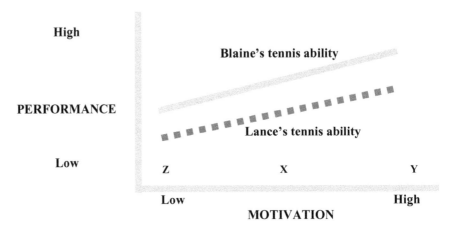

Figure 5.1   The interaction between procedural and outcome justice

a match every day. Blaine Davis is one of Lance's regular weekly matches. Every Wednesday afternoon they play and Blaine usually wins. It is especially frustrating to Lance because Blaine hardly practices and plays only twice, at the most three times, each week.

This example illustrates that performance (or results) is a function of two things: motivation and ability. This is the basis of a very fundamental relationship for understanding human performance in organizations and is shown in the formula below:

$$\text{Performance} = f(\text{Ability} \times \text{Motivation})$$

Figure 5.1 shows how these three factors are related. On one axis is performance and on the other, motivation. The lines in the figure represent the abilities of both men. They show that Lance has less tennis ability than Blaine. Therefore, if both are equally motivated (say at point X), then Blaine will always win. Lance will only win when he has high motivation (at point Y) and Blaine is less motivated (near point Z).

THE FUNDAMENTALS OF MOTIVATION AND PERFORMANCE

What do we mean by performance?

Job performance turns out to be a pretty complicated concept because most jobs have several distinct elements and therefore require several different types of performance. These different elements are called **performance components**, relatively discrete subtasks or behaviors which require different abilities and which might have different motivational predispositions. Jobs, as we discussed in chapter 1, have task performance, contextual performance, and ethical performance components.

- **Task performance components** are what you do to complete the work itself. For example, a plant manager must have the ability and the motivation to manage production and quality levels, prepare work schedules, order supplies, deal with subordinates, and run departmental meetings.

- **Contextual performance components** go beyond task performance and are essential if organizations are to excel, because success depends on employees going beyond formal task performance requirements [1].

- **Ethical performance components** focus on doing the "right" thing in your job.

The role of ability

Ability is the capacity to carry out a set of interrelated behavioral or mental sequences to produce a result. For example, to play the piano requires that you are able to read music, understand chord structures, and have the manual dexterity to finger the keyboard. Generally, it is easy to see ability differences between two individuals; it is often apparent among individuals who perform similar jobs.

It is also important to remember that individuals have different abilities. A person may be a highly skilled architect but have very low communication skills. Since most job performance is multidimensional, it follows that the person who is assigned to do the job must have adequate ability for each different performance component. For example, the plant manager's job involves scheduling work, dealing with subordinates (handling grievances, supervision, etc.), and running departmental meetings. Each of these separate activities requires different skills and a person can be good in some and poor in others.

Ability also differs by level, or how much ability that they actually have. There are different levels of competencies of the type we discussed in chapter 1.

The role of technology

Technology interacts with ability to affect performance, but in different ways. **Technology** refers to the methods, tools, facilities, and equipment a person uses in performing a task. Workers in an auto plant "use" a complex production system with highly independent activities to manufacture a car. An artist's technology may be a canvas, paint, and brushes.

We think it helps to think of any specific task as being either skill-dominated or technology-dominated. In **skill-dominated tasks**, individual skill is the most important factor. A clothing designer's job is an example of skill-dominated work. Giving a designer better equipment is likely to have only a marginal effect on performance, just as giving Blaine and Lance, our tennis players, better rackets and shoes will probably not improve their game very much because tennis, like most sports, is a skill-dominated task.

There are several important things to learn when viewing performance in this way.

1   Specific and different abilities are required for the various parts of a job. A person may be more talented in one performance component and less in another. A quarterback for a football team may be an excellent passer but a very poor runner.
2   A person may be more motivated (willing to put forth more effort) for one performance component than others; the plant manager, for example, might prefer to manage production and quality than spend time in dealing with subordinates.
3   Technology and human skill may be interchangeable. When technology is substituted for human skill, it often leads to more predictable and dependable performance. Take a task so simple as making coffee. Until the introduction of automatic coffee-makers, making a good cup of coffee required a great deal of skill. With the automatic technology, it is a task that a child can do.

What do we mean by motivation?

Motivation has both a psychological and a managerial connotation in the field of organizational behavior. The **psychological meaning of motivation** is the internal mental state of a person that relates to the initiation, direction, persistence, intensity, and termination of behavior [2]. The **managerial meaning of motivation** is the activity of managers to induce others to produce results desired by the organization or, perhaps, by the manager. In this latter context, we might say, "The role of every manager is to motivate employees to work harder or to do better."

Classes of motivation theories

Any motivation theory attempts to account for the reasons why people behave as they do and the processes that cause the behavior.

- Those theories that focus on "what" motivates behavior are called **content theories of motivation**.
- Those theories that focus on "how" behavior is motivated are called **process theories**.

This distinction between content and process theories of motivation highlights the main orientation of a particular formulation about motivation. However, as you will see, content theories have some process orientation and process theories usually have some content dimensions.

MOTIVATION: THE CONTENT THEORIES

Content theories of motivation emphasize the reasons for motivated behavior, that is, "what" causes it. A content theory would explain behavioral aspects in terms of specific human needs or specific factors that "drive" behavior. For example, you might say that "Joan is motivated to work for higher pay" or "John did that because he has a high need for power." In this chapter, we discuss the following content theories:

- Need theories
- Herzberg's two-factor theory
- The job characteristics approach
- McClelland's achievement-power theory.

Need theories

Need theories of motivation assume that people act to satisfy their needs. A need (or a motive) is aroused when the person senses that there is some difference between the present (or, perhaps, a future) condition and some desired state. When a "need" is aroused (say you need to advance at work), you feel some tension and act to reduce it. One way would be to work harder so that you might be promoted. Then the need is satisfied. If it doesn't happen, the desire for promotion may be suppressed and lead to frustration or you might decide to seek a job elsewhere to be promoted.

Maslow's need theory

The most popular need theory of motivation by far is the one developed by Maslow [3]. He believed that human needs could be categorized into five categories:

1 **Physiological needs** are the basic requirements for survival. Humans must have food to live, and shelter is necessary before anything else can assume importance for a person.
2 **Safety needs** reflect a desire for protection against loss of shelter, food, and other basic requirements for survival. Security needs also involve the desire to live in a stable and predictable environment. They may also involve a preference for order and structure.
3 **Belonging needs** reflect the person's desire for love, affection, and belonging. The need to interact with others and have some social acceptance and approval is generally shared by most people. For some, this need may be satisfied by joining groups. Others may find sufficient affection from their family members or other individuals.

73

Figure 5.2   Maslow's Hierarchy of Needs

4   **Esteem needs** are those human desires to be respected by others and for a positive self-image. Individuals strive to increase their status in the eyes of others, to attain a good reputation or a high ranking in a group. Self-confidence is increased when self-esteem needs are satisfied. When self-esteem needs are thwarted, feelings of inferiority or weakness often result.

5   **Self-actualization needs** are the individual's desire to do what he or she has the potential of doing. The desire for self-actualization is called the "highest-order need."

These basic needs are arranged in a **hierarchy of needs** as shown in figure 5.2.

Unsatisfied needs dominate the individual's thoughts and are reflected in what the person is concerned about. The higher-order needs (belonging, esteem, and self-actualization) are not important until the primary, or lower-order needs (safety and physiological) are at least partially satisfied.

Maslow also felt that a person is not motivated by a need that is satisfied. Once a need is satisfied, the person is concerned with the next level of the need hierarchy. A person seeks to move up the hierarchy of needs, generally striving to satisfy the need deficiency at the next-highest level.

Erg theory

ERG theory is similar to Maslow's approach, though there are important differences. In ERG theory there are three, not five, basic need categories [4]. They are existence needs, relatedness needs, and growth needs (hence the label ERG).

- **Existence needs** encompass Maslow's physiological and security needs for material things.
- **Relatedness needs** include security needs for interpersonal matters, love and belonging needs, and needs of an interpersonal nature.
- **Growth needs** focus on the need to confirm personal esteem and self-actualization.

Like Maslow's theory, ERG theory states that unsatisfied needs will dominate behavior and that once a need is satisfied, higher-order needs are desired, but there are two further points [5]:

- The less relatedness needs are fulfilled, the more existence needs will be desired.
- The less growth needs are fulfilled, the more relatedness needs will be desired.

This implies that if a person is deprived of a higher-order need or does not have the potential to satisfy it, he or she will continue to focus on lower-order needs and regress on the need hierarchy.

Herzberg's two-factor theory

It is a problem to translate need theory into managerial practice: a particular need may be satisfied in different ways for different people. Herzberg [6] provided some guidance for managers in solving this problem. They challenged a long-held assumption about how a person's work satisfaction affected performance and motivation. Before, it was assumed that if a person was dissatisfied with part of the job (for example, pay) all that had to be done was to improve the factor (increase pay). This would lead to higher satisfaction, greater motivation, and higher performance. However, Herzberg and his co-workers concluded that there are two sets of factors (hence the name "two-factor" theory) that affect people in the workplace, each of which worked in different ways. They are hygiene factors and motivating factors.

Hygiene factors

Hygiene factors create dissatisfaction if they are not present. If they are present in a job setting, dissatisfaction will be lower, but satisfaction will not be high. Hygiene factors are associated with the context of a job. They include:

- Technical supervision
- Interpersonal relationships with peers
- Salary
- Working conditions

- Status
- Company policy
- Job security
- Relationship with supervisors.

According to the two-factor theory, providing fringe benefits, nice offices, and good vacation plans serve mainly to minimize dissatisfaction and to keep people in the organization; they do not lead to higher motivation or better performance.

Motivators

Motivators create high satisfaction and willingness to work harder. When motivators are present, they result in more effort, but if they are absent, it will not produce dissatisfaction in most people. Motivators are associated with the content of the job. They are:

- Responsibility
- Achievement
- The work itself
- Recognition
- Growth opportunities.

Therefore, a person in a challenging job is likely to be satisfied and motivated to perform better. However, the lack of challenging work does not cause dissatisfaction, merely the absence of satisfaction. A person who is well paid will not be dissatisfied; however, high pay will not lead to motivation and higher performance. To improve performance the manager must work on the motivators, and this means changing the nature of the work to make it more challenging and **intrinsically rewarding**. That means that the person experiences good feelings of growth and status as a result of doing a good job.

The job characteristics approach

Herzberg's work has been the subject of much research and controversy [7] but it did one important thing: it directed attention in a very dramatic way to the role of the work itself as a factor that affects worker motivation and performance. This idea is the basis of the **job characteristics approach**, also called the **job design approach**. This theory is based on the idea that the nature of the work itself is a factor that affects motivation and performance: when specific job characteristics are present "employees will experience a positive, self-generated response when they perform well and that this internal kick will provide an incentive for continued efforts toward good performance" [8]. There are four key elements in the job design approach as depicted in figure 5.3 [9]:

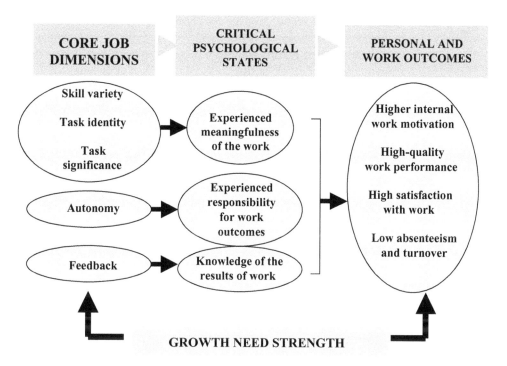

Figure 5.3   The Job Characteristics Model

1   **Work outcomes** are the result of the work activities. They are:

- **Internal work motivation** is how motivated the person is by the work itself, rather than external factors such as pay and supervision.
- **Quality of work** results from people having meaningful jobs. Individuals will produce fewer errors, lower numbers of rejected parts, and lower scrap rates. The job characteristics approach does not suggest that people will produce more, although productivity may increase if an output level is maintained and work quality is improved.
- **Job satisfaction** is a third outcome that is affected by the characteristics of work.
- **Absenteeism and turnover** is the final set of outcomes in the job characteristics model. Both absenteeism and turnover can be quite expensive for firms when they are high and out of control.

2   **Critical psychological states** are what give the person a kick out of doing the work when performing well in a job. These are:

- **Meaningfulness of work** occurs when the person believes that it counts for something, i.e. that is important either to the person or to someone else. For instance, most Peace Corps volunteers believe that their work is "the toughest job you will ever love."

77

- **Experienced responsibility for outcomes** of work occurs when a person believes that he or she is personally accountable for the results of work.
- **Knowledge of results** is when a person can personally judge the adequacy or inadequacy of work performance. Obtaining knowledge of results is not as simple as it sounds. For instance, the project director for the Mars Pathfinder Mission that successfully landed the Sojourner Walker on Mars in July, 1997 only had feedback about how well he did when the vehicle itself was on Mars and began transmitting pictures. For the years that he and his team worked on the project, they had no idea about the success of the project.

3 **Core job characteristics** that determine the critical psychological states are: high levels of meaningfulness, responsibility, and knowledge of results. These exist when five core job characteristics are present:

- **Skill variety** is how many different abilities and capacities are required for the performance components that make up the person's job. A clerk in a secretarial pool who only types outgoing letters has a job that is of a low skill variety. A personal secretary to the CEO, however, may use several different skills, such as typing and dealing with different people from both inside and outside the organization.
- **Task identity** is the extent to which a person is responsible for the whole job, from beginning to end.
- **Task significance** is the effect that work has on others, either in their work or in their lives. This occurs when the person can link his or her task to some value created for the customer.
- **Autonomy** is the freedom that you have in the job. High autonomy is the freedom to determine when, how, and where a job is to be done. When autonomy is high, so are perceived feelings of responsibility.
- **Feedback** is the information that a person receives about the results of the job. One source of feedback is from other workers or supervisors. Another form of feedback may be from the job itself; a basketball player has immediate feedback – when a shot goes through the hoop or it misses.

These core job characteristics contribute to different psychological states. Work meaningfulness is affected by skill variety, task identity, and task significance. Experienced responsibility is a function of autonomy. Knowledge of results is determined by feedback.

4 **Growth need strength** determines how these job characteristics affect the person. Growth need strength is the extent to which a person desires to advance, to be in a challenging position, and, generally, to achieve. If you have high growth need strength and have a job high on the core dimensions, you are more likely to experience high internal motivation, high satisfaction, high work quality, and low turnover and absenteeism than if you have low growth need strength [10].

McClelland's achievement-power theory

McClelland [11] developed an important motivational model, particularly useful in understanding leadership. There are three needs, or motives, that are at the center of this approach:

1   The need for achievement
2   The need for power
3   The need for affiliation.

These motives are arranged in a hierarchy of strength and importance within a person and emerge as the personality develops [11]. The idea is that, for a particular person, one of these motives is more likely to be dominant, or have the highest position in his or her hierarchy, and that motive will have the strongest effect on behavior. The two most important for you to understand are the achievement motive and the power motive.

The **achievement motive** is the extent to which success is important and valued by a person. For the high achiever, the achievement motive is toward the top of the motive hierarchy and only minimal achievement cues are necessary to generate the positive feelings of potential success and, therefore, increase the likelihood of trying to succeed [11].

If you have a high achievement motive you want to succeed in everything. Here are the sorts of cues and conditions that activate achievement motives:

* Success must come from your own efforts, not from those of others or from luck.
* The situation must have an "intermediate level of risk." This means that it will be challenging, but not impossible.
* You want concrete feedback about success, because you want to keep track of how well you are doing. You would try to avoid situations where there can be any doubt about achievement.

Successful entrepreneurs have high achievement motives – those high in achievement motives play a "one-man game that need not involve other people." Entrepreneurs know that if they win or lose, they are responsible, accountable, and in charge.

The **power motive** is the need to have an impact on others, to establish, maintain, or restore personal prestige or power [12]. It was discovered that many top-level executives did not have high achievement motivation, but instead, they had high power motives [12]. The power motive can show up in three different ways:

1   You could take strong aggressive actions towards others, give help to others, try to control or persuade others or try to impress them.
2   You might act in a way that results in strong emotions in others, even though the act itself is not strong.
3   This motive can be reflected by a concern for your reputation and, perhaps, doing things that would enhance or preserve it.

The power motive may take one of two different forms: personalized power and socialized power. **Personalized power** is adversarial. Those with a personalized power orientation prefer person-to-person competition in which they can dominate. To them, life is a win-lose game and the law of the jungle rules; the strong survive by destroying the weak. They drink somewhat heavily and gain considerable satisfaction from power fantasies while under the influence of alcohol. These persons are high in the power motive but low in self-control and inhibition [12].

A person with a **socialized power** orientation wants to exercise power for the good of others, to be careful about the use of personal power, plan carefully for conflict with others, and know that someone's win is another person's loss. They have high self-control and prefer a more disciplined expression of their power motivation than those who have a personal power orientation. People with strong socialized power motives, low affiliation needs, and high self-control have a configuration of motives called the "leader motive pattern" [12].

MOTIVATION: THE PROCESS THEORIES

Process theories of motivation focus on how behavior change occurs, or how a person comes to act in a different way. There is less emphasis on the specific factors (or "content") that cause behavior. As you come to understand the concepts in these theories, you will see the dominant process orientation and the less prominent, but still present, content aspects of each. Four process theories are discussed in this section:

1 Reinforcement theory
2 Expectancy theory
3 Goal-setting theory
4 Organizational justice theories.

Reinforcement theory

Reinforcement theory is one of the most important and, perhaps, most complicated of the motivation theories. It is very useful to managers because it can help them to understand how rewarding or punishing behavior affects performance and satisfaction. There are two key concepts in reinforcement theory:

1 The types of reinforcement consequences
2 Reinforcement schedules.

Types of reinforcement consequences

There are several different types of reinforcement consequences (see figure 5.4) and each has a different effect on the probability of a behavior recurring.

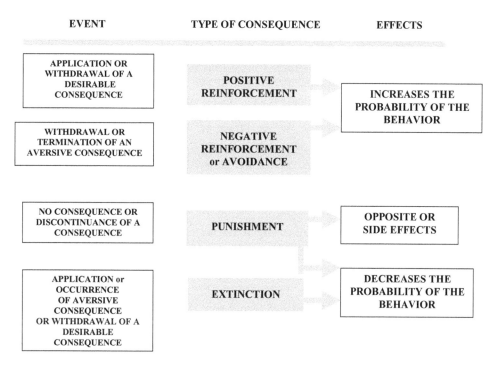

Figure 5.4   Types of consequences and their effects

- **Positive reinforcement** occurs when desirable consequences are associated with a behavior. A positive reinforcer increases the likelihood that the behavior will recur in the future. Positive reinforcement could be something as simple as praising an employee for good work to more sophisticated uses of rewards. The use of rewards to reinforce certain behaviors requires a careful understanding of reinforcement theory as well as many of the related theories contained in this chapter.
- **Negative reinforcement** occurs when an undesirable consequence is removed. It also increases the likelihood that the behavior will occur again. Suppose that you work in a very noisy plant and find that wearing earplugs reduces your discomfort from the noise. This should lead you to associate noise (in the plant) and the use of earplugs, so use the earplugs to avoid a negative effect. Just as you stop at a red light to avoid a ticket and fine, so at work you may work hard to meet job standards to avoid negative consequences.
- **Punishment** can take two forms. Negative consequences (undesirable things) can be applied to a response, or positive consequences (desirable things) can actively be taken away. For example if your reports are not well done, your boss may be very critical and reprimand you. Or, punishment can be applied by withdrawing positive consequences. For example, the result of a low-quality report could be taking away your extra break privileges. In both instances, the response, "poor reports," should decrease.

81

Some managers think that negative reinforcement and punishment are good ways to manage people at work; that is, employees who engage in undesirable behavior should expect something to happen to them. However, there can be some difficulties with this approach. There should be a last resort. Reprimands and firing may have to occur, but it is best to try to correct the behavior first. Positive reinforcement is a much better alternative, and many examples exist of its effective use in improving performance and attendance [13].

• **Extinction** is another way to change behavior. It involves stopping a previously established reinforcer, either positive or negative, that is maintaining a behavior. Managers may extinguish a response of a worker by not reinforcing it for an extended period of time; the response then becomes less frequent and eventually stops. Managers should be very sensitive to the wide array of possibilities of extinction in the workplace. Employees should not learn that good behaviors have little or no consequences. For instance, when there is no distinction between rewards for average performance and outstanding performance, you soon learn that high levels of performance do not pay off.

Reinforcement schedules

Reinforcement schedules refer to the timing and frequency with which consequences are associated with behavior. They are important because they affect how long it takes to learn a new behavior and how resistant the behavior is to

Guide for Managers:
USING REWARDS EFFECTIVELY

While positively reinforcing behavior seems a simple concept, the practice of effectively linking rewards to behavior is often complex. Managers encounter many common problems in administering rewards that are the result of an ineffectively designed system. This may include rewarding behaviors other than those intended, rewarding average (or sometimes even poor) performance, and using rewards that have little value to those whose behavior is to be affected. Here are some guides for improving reward systems.

Link the reward to the behavior. This can be accomplished by first clarifying what might constitute outstanding performance. The connection can also be made by rewarding very soon after performance or by verbally explaining why the employee is being reward.

Fit the magnitude of the reward to the magnitude of the behavior. A small reward such as a brief word of praise is insufficient for a rather substantial contribution by an employee. It is also possible to over-react to performance, such as putting a story about the employee in the company newspaper and throwing a party when the performance was not sustained or outstanding. This rule requires some judgment.

change. Reinforcement schedules break down as follows:

1 In a **continuous reinforcement schedule**, a response is reinforced (or punished) each time it occurs. For example, when someone is learning a new job, an instructor may be constantly present to respond in a reinforcing manner each time a worker does the right thing.

2 In a **fixed-interval reinforcement schedule**, a response is reinforced after a fixed amount of time has elapsed. These schedules result in irregular performance rates, with behavior at its highest rate closer in time to when the reinforcement occurs. For example, when performance appraisals are scheduled every six months, employees are likely to work harder as the time for appraisal nears. Pay is another example because it is generally given at a regular time of the week or month.

3 In a **variable-interval reinforcement schedule**, the period of time between reinforcements is not constant. Variable-interval schedules are common in work settings. Supervisors often visit work sites at irregular intervals. Consider the example of a security guard who dare not leave his post because he does not know when the post might be checked by a supervisor.

4 In a **fixed-ratio reinforcement schedule**, a certain number of responses must occur before a reinforcement follows. A piece-rate payment system is an example of a fixed-ratio schedule at work. The employee is credited with additional pay for increments of productivity.

Better performers should be rewarded more than average performers. Who complains when every employee gets the same reward treatment? The best performers do, and there is not much that can be said to the best employees when they have not been differentially recognized. Who complains when the best employees are rewarded better? The poorer performers are more likely to make inquiries. Thus, when using such discrimination in rewards, the manager needs to prepare for questions raised by the poorer employees and attempt to improve their performance.

Reward more often. Many managers are stingy with rewards either because they are embarrassed to give them or because they fear the employee might become "spoiled." Good rewarding does not mean giving employees whatever they want whenever they want it. Good rewarding is based on the existence of performance standards, and if the reward is linked to performance, it need not have a spoiling effect.

Reward after performance. Avoid rewarding before the behavior takes place. For example, suppose a supervisor grants a merit raise to an employee and explains to the employee that the raise is an act of good faith and that the employee will improve on unacceptable performance in the future. This might work on the rare occasion that the employee agrees he or she needs to

Fixed-ratio schedules can produce high rates of response that continue so long as the reinforcement remains powerful.

5 With a **variable-ratio reinforcement schedule**, the number of behaviors necessary for a reinforcement varies. This produces a very high and steady rate of response, typically without predictable pauses or bursts of behavior. Gambling and fishing are good examples of variable-ratio schedules. The payoff occurs at unpredictable times and sustains behavior over long periods. Variable-ratio schedules occur at work when managers reward irregularly, either by accident or design. Some companies have tried to implement them formally by using lotteries to reduce absenteeism, For example, at Continental Airlines, employees with perfect attendance records for six months were eligible for a drawing in which a new car is the prize.

One approach to changing behavior, called **behavior shaping**, involves reinforcing small increments of behavior that are in the direction of desired behavior until a final desired result is achieved. Behavior shaping can be used in all kinds of learning, not just when we are trying to extinguish or overcome old habits. Shaping requires that we break down a desired response into components and think of the desired behavior as a sequence of the components. Then if we can encourage a part of the behavior anywhere in the sequence, it can be reinforced. This continues until the complete behavior is learned.

shape up and really respects the supervisor. Usually, however, the reward will act as a reinforcement for past behavior. The employee might conclude that his or her behavior couldn't have been that bad, or the boss would never have granted the merit pay.

Reward people with what they value. It is important to remember that individuals differ in what they value. A group of employees may have a wide range of preferences. Knowing what those preferences are, the manager may be able to tailor some rewards to the specific values of employees and, unless someone values a reward, it is not likely to affect their behavior. There are several ways to discover what people value. One is to use consequences that are widely valued, such as praise, a smile, or recognition. Another is to ask people. A third is to observe how a person uses free time on and off the job to find out what they like or dislike.

Expectancy theory

The basic idea of **expectancy theory** is that you will work (put forth effort) to do those things that will lead to the results (outcomes) that you desire. This is a rational approach to motivation that implies that people make an assessment of the costs or benefits of the different alternatives that they have and then select the one with the best payoffs [14]. Suppose you sell architectural tile and over the years of your experience you have developed two different ways to approach your customers:

- You could spend a lot of time telephoning prospective buyers.
- You could make personal sales visits to the architects' offices.

What you do depends on your preference for certain outcomes and the expectations about those outcomes. If you estimate that personal sales visits have a high probability (an expectancy) of earning a substantial bonus and a low expectation of earning the bonus if you telephone them, the motivation to visit the offices is much higher. According to expectancy theory, you would decide to make personal sales visits to the offices.

An **expectancy** is an individual's estimate, or judgment, of the likelihood that some outcome (or event) will occur. It is a probability estimate and can range from 0 (impossible) to 1 (certain). If you believe that to sell to one customer it is necessary to personally call on five potential buyers, the expectancy is 0.20.

There are two kinds of expectancies (see figure 5.5):

1 The **effort-performance expectancy** $(E \rightarrow P)$ is the person's belief about the level of effort made and the performance that it will lead to. For you, in the above example, the effort-performance expectancy is the relationship between "How hard I work to sell tiles," and "How many tiles I sell."

2 The **performance-outcome expectancy** $(P \rightarrow O)$ is the expecta-

Guide for Managers: USING MOTIVATION THEORIES AT WORK

There are several useful ideas for managers in this chapter. Perhaps the most important is that they must recognize that their primary role is to manage performance, and that low levels of motivation can be one of many factors that contribute to poor performance. Here are some general guides to effectively using motivation theories at work.

Create an intrinsically rewarding work environment. This can be accomplished by making the job more challenging and interesting while at the same time increasing the autonomy and responsibility of workers.

Define clear and challenging work goals. The manager should ensure that subordinates know what level of performance is expected in some measurable, quantifiable terms if possible. These goals must be attainable. Unattainable goals have an $E \rightarrow P$ expectancy of zero, and very difficult goals have low $E \rightarrow P$ expectancies.

Remove barriers to performance. By providing adequate resources, training workers, or removing unnecessary bureaucratic constraints, the $E \rightarrow P$ expectancy can be increased.

Clarify what is appropriate performance. There are often several ways to achieve a goal. For example,

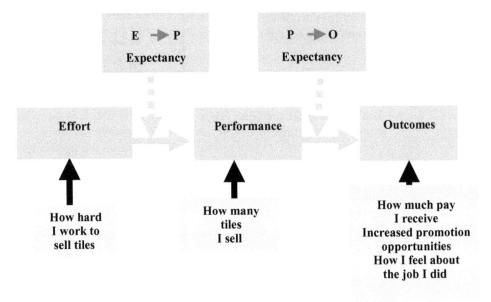

Figure 5.5   Effort-performance and performance-outcome expectancies

tion that achieving a given level of work performance will lead to certain outcomes. High P → O expectancies, particularly with respect to attaining rewards, are necessary for high performance. This is called the **performance-reward linkage**, and if it is not made, then we should not expect a person to make an effort.

Not all outcomes are equally valued by a person. The strength of the person's preferences is called valence. **Valences** are anticipated satisfactions (or dissatisfactions) that result from outcomes, or the different degrees of pleasantness (or unpleasantness) of outcomes. So when an outcome has a low positive valence, you will not exert much effort to attain it. You may have a strong desire for some outcomes but not for others. You may, for example,

cost reduction might be achieved by effective control of all costs or by omitting preventive maintenance programs. A subordinate should know what is considered the preferred way to achieve reduced costs. Clarifying such performance level expectations for subordinates is an important aspect of the coaching role of the manager.

Reward performance. Extrinsically rewarding good performance can modify the P → O expectancy of a person. Extrinsic rewards are administered by someone else and are, for example, pay, advancement, and fringe benefits. To the extent that high rewards follow good performance, one can expect an employee to engage in that performance more frequently. Other tips on the use of wish to have the pay increase and the advancement but wish to avoid antagonizing co-workers who may be jealous.

rewards were provided earlier in the chapter where we provide greater detail on using rewards to positively reinforce desired behavior.

Goal-setting theory

Goal-setting theory is based on a simple premise: the level of performance is caused by what a person is trying to accomplish or intends to do, and according to this theory, people will do what they are trying to do [15]. What follows from this is quite clear:

- A person with higher goals will do better than someone with lower ones.
- If someone knows precisely what he or she wants to do, or is supposed to do, that person will do better than someone whose goals or intentions are vague.

These are the two basic ideas that underlie the four propositions of goal-setting theory, which are:

1 There is a general positive relationship between goal difficulty and performance except for extremely difficult goals beyond one's ability [15].
2 Specific goals lead to higher performance than general goals. This is a particularly important point to remember because managers have a tendency to set goals that are too general for their subordinates [16].
3 Participation in setting goals is related to performance through goal acceptance and commitment, and information-sharing. Participation can increase goal commitment and, ultimately, performance, particularly if it leads to some real choices about the way to achieve a goal as well as information about the goal and the task [17].
4 Feedback about performance with respect to goals is necessary. A person must know whether the desired level of performance has been achieved.

Organizational justice theories

Organizational justice approaches to motivation are based on perceptions of how justly or fairly you are treated at work. **Distributive justice** is the degree to which persons believe that they are treated fairly and equitably with respect to work outcomes, or how much they put into work and how much they gain from it. This is the basis for equity theory. **Procedural justice** is the extent to which people believe they are treated fairly in terms of *how* decisions are made about things that affect them in the workplace.

Outcome justice theory

Equity theory states that people are motivated to maintain "fair relationships with others and to rectify unfair relationships by making them fair" [18]. A fundamental premise is that individuals compare themselves to others and want their efforts and achievements to be judged fairly relative to them. This means that the concern in equity theory is **outcome justice,** or how you perceive your organizational outcomes relative to the contributions that you, and others, make to gain them. There are three key factors used in explaining and understanding motivation in equity theory:

1 **Inputs** are what you bring to the job, such as age, experience, skill, and seniority, and contributions to the organization or group. They can be anything that you believe is relevant to the job and that should be recognized by others.
2 **Outcomes** are things that you perceive to be received as a result of work. Outcomes may be positively valued factors such as pay, recognition, promotion, status symbols, and fringe benefits. They may also be negative: unsafe working conditions, pressure from management, and monotony.
3 **Referents** are the focus of comparison for the person – either other individuals or other groups. For example, as a department manager, you might compare yourself to one of the other department managers, say Paula Dawkins, or to all the department managers in your firm.

Perceived inequity (or equity) is based on the comparison of two ratios of outcomes to inputs. Equity occurs when your ratio of outcomes to inputs is equal to the ratio of the referent (Paula), as shown in the following equation:

$$\frac{\text{Outcomes (yours)}}{\text{Inputs (yours)}} = \frac{\text{Outcomes (Paula's)}}{\text{Inputs (Paula's)}}$$

Underpayment inequity occurs when you believe that your inputs are at least equal to Paula's but your outcomes are less than hers. You gain less from the job than does Paula, relative to what you both contribute. This underpayment results in dissatisfaction that stems from anger at being under-rewarded and is likely to lead to a reduction in the quality of work [19, 20], counter-productive behavior such as theft [21, 22], and lower performance [23].

There is also **overpayment inequity**. If Paula assesses her outcomes in the same way that you evaluate them, she experiences overpayment inequity. This means that she believes that she gains more from the job relative to her referent (you, in this case). Overpayment inequity leads to dissatisfaction, just as does underpayment inequity, but, in this case, the dissatisfaction results from feelings of guilt that the person (in this case, Paula) develops. The dissatisfaction, whether it arises from guilt or anger, will cause the person who experiences it to do something to bring the situation into a state of equity. For example, when a group of managers were assigned higher-status offices than their current position warranted, they increased their performance [23]. Also, if co-workers were terminated because of low performance, those remaining thought that they had performed more favorably on the assignment than those terminated. When co-workers were terminated on a random basis, the remaining workers worked harder, increasing their inputs, as equity theory predicts.

When inequity is perceived, a person is likely to take some action to restore equity, and thus to bring these ratios into balance. This is especially so for those who have strong moral values, a strong conscience, and high ethical standards [24]. Here are some of the different ways of achieving an equitable balance:

1 **Change the inputs**. One way for you to restore equity is to reduce your inputs by lowering organizational commitment, working fewer hours, and having less concern with quality, returning to as you had been in the past.
2 **Change outcomes**. Another way to reduce your feelings of inequity is to try to get a pay raise, to increase your power, or seek more privileges.
3 **Rationalize the inputs and outputs and psychological distortion**. You could psychologically distort inputs by changing your attributions about how much effort you put into the job, believing that you do less than you believed before. Workers who were forced to take a pay cut but remained on the job elevated the perceived importance of their own work [25].
4 **Leave the situation**. You may decide to move to another job. Then, in the new setting, you escape the inequity and may find a fairer situation.
5 **Act against the other person**. You might try to convince Paula to work harder, thus increasing her inputs, or try to undermine the confidence others have in her, so that she leaves the company.
6 **Change the referent**. You may find it easier not to compare yourself to Paula. If you can find another person in the firm who seems to have a similar ratio of outcomes to inputs as you, you will reinstate a sense of equity, your satisfaction will increase, and your anger will decrease.

Procedural justice theory

Procedural justice theory focuses an another facet of justice that affects motivation and satisfaction: how you make judgments and your perceptions about whether you believe that the *way* that decisions are made is fair. Perceptions of procedural justice are related to higher levels of organizational commitment, job satisfaction, and higher levels of organizational citizenship behavior, or contextual performance [26, 27].

Procedural justice theory is a relatively new motivational approach, but an important one. If you think about it for a minute, you will realize that decisions that affect you, decisions about your pay, your advancement, your work assignment, and so on are made in the organization where you work. There are organizational systems of rules, policies, procedures, and operating systems through which these decisions are made and then implemented. Some managers believe that, if they follow specified rules and procedures to make a decision, those affected by the decisions will view them as reasonable and equitable.

There could be nothing further from the truth. Though managers might think that the use of standard procedures and policies is fair, there are still feelings of unfairness when managerial action does not result in an outcome favorable to the person, or when the procedures are seen us unfair. Three factors have to be present to give a sense of procedural justice:

1 **Process control**, or the extent to which you believe that you are allowed to present your position and justify your case before a decision is made. For example, in unionized organizations, the grievance procedure permits you some level of process control since you are allowed to provide evidence favoring your position at every step in the process.
2 **Decision control**: the amount of influence you have in the decision-making process.
3 **Interactional justice**: whether the decision and the decision-making process are fully explained to you and whether you are treated with respect and dignity during the decision-making process [28].

The interaction of outcome justice and procedural justice

It is quite obvious that the effects of procedural justice on personal reactions depend on whether the result (the outcome) is favorable or unfavorable and, vice versa, that the favorability of any outcome will have an effect on the perceptions of procedural justice [28]. Figure 5.6 shows how these two different justice concepts are related

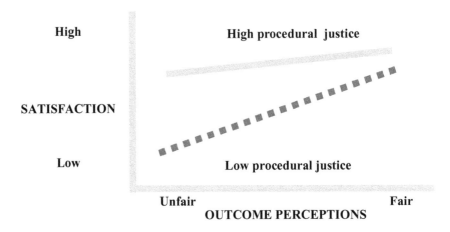

Figure 5.6 The interaction between procedural and outcome justice

to each other and how they affect the satisfaction of those affected. When the outcome is favorable to a person, then there is high satisfaction, whether or not the procedure was fair. When there are unfavorable outcomes, figure 5.6 shows that if the procedure is unfair, then you will have much lower satisfaction.

SUMMARY

Several motivation theories have been discussed in this chapter. Need theories, a class of content theories, suggest what motivates people. They give clues to managers about what they can change so that increased employee performance and satisfaction as well as organizational effectiveness can result. It is important to note here, though, that there is no one best theory of motivation and some seem better suited to deal with certain topics than others [2]; need theories are most widely used to study satisfaction and work effort; reinforcement theory focuses on effort, performance, and absenteeism and turnover; expectancy theory can be used to predict job and organization choices and withdrawal behavior; goal-setting theory has been related to choice behavior and performance.

Further, since these different theories have psychological bases and concern the same variable, human behavior, it is only logical that they can be related to one another. Expectancies, for example, develop as a result of previous learning experiences. Learning theory may also explain the development of particular motives. Strong achievement needs may result from the positive reinforcement of success experiences in early life. In fact, this is exactly the point we made in the discussion of learning and personality. In the final analysis, understanding each of these different approaches is useful because it gives the manager several ways to look at problems. As a result, he or she may arrive at better solutions more quickly and effectively.

REFERENCES

1 Borman, W. C. and S. J. Motowidlo. 1993. Expanding the Criterion Domain to Include Elements of Contextual Performance. In N. Schmitt and W. C. Borman, eds., *Personnel Selection in Organizations*, 71–98. San Francisco: Jossey Bass.

2 Landy, F. J. and W. S. Becker. 1987. Motivation Theory Reconsidered. In L. L. Cummings and B. M. Staw, eds., *Research in Organizational Behavior*, 1–38. Greenwich, CT: JAI Press.

3 Maslow, A. H. 1943. A Theory of Human Motivation. *Psychological Review*, **50**: 370–96.

4 Alderfer, C. 1972. *Existence, Relatedness, and Growth: Human Needs in Organizational Settings*. New York: Free Press.

5 Miner, J. B. 1980. *Theories of Organizational Behavior*. New York: Macmillan.

91

6 Herzberg, F. A., B. Mausner, and B. Snyderman. 1959. *The Motivation to Work*. New York: John Wiley.

7 House, R. J. and L. Wigdor. 1967. Herzberg's Dual Factor Theory of Job Satisfaction and Motivation: A Review of the Evidence and Criticism. *Personnel Psychology*, **20**: 369–89.

8 Hackman, J. R. and J. L. Suttle, eds. 1977. *Improving Life at Work: Behavioral Science Approaches to Organizational Change*. Santa Monica, CA: Goodyear Publishing.

9 Hackman, J. R. and G. R. Oldham. 1976. Motivation through the Design of Work: Test of a Theory. *Organizational Behavior and Human Performance*, **16**: 250–79.

10 Spector, P. E. 1985. Higher-Order Need Strength as a Moderator of the Job Scope–Employee Outcome Relationship: A Meta-Analysis. *Journal of Occupational Psychology*, **58**: 119–27.

11 McClelland, D. A. 1965. Toward a Theory of Motive Acquisition. *American Psychologist*, **20**: 321–3.

12 McClelland, D. A. 1975. *Power: The Inner Experience*. New York: Irvington.

13 Locke, E. A. et al. 1981. Goal Setting and Task Performance: 1969–1980. *Psychological Bulletin*, **90**: 125–52.

14 Vroom, V. H. 1964. *Work and Motivation*. New York: John Wiley.

15 Locke, E. A. and G. Latham. 1990. *A Theory of Goal Setting and Task Performance*. Englewood Cliffs, NJ: Prentice-Hall.

16 Carroll, S. J. and H. L. Tosi. 1973. *Management by Objectives: Applications and Research*. New York: Macmillan.

17 Erez, M., P. C. Early, and C. Hulin. 1985. The Impact of Participation of Goal Acceptance and Participation. *Academy of Management Journal*, **28**(1): 50–66.

18 Baron, R. A. 1983. *Behavior in Organizations: Understanding and Managing the Human Side of Work*. Boston: Allyn & Bacon.

19 Kanfer, R. 1990. Motivation Theory and Industrial and Organizational Psychology. In M. D. Dunnette and L. Hough, eds., *Handbook of Industrial and Organizational Psychology*, 75–170. Palo Alto: Consulting Psychologists Press.

20 Cowherd, D. M. and D. I. Levine. 1992. Product Quality and Pay Equity Between Lower-Level Employees and Top Management: An Investigation of Distributive Justice Theory. *Administrative Science Quarterly*, **37**(2): 302–20.

21 Greenberg, J. 1990. Employee Theft as a Reaction to Underpayment Inequity: The Hidden Costs of Pay Cuts. *Journal of Applied Psychology*, **76**(5): 562–9.

22 Greenberg, J. 1993. Stealing in the Name of Justice: Informational and Interpersonal Moderators of Theft Reaction to Underpayment Inequity. *Organizational Behavior and Human Decision Performance*, **54**(1): 81–104.

23 Greenberg, J. 1988. Equity and Workplace Status. *Journal of Applied Psychology*, **73**(4): 606–14.

24 Vecchio, R. P. 1981. An Individual Difference Interpretation of the Conflicting Predictions Generated by Equity Theory and Expectancy Theory. *Journal of Applied Psychology*, **66**: 470–81.

25 Greenberg, J. 1989. Cognitive Reevaluation of Outcomes in Response to Underpayment Inequity. *Academy of Management Journal*, **32**(1): 174–85.

26 Folger, R. and M. Konovsky. 1989. Effects of Procedural and Distributive Justice on Reaction to Pay Raises. *Academy of Management Journal*, **32**(1): 115–30.

27 Ball, G., L. K. Trevino, and H. Sims. 1994. Just and Unjust Punishment: Influences on Subordinate Performance and Citizenship. *Academy of Management Journal*, **37**(2): 229–323.

28 Brockner, J. and B. Wiesenfeld. 1996. An Integrative Framework for Explaining Reactions to Decisions: Interactive Effects of Outcomes and Procedures. *Psychological Bulletin*, **120**(2): 189–208.

Block III:
The Context of Organizational Behavior

BLOCK I
INTRODUCTION

BLOCK II
A FOCUS ON THE INDIVIDUAL

BLOCK III
THE CONTEXT OF ORGANIZATIONAL BEHAVIOR
Chapter 6   Group and Team Performance
Chapter 7   Culture: National and Organizational
Chapter 8   Organizational Structure and Design

BLOCK IV
INTEGRATING BEHAVIORAL THEORY INTO EFFECTIVE MANAGEMENT AND LEADERSHIP

CHAPTER 6

Group and Team Performance

THE FUNDAMENTALS OF GROUPS AND TEAMS

GROUP DEVELOPMENT

TEAM EFFECTIVENESS ISSUES

GROUP PROCESSES

GROUP DYNAMICS

SOCIAL INFLUENCES ON BEHAVIOR

VIRTUAL TEAMS

Rebecca stared at the computer screen in disbelief. She read the e-mail again:

From: Tom Martinez, Vice-President for Operations

To: All Members of Team Thunderbird

After conferring with divisional managers, I have decided to disband the activities of Team Thunderbird effective immediately. Like most of you, I had high expectations for the team and was confident that the team would be able to improve the efficiency of the design and production process. Unfortunately, two years after its inception Team Thunderbird has failed to make a significant impact in our process and the recent delays in development of our Thunderbird product-line have led me to conclude that using an integrated team for this purpose is inappropriate. I would like to thank the members of this team for their efforts.

Tom Martinez

Rebecca had been the team leader for Team Thunderbird, an assignment for which she held high anticipation. From the beginning, organizing Team Thunderbird was a struggle. At the initial meeting, Rebecca became aware that divisional managers had not assigned their strongest people to the product team. Despite Tom's "encouragement" to them to give Team Thunderbird their "best and brightest," Rebecca found that many original team members had been in disfavor with their divisional manager and several were within a year or two of retirement. When Rebecca convinced Tom to encourage division managers to assign their rising stars to the team, he did so only after agreeing that these individuals would continue to report to their divisions. From there, things only got worse. Divisional managers wanted the right to "review" all team suggestions, and Rebecca found that whenever an update on the team's progress was presented to Tom, many division managers brought with them well-developed rebuttals of the team ideas. Despite the obstacles, Rebecca was quite proud of the recent team report that had provided a comprehensive plan for manufacturing and marketing the Thunderbird product-line. Their plan included over 500 suggestions from employees on issues ranging from design of manufacturing workstations to the placement of products in retail outlets. Key to their plan was the implementation of an integrated Thunderbird Product Division that would be made up of personnel from all divisions, including R&D, manufacturing, and marketing. A product team, Rebecca thought, is what we need. She again looked at the line in Tom's memo "using an integrated team for this purpose is inappropriate" and wondered, "Why is it that some managers view teams as a threat?"

In countless organizations around the world, teams and teamwork seem to be a part of the US corporate strategy to become more productive and competitive. Self-managed teams, cross-functional teams, product teams, and virtual teams, teams that rely on information technologies for communication and may never meet face to face, are all commonly used in the modern workplace. However, the use of this potentially powerful management tool has met with mixed effectiveness and often with cynicism. Some managers have said that half of the decisions reached by teams are never implemented and the other half should not have been implemented.

Why are some teams effective and other teams ineffective? What can leaders do to improve the effectiveness of their teams? In this chapter we review what we know about group and team effectiveness.

THE FUNDAMENTALS OF GROUPS AND TEAMS

Groups and teams: definitions

The concept of "group" is broader than the concept of "team," though researchers who study groups often use this term when studying the same processes. A **group** is defined as two or more people who interact and are dependent upon each other to achieve some common objective. Patients in a doctor's waiting room or passengers on an airplane do not constitute a group because while they may have some interaction, they do not depend on each other. **Teams** are a special form of group that have highly defined tasks and roles, and demonstrate high group commitment [1]. In this chapter, we use the terms team and group interchangeably.

Why groups form

People join groups for a variety of reasons and are often willing to endure great hardships and financial costs to belong. However, in many common organizational situations, individuals often have little choice about the groups and teams to which they are assigned. Understanding the basic theories of group formation can help us to understand groups we associate with willingly and more carefully analyze those we associate with because of our job requirements.

Personal characteristics

Our social groups, which we usually join willingly, are often formed with those who share our beliefs, values, and attitudes. It is much easier to interact with those who share our attitudes: it permits us to confirm our beliefs, to deal with others with minimal conflict, and to express ourselves with less fear of contradiction. In our earlier discussion of the development of our beliefs, attitudes, and values, we discussed the role that association and interaction with others have in reinforcing these structures.

Interests and goals

Shared goals that require cooperation are a powerful force behind group formation. Managers organize employees around functions such as sales, production, accounting, or maintenance. If people in these groups also have similar characteristics, the basis for group formation and cohesiveness may even be strengthened.

Potential to influence

Many managers have been approached by a group of workers with a complaint or a request. The work group knows that a manager might be more prone to listen when any complaint is prefaced with a "we" instead of an "I." Co-worker support may be necessary to gain attention and action. One formal group found in many organizations is a **union**. People from diverse groups and backgrounds who share a common interest often form unions or join them based on the common goals of protecting their rights and increasing their influence in the workplace.

Opportunity for interaction

Individuals often form groups with others just because their jobs force them to be in close contact with others. Physical proximity and interaction permit relationships like these to develop and this can lead to friendships and group formation. Lifetime friendships are often formed among individuals who have been placed together due to work or living circumstances. The military has traditionally placed new members into close environments to facilitate interaction among members and team-building.

Types of groups

We are all members of some type of group. Since birth, most of us were members of a common group, our families. As we grew, we participated in groups or teams formed in our schools, neighborhoods, and work organizations. In each group we added to our knowledge of how to behave in groups and we learned that roles and expectations may differ, based on the type of group or team and its objectives. In this section we will consider two particular types of groups that are common in organizations, formal and informal groups as well as introduce virtual teams as a form of group seen increasingly in the workplace.

97

Formal groups

Formal groups are created as part of the formal organization structure. The formal organization is the hierarchical structure and the various departments that exist within that structure. Formal organization is reflected in the goals, policies, rules, and procedures that are designed to accomplish the organization's tasks. Any group that is purposely designed into this configuration is a formal group.

There are different types of formal groups, including functional and task groups. A **functional group** is comprised of individuals who accomplish similar tasks within the organizational structure. Functional groups exist for an unspecified period of time. Many organizations organize around functional groups assigned to related work activities such as accounting, marketing, production, and research and development (R&D). **Task groups** are used to accomplish a specific organizational goal. They are usually established by the organization and exist for a specified period of time. In task groups, social benefits for members are secondary or may even be absent. Committees, project teams, and employee participation teams are all organizational task groups. They usually have a defined purpose, deadlines to meet, specific work assignments, and a reporting relationship in the organization.

Informal groups

Informal groups arise out of individual needs and the attraction of people to one another. While outside of the normal structure of the organization, these groups can have a significant effect on organizational performance. Membership is usually voluntary and is based on common values and interests. Sometimes the origin of these groups is social in nature. They might consist of people who also like and trust each other and perhaps interact outside work in a church group or neighborhood. On other occasions, an informal group develops in response to some organization action, such as when workers band together to protest an unpopular management action. These groups may develop to bypass company rules or to enhance the members' power.

Because informal groups develop outside of managerial control and are an important part of the informal structure of an organization, managers should understand this type of group. Informal groups in organizations can be both effective and powerful and managers often view them with doubt and suspicion. They tend to see informal groups as disruptive and potentially harmful to the formal organization. Some managers seek ways to gain the support of informal groups and informal leaders to reduce their threat or to enhance some company purpose. Since informal groups are an inevitable component of behavior in organizations, as managers, we should attempt to work with these groups so that they contribute to, rather than subvert, organizational goals.

Informal groups serve basic needs for employees and are just as important, enduring, and rewarding as the relationship that employees have with the formal organization. The informal group can become a problem when it conflicts with some formal purpose, but even this is not necessarily bad. It may signal some error on management's part or be a symptom of a poor relationship with employees.

Virtual teams

Virtual teams are comprised of geographically or organizationally dispersed members [2]. Collaboration among virtual team members is done using some electronic form of medium such as e-mail, chat, bulletin boards or software designed specifically to support group interaction and decision-making.

GROUP DEVELOPMENT

One factor that may strongly influence the effectiveness of a group is the level of group maturity. Group maturity can be thought of similarly to individual maturity. As individuals, we develop confidence in ourselves and increase our emotional stability over time, partly through our education and interaction with others. Like individuals, some groups are slower to mature; some never reach full maturity. It takes considerable skill from both members and leaders to bring a group to full maturity. Mature groups can be recognized by the following characteristics:

1 The group accepts feelings in a non-evaluative way.
2 The group members disagree over real and important issues.
3 The group members make decisions rationally and encourage dissent, but do not force other members or fake unanimity.
4 All group members have an awareness of the process.
5 Members understand the nature of their involvement.

To achieve maturity, groups must go through certain stages of development [3, 4]. These stages are shown in figure 6.1 and include:

1 **Forming**. The early stage of any group activity, called forming, focuses on getting organized. At this point group members may have more questions than answers about the group. "What is our purpose?" "Will I fit in with the members of my group?" As a result, initial group activities seek to define the purposes of the group and begin to establish its activities and priorities. Early discussion and meetings among group members will focus on basic questions about group goals and objectives. A general demeanor of politeness often characterizes this stage, as there is little to disagree about.

2 **Storming**. The politeness of the forming stage continues until the group is forced to tackle the more difficult issue of group structure, including the roles of

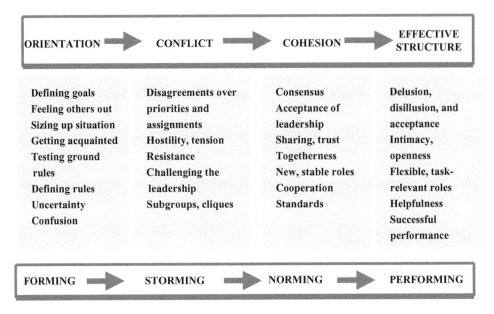

Figure 6.1   Stages in group development

individual members. The process of selecting and/or accepting the leader (if a formal leader is appointed or one emerges) and establishing goals and purposes leads to a stage of increased conflict, called storming. The leader is often challenged and the group may divide over these issues and form two or more subgroups rather than attempt to restructure the group or change the leadership. Some groups never make it through the conflict stage. Disagreements and resistance prevail and energy goes into more conflict. Occasionally some members may leave and others may stay but psychologically withdraw, exhibiting silence and lack of commitment.

3   **Norming**. If a group successfully resolves these early conflicts, individuals will begin to feel more cohesive and will express a readiness to move into a cohesive stage called the norming stage. At this stage, consensus develops around goals and leadership and a sense of liking and trust develops. In this stage, group members accept performance standards, norms, and their individual roles within the group.

4   **Performing**. If a group survives forming, storming, and norming its members move into the performing stage, dealing with problems concerning the structure of the group. A sign that the group is maturing beyond the conflict stage is when acceptance is achieved. Here, subgroups become less prominent, communication increases, and the needs of individuals are more freely expressed. When the task and the emotional needs of group members are handled well, the group has achieved full maturity. However, it is very rare to see a fully mature group; they are not that common.

TEAM EFFECTIVENESS ISSUES

Very often managers implement teams only to find that they fail. Within the organization, there are several factors that could influence group or team success. Also, many factors that influence group or team effectiveness are outside of the control of the members. Teams established with unclear goals and objectives in an environment where rewards are based on individual performance may be doomed. Among the important factors are the design of the task, the reward structure, training, and the size and composition of the group.

Task design

Task design refers to the nature of the work assigned to the group or team. One component of task design is the clarity of the goals and tasks that are either assigned to the group or that the group or team itself establishes. Groups are often formed with specific goals such as improving the quality of a particular product or resolving a specific problem. Groups can also be formed with less specific goals such as improving the general quality of work life or improving conditions in the workplace. Just as in individual goal-setting, group performance is improved when it is handed specific and difficult goals.

A second component of task design considers the coordination the group must have with others in achievement of its assigned tasks. Two key factors are interdependence and autonomy. **Interdependence** is the amount of coordination with, or approval from, others that the team needs to complete its assigned tasks. **Autonomy** refers to the degree of freedom and independence that the team has to conduct its activities. Teams that operate autonomously are often called self-managed teams.

Reward structure

Another factor controlled by the organization is the reward structure. Does the organization have a system of rewards that encourages the cooperation required for successful team performance? There is considerable debate as to whether individual rewards are more appropriate to encourage team performance or whether team reward systems should be used. Organizations can effectively use a wide variety of monetary and non-monetary rewards in team contexts and these rewards are often linked to improvements in customer satisfaction or other measures of overall product quality [5]. These rewards can often provide significant incentives for teams as some compensation systems put as much as 10 percent of the team's overall compensation at risk based on its effectiveness [6].

Training

Many of the activities in which we participate, both at work and away from work, are organized into teams or groups. However, despite their pervasiveness in life, it is a mistake for managers to assume that the skills necessary to be an effective member are common. While members may have important technical skills to contribute to the team, their placement on the team may have dysfunctional consequences if they lack these appropriate team skills. Many lack the skills necessary to be effective team members, often because of lack of experience or cultural differences. Training programs provided by the organization can include team-building activities to build member confidence and trust in each other, conflict resolution skills, or a variety of other useful skills.

Group size and composition

Another important factor in the group performance environment that influences team effectiveness is the composition of the group itself. Social groups have much more discretion in selecting their members than do members of a group within a typical organizational setting. Factors such as group size and group member diversity are important factors that influence overall group effectiveness.

Small groups are of interest because many of the teams found in organizations are small groups for our purposes: a small group has a membership from four to 15 members. If groups are much larger, it is much more difficult for people to interact. Fewer than ten people can conduct a discussion quite adequately. In larger groups, individuals sense the interaction problems and may become less involved and withhold their ideas.

There are several considerations in determining the optimum size for group effectiveness. There should be an odd number of members, as even-numbered groups are more likely to have deadlocks. Because of this, groups of five, seven, or nine members are more effective. In larger groups, there is less opportunity to participate. In addition to the natural inhibitions that people experience in groups, the amount of time available to a person to talk is reduced as size increases. Consider your experience in large classes. Do you notice that class members often avoid speaking up because they intuitively know everyone cannot do so?

People in smaller groups are also generally more satisfied. Other positive aspects of group participation, like increased interaction and shared goals, all positively relate to member satisfaction. One reason for this is because in smaller groups, it is easier for members to feel they contributed to the group's success.

To manage a larger group, it must often be broken down into smaller subgroups. This is a natural tendency that occurs as group size increases. Control also becomes a problem as groups grow in size, so it is natural for norms and rules to develop. Larger groups often formalize communication by using written memos to supplement face-to-face discussion.

102

Another issue managers should consider is the diversity of individual members of the group. Members of **homogeneous groups** have similar characteristics and perhaps similar beliefs, values, and attitudes. While these groups may have less conflict and be more effective at achieving consensus, they may also be limited in creativity and innovation. **Heterogeneous groups** are those where group members vary widely in terms of individual characteristics such as age, race, ethnicity or gender. Or, there could be differences in terms of personalities, skills, or backgrounds.

Research shows that the effects of **group diversity** on performance are conflicting. When group members differ in terms of personalities, gender, attitudes, and background, there is a positive effect on creativity and decision-making [7]. However, when there are cultural or ethnic differences, initial performance is often poorer. Perhaps diversity of this type may initially cause a group difficulty as it deals with values, beliefs, and attitudinal differences during the initial stages of group development. Perhaps diverse groups may be less efficient in the short term but may improve performance in the long term [8].

GROUP PROCESSES

There are processes that occur within groups and teams that can also influence their success. Two of these are the development of norms and the development of group cohesiveness.

Development of norms

Norms are reflections of the "oughts" and "shoulds" of life, both inside and outside the organization. They develop and become strong in the "norming" stage of group development. Norms are also the ways we express values, attitudes, and beliefs. When we believe someone should do something, we are expressing what we feel is right, good, or useful. Norms provide groups with control and predictability, and give members a sense of security and comfort. Norms are expectations about behavior and involvement in the group that apply to all members, though not always equally. For example, we might expect all members to be on time for a meeting but excuse one member under special circumstances.

Many norms in organizations originate from management expectations or from work rules and formal procedures and policies. They develop and operate, as well, in informal groups. A new employee's introduction to an organization requires the learning of its varied norms. Norm may form one basis on which employees are evaluated, and violation of the norms can be personally costly. Sometimes individuals choose to deviate from the norms of the group. They are more likely to be successful in doing this if they are highly competent, and therefore hard to replace, or they have some political clout to withstand the consequences of ignoring norms.

Norms put boundaries on member behavior that may be narrow or wide. For example, at a religious service, very little deviance from norms is tolerated. Organizations can also have narrow norms, such as a company with rigorous dress standards. If an employee were to wear jeans to work at a company with a norm of business dress, not only might the supervisor quickly rebuke him or her, but also others in the firm will apply some sort of sanction. To improve the organizational climate, many organizations have instituted a "dress-down" day that allows employees to wear more relaxed clothing on a certain day of the week or month. You might expect though that when a program like this is implemented, employees would quickly look to their supervisors and others to understand the new dress standards that would become the new norm for this activity!

The power of norms lies in two things. First, they sensitize us to expectations of others. Second, the power of norms is a function of our ability and willingness to act in a way consistent with those norms. A norm's power to control us depends on how we feel about the consequences of violating it. If we value our membership in a group, we can protect that membership by complying with norms. Some people also have higher needs to be accepted and approved by others, making them more susceptible to group norms.

Many central work group norms revolve around productivity. Norms can put lower and upper limits on productivity. A **ratebuster** is an individual who performs at a level higher than the group will tolerate. Ratebusters can cause serious problems because workers in a group often have strong norms about what constitutes a fair day's work. Controlling productivity not only spreads the work out to more people for a longer period, but also prevents management from raising its expectations. This ratebusting norm can be often seen in college classrooms. Have you ever noticed in your classroom how a group of students may try to control the participation of other students? Making sarcastic remarks or laughing after an active student has made a comment are ways members of a classroom control the behavior of ratebusting students.

Management can do much to foster norms affecting work quality, helpfulness, or customer relations that contribute to organizational success. For example, managers in some supermarket chains who want to develop norms of customer service do so by encouraging specific behaviors such as responding to customer requests for directions to a particular product by taking the customer there rather than just telling them where the product can be found. This "extra step" in providing customer service facilitates the development of a norm of excellent customer service.

Group cohesiveness

Group cohesiveness is the degree to which members of a group are attracted to one another and to group membership and can resist threats. Cohesive groups have a higher **level of interaction**. Members share needs and problems in cohesive groups

104

more than they do in less cohesive groups. Similarity in interests, common goals, personal attractiveness, and size all contribute to these increased interactions.

Cohesive groups can exert a great deal of **power and influence** over members. Member of highly cohesive groups will respond more readily to demands than in low cohesive groups. However, high susceptibility to influence can be a problem. If members cannot express opinions or feelings for fear of losing acceptance or membership, individualism and self-respect may be reduced. **Groupthink**, the tendency for group members to not criticize the ideas and suggestions of others, is a phenomenon found in highly cohesive groups. As a result, the group may lose the benefit of fresh ideas, and authenticity and honesty can suffer. This is an important phenomenon which we discuss in greater depth in chapter 11 in our discussion of decision-making.

Members of cohesive groups are more satisfied than members of less cohesive groups. The sources of satisfaction are friendliness, support, opportunity to interact, success, and protection against outsiders. Because cohesive groups can pull together against outside threats, satisfaction also grows out of a feeling of security. Finally, in some contexts cohesiveness can positively influence group member **productivity**. Individuals enjoy the strong bonds that form among members of cohesive groups and members are often focused on a common goal. As a result, highly cohesive groups have a high degree of success in achieving their goals. Unfortunately, those goals may not always be consistent with organizational goals.

Factors that foster group cohesiveness

The conditions leading to **group formation** that we discussed earlier contribute to cohesiveness. When people are similar to one another and when they share common goals and interests, the foundation for cohesiveness is laid. The more important group goals are to each member and the more they perceive the need to work together to accomplish these goals, the higher the cohesiveness. Cohesiveness is also increased when there are difficult entry requirements. Members are carefully selected and there may be elaborate rites of entry. An elitist feeling or attitude can develop that contributes to the spirit and cohesiveness of the group.

Perhaps the strongest factor that influences group cohesiveness is **group success**. When a group achieves a meaningful and shared goal, cohesiveness usually increases. Members experience a sense of accomplishment and pride. Nowhere is this more obvious than on sports teams. Members of successful teams often discuss team unity and attribute success to group members "stepping up" when there is a need. Even though the personalities are similar, when teams are not performing well we often see arguments, infighting, and other evidence of a lack of team cohesiveness.

Group cohesiveness can also increase dramatically when group members perceive an **external threat** to member goals and interests. Differences between members become less important as they pull together to protect the group and resist the threat.

The threatening party will feel less chance of success when faced with a unified response.

Fair rewards allocation can also influence group cohesiveness. Cohesiveness is facilitated when rewards are allocated fairly or evenly. To be fair, rewards must be either equivalent to the contribution a person has made or consistent with a person's status level. Equal distribution of rewards can grow out of a group agreement to do so. Cohesiveness suffers when a member is given rewards inconsistent with what others may feel he or she deserves.

GROUP DYNAMICS

As groups develop there are forces, or dynamics, that can influence both individual and subgroup behavior and overall group effectiveness. These dynamics are common in groups in all contexts and when managed properly can improve a group's effectiveness.

Cooperation and competition

Members of a group have choices about whether to cooperate or compete with other members. Cooperation means more than just helping; it includes giving support to others, and contributing time and effort in situations where people jointly work together toward some end. Typically, the whole group can benefit from cooperation. As mentioned earlier, factors within the group performance environment can have an effect on cooperative behaviors. Sometimes, it occurs as a direct result of how tasks are designed. For example, the layout of a factory or office can be designed for cooperative effort. Cooperation is also a common consequence of team sports such as baseball or basketball. When we use the term "teamwork," we are referring to cooperative activity.

In addition to cooperation, some groups also experience **competition** among members; members become more concerned with their own welfare, sometimes at the expense of others. Competition can impact cohesiveness and encourage group member behavior that may detract from accomplishment of group or organizational goals. Whether it is a basketball player who wants to score the most points and "hogs the ball," or the salesperson who keeps important sales information from colleagues in order to be the top salesperson, competition can have negative consequences for groups in which successful performance is determined by high task interdependence.

Competition can also lead to some benefits. Salespeople often compete among each other in rewards programs designed so that both they and the company gain from improved performance. If awards go to winners, the losers may suffer some, but the gain to the whole group may more than offset it. Therefore, whether

---

Guide for Managers:
CREATING A GOOD TEAM ENVIRONMENT

Here are some specific suggestions for creating a good team environment.

- **Instill within the organization the value of teams and groups to organizational success**. Organizations that use teams successfully have embedded the use of teams within the company's culture. Supporting the use of teams through vision statements, allocation of resources, and developing team-based reward systems all contribute to team success.

- **Develop selection mechanisms for all employees that value team skills in newly hired employees**. Many organizations focus on technical skills but we suggest you also consider interpersonal and team skills as part of your selection criteria.

- **Implement organizational training programs to ensure team skills are taught to employees who may participate on teams or groups**. Behaviors required in team environments are quite different than those needed in other environments. Don't assume employees are aware of the tools needed to be a successful team member or team leader.

- **Develop reward structures that reward team performance or encourage team-oriented individual behaviors**. Compensation programs that provide individual incentives are likely to foster competition rather cooperation.

- **Provide clear, specific, and difficult goals for the team or group**. Teams need to understand what they are being asked to do. Where possible, clearly identify effectiveness metrics that will be used to measure team performance.

- **Provide groups with as many opportunities for success as possible**. Participation in goal formation, special assignments, and other methods can give groups a sense of involvement. Successful achievement has a powerful impact on all aspects of group effectiveness. Opportunities for success are especially useful for newly forming groups: success helps keep them on a track toward maturity as opposed to dissolution.

- **Empower teams to be more responsible, more self-sufficient, and self-managing**. Expect teams to identify, select, and solve problems as much on their own as possible, and to evaluate the quality of their own work. Minimize supervisory interventions.

---

competition is damaging or not depends on the balance of benefits and costs that result.

Several factors can tilt individuals and groups toward either competition or co-operation. **Individual differences** affect a person's tendencies toward cooperation or competition. For example, on average, men are more competitive than women. People high in achievement needs are also highly competitive [9]. There are also cross-cultural differences in cooperativeness and competitiveness. For example, those

107

in a collectivist society such as China are less competitive than people from an indi-vidualistic society like the United States [10].

Groups usually have norms related to whether cooperative or competitive behav-ior is acceptable. In some situations, competition is the norm, such as in sports or in the business world. If, however, groups within organizations compete for the same pool of resources, then balancing cooperation and competition in organizational settings is a delicate and difficult issue.

Goals and rewards also influence whether group members cooperate or compete. Cooperation is more likely to occur where there are common goals that are under-stood, accepted, and believed to be obtainable. Traditional wisdom suggests co-operation is more easily achieved when employees perceive some chance of earning a valued reward. Within work groups, cooperation is maximized when members within the group share rewards equally. Group incentive plans have this attribute. Regardless of individual contributions, the group's product is assessed and rewarded. Group incentives, compared to individual incentives, encourage cooperation and sharing of ideas, and members are more willing to help and give each other feed-back. However, not all data supports the contention that rewarding the entire group is the best way to reward team performance. Some argue that individual behavior should be rewarded, with one aspect of that behavior being how the person con-tributes to the team. This suggests that effective teams may develop as a result of an effective system of rewards that facilitates an appropriate level of competitiveness among group members.

The characteristics of the task can affect whether the group members cooperate or compete. With complex tasks, people need to give and receive more information. Complex tasks have more elements than simple tasks. Less is known about how to perform them, and more problems can arise. **Task complexity** can also mean that it is difficult to give someone a clear job description. All this increases the need for interaction and cooperation.

Consider the differences between a sales team and a product development team. The sales team is assigned to contact individual customers to sell a new product while a product development team may be responsible for developing a new product. Each member of the sales team can work alone in a separate location, and interac-tions between members are not necessary to do the work. The product development team, however, is more likely to have a complex task. Product feasibility, production issues, marketing questions, and technological problems are all woven together, and team members are highly interdependent at all stages of work. Without inter-action, these team members would not know about the work of others, and this may result in duplication and wasted effort. When conditions change, members of the product development team must keep each other informed; they hold frequent meetings and use a variety of communication methods to facilitate cooperation.

Both cooperation and competition can be useful in improving group effectiveness, depending on the nature of the task performed by the group. Improving coopera-tion can result in better performance for group tasks that require interdependent action. For example, interaction and communication are critical to the success of the product development team because team members must share information, coordinate their plans and activities, and help each other. This is in contrast to the sales team, that might be more productive under moderate competition. The productivity of salespeople is possible with minimal interaction with one another. Care must be taken, however, so that lack of cooperation is not damaging to groups such as these. Competition might result in behaviors such as withholding critical information, which could damage the entire sales effort.

SOCIAL INFLUENCES ON BEHAVIOR

In this section we focus on the social influences that can have functional or dysfunctional consequences in group and team environments. For influence to take place, other people do not have to offer judgments, give orders, or otherwise exert direct pressure: their mere presence, without active involvement, is sometimes all that is necessary to arouse or sensitize us. **Social facilitation** occurs when performance improves in the presence of others. This happens with easy or previously learned tasks. **Social inhibition** occurs when performance is worse in the presence of others. This happens when the person is performing new, not yet learned tasks in the group. This is an important principle for managers who are attempting to increase the use of groups and teams within their organization to understand. It suggests using groups or teams may improve performance when they do work at which they are proficient. Conversely, when a person is learning new tasks, the principle argues for giving employees a place to learn or practice alone, away from others.

How does this social influence operate? Many of us become apprehensive when we are observed and evaluated. We also become distracted by the presence of others, and this can interfere with our performance. Another explanation lies in individual differences. Some of us are more affected by others, regardless of the task. Some people are simply more aware of others; they are more concerned about others' reactions, and have a greater desire for social acceptance or approval.

There are also positive social influences in groups that may lead to **helping behaviors**. Team or group members have many opportunities to exhibit helping behavior. They can assist a teammate with a task or a personal problem, volunteer extra effort, or suggest improvements. These behaviors, called prosocial or **contextual performance** in chapter 1, are actions that, in many ways, are not exaggerated, not extreme or heroic. They may seem even trivial and mundane yet they contribute in an important way to the effectiveness of the organization. People differ in their willingness to help others and there are several factors that influence the presence of helping behaviors in group and team members. The existence of role models, extrinsic or intrinsic rewards, or group and team norms can all facilitate helping behavior.

Social loafing occurs when a member of the group does not contribute fully to the group's work and expects others to pick up his or her load. This happens in larger groups because, with other people present, we assume that someone else will do what is needed and thus relieve us of the task. People seem willing to pass the buck even though nothing will be achieved if everyone loafs [11]. Social loafing helps us to avoid being the one who contributes a lot while others escape with doing less. It also protects us from failing, and it is difficult to fix responsibility or blame when other people are present. When people believe that individual contributions can be evaluated, however, social loafing is sharply reduced [12]. Unproductive people do not enjoy being exposed. When contributions to a group are made public, team members are less likely to loaf than when only the group performance is displayed. Individual visibility increases the pressure to perform [13].

Social loafing can be a serious problem in work groups and teams. Helping and individual effort might decline because of the presence of others. These effects can be overcome with norms and incentives which help to discourage social loafing, by making individual contributions more visible, and by fostering a culture where individualism and self-interest are replaced by a spirit of commitment to group effort [14].

VIRTUAL TEAMS

Modern organizations rely increasingly on virtual work arrangements. These involve work that is done by telecommuting or telenetworking using electronic communications. Members of virtual teams may work in different buildings or even different countries. While we suspect much of what we know about groups and teams will apply to virtual teams, it is clear that the very nature of this form of team structure creates new management challenges.

Advantages and disadvantages of virtual teams

Virtual teams have several advantages [2]. First, they span **time and distance constraints**. For example, a virtual team meeting is not subject to limitations of having to ensure that everyone is in town on the day of the team meeting. Team members can "virtually" be anywhere and still be active participants in meetings. Second, the virtual team **takes advantage of an individual's expertise who may work in another location**. Suppose that the production line of a manufacturing plant in Toledo has had a history of frequent breakdowns. In response, plant management has appointed a virtual task team with the specific purpose of developing plans to improve equipment reliability. Because this is a virtual team, team members include a troubleshooter who represents the company that made the manufacturing equipment as well as a foreman from a similar plant in Germany that has had the same problems. This would be impossible to do in the short run because of the time that it would take to get several people together in the same place. Third, virtual teams can **significantly reduce costs**. The travel costs for members who are geographically separated could be quite expensive. Fourth, virtual teams can lead to **improvements in the processes used to create team communications and reports**. In traditional teams trying to prepare a final report, the process can be cumbersome and time-consuming. This has typically meant sending a copy of a document to all team members and then having one person consolidate all of the inputs. With virtual technologies, all members can have both synchronous and asynchronous access to documents. A virtual team with members from Detroit and Tampa could simultaneously work on a document and that same document would be available for their team member to work on in Tokyo the next day.

One of the major disadvantages of virtual teams is the **lack of physical interaction** so that many key elements of effective communication are not present. Verbal and nonverbal cues are missing and, as a result, information we traditionally rely on to infer meaning from communications is also missing. As a result, virtual teams may have difficulty developing the level of trust necessary to become high-performing teams. Virtual teams that do develop higher levels of trust have three things in common. First, there is a social period where members introduce themselves and provide background information. Then, they develop clear roles for members. Finally, virtual team members demonstrate positive attitudes toward the team's tasks [15].

Improving performance of virtual teams

Virtual team members require many of the same skills as those necessary for traditional teams. However, because of the use of technology, managers need to understand the limitations and advantages of virtual technologies as a communication medium. Training is a key to performance on virtual teams. Team members need to know how to use the specific technologies that support team activities. Whether it is the technology used for communication or for decision support, team members need to feel comfortable with the medium. Members also need to be trained in behaviors relevant to the virtual environment. Given that traditional communication cues are limited in the virtual environment, members may need to learn new skills to communicate effectively as part of a virtual team.

Skills necessary for the virtual team environment fall into three areas; collaboration, socialization, and communication [15]. Collaboration skills are behaviors such as exchanging ideas without being critical, and ensuring that member ideas and input are tracked and summarized for accuracy. Socialization skills include using team member names in electronic greetings, soliciting feedback on process, express appreciation for ideas of others, and volunteering for necessary roles. Communication skills include responding in a timely manner to e-mail, using chat functions when available, addressing the entire team in communications, and ensuring that local translators are used when language issues are a factor.

111

SUMMARY

Much of your professional life will be spent working in teams. As a result, it is important to understand the factors that influence group effectiveness. Group performance is strongly affected by the context within which the group operates. Organizational culture, systems of reward, and training are all critical factors to group success. Performance also depends on the patterns of group development. Early in its life, a group has to establish goals as well as resolve questions of leadership and personal commitment. Conflicts that surface must be resolved if the group is to become cohesive. Members must also deal with questions of intimacy and openness. Group members can delude themselves into feeling all is well, but when this is not the case, the members become disillusioned and struggle further before the group can mature.

We have all been members of groups or teams in our personal and social lives. If you have not been part of a group or team in your professional life, you probably will be in the future. Understanding the issues important to group and team effectiveness is an important aspect of insuring that this experience will be a positive one.

REFERENCES

1 Katzenback, J. R. and D. K. Smith. 1993. *The Wisdom of Teams: Creating the High Performance Organization*. Boston, MA: Harvard Business School Press.

2 Cascio, W. F. 2000. Managing a Virtual Workplace. *Academy of Management Executive*, **14**(3): 81–90.

3 Bennis, W. G. and H. S. Shepard. 1965. A Theory of Group Development. *Human Relations*, **9**: 415–57.

4 Tuckman, B. W. and M. A. Jensen. 1977. Stages of Small-Group Development Revisited. *Group and Organization Studies*, **2**: 419–42.

5 Balkin, D. B. 1997. Rewards for Team Contributions to Quality. *Journal of Compensation and Benefits*, **13**: 41–6.

6 Overman, S. 1995. In *HR Magazine*, 72–4.

7 Jackson, S. E., K. E. May, and K. Whitney. 1995. Understanding the Dynamics of Diversity on Decision-Making Teams. In R. A. Guzzo and E. Salas, eds., *Team Decision-Making Effectiveness in Organizations*, 204–61. San Francisco: Jossey Bass.

8 Cohen, S. G. and D. E. Bailey. 1997. What Makes Teams Work: Group Effectiveness Research from the Shop Floor to the Executive Suite. *Journal of Management*, **23**: 239–90.

9 McClelland, D. A. 1965. Toward a Theory of Motive Acquisition. *American Psychologist*, **20**: 321–3.

10 Hofstede, G. 1980. *Culture's Consequences: International Differences in Work-Related Values*. Beverly Hills, CA: Sage Publications.

11 Baron, R. A. 1983. *Behavior in Organizations: Understanding and Managing the Human Side of Work*. Boston: Allyn & Bacon.

12 Williams, K., S. Harkins, and B. Latane. 1981. Identifiability as a Deterrent to Social Loafing:

Two Cheering Experiments. *Journal of Personality and Social Psychology*, **40**: 303–11.

13 Nordstrom, R., P. Lorenzi, and R. V. Hall. 1990. A Review of Public Posting of Performance Feedback in Work Settings. *Journal of Organizational Behavior Management*, **11**: 101–23.

14 Albanese, R. and D. D. Van Fleet. 1985. Rational Behavior in Groups: The Free-Riding Tendency. *Academy of Management Review*, **10**: 244–55.

15 Jarvenpaa, S. L., K. Knoll, and D. E. Leidner. 1998. Is Anybody Out There? Antecedents of Trust in Global Virtual Teams. *Journal of Management Information Systems*, **14**(4): 29–64.

CHAPTER 7

Culture: National and Organizational

THE HOFSTEDE MODEL OF NATIONAL CULTURE

ORGANIZATIONAL CONSEQUENCES OF NATIONAL CULTURAL DIFFERENCES

ORGANIZATIONAL CULTURE

THE MODAL PERSONALITY OF TOP MANAGEMENT AND TYPES OF ORGANIZATIONAL CULTURES

ORGANIZATIONAL SUBCULTURES

ORGANIZATIONAL CULTURE: SOME SPECIAL CASES

How important is it to recognize the different cultures that we are exposed to in our professional lives? Just in the USA, there are more than 100,000 firms that are involved in global ventures of more than $1 trillion dollars, and one in five of all US workers is employed in a firm with international activities. One example is Colgate Palmolive; with 35,000 employees, it has 75 percent of its $9 billion in sales from markets in 200 countries and territories. In the terrorist attack on the World Trade Center on September 11, 2001 the victims in that one complex included citizens from 80 different countries. These figures just begin to illustrate the issue of national culture. When you consider the numerous different cultures that exist within our organizations and even the subcultures within those organizations, it is clear that all managers need an understanding of the influence of these different conceptions of culture on organizational behavior.

Culture, in the broad sense, refers to the social context within which humans live. It affects the very nature of organizations in which people work, and how individuals perceive and respond to the world. There are different ways to characterize national cultures, and perhaps the most common is to think of them in terms of cultural stereotypes. Think about your views of Israelis, Turks, the French, and the English. All of these national groups emerge in our mind as pictures and concepts that reflect what we believe about them. One interesting approach to classifying cultures, a variation of the stereotype approach, is the use of **cultural metaphors** [1]: situations, events, or circumstances that occur in a culture and that capture and clarify its essential elements. For example, the symphony orchestra is the metaphor for Germany. Not only is Germany a musical nation with many orchestras, but the country operates like one. In a symphony orchestra, conformity is valued, rules are established, and each person is expected to work for the good of the whole. In business, as in the orchestra, strong leadership is preferred, but it should be exercised in such a way that there is considerable delegation of power and decision-making to subordinates. The opera is the metaphor for Italy, a country in which drama and emotions are so often intensely felt that they cannot be easily contained within the individual. Among other cultural metaphors are the Japanese garden, the Turkish coffee-house, and the Israeli kibbutz.

THE HOFSTEDE MODEL OF NATIONAL CULTURE

Perhaps the most important model of the way culture affects organizations and work is the **Hofstede model of culture** [2, 3, 4]. Culture is the patterned ways of thinking, feeling, and reacting, acquired and transmitted mainly by symbols, constituting the distinctive achievements of human groups including their embodiments in artifacts. The essential core of culture consists of traditional . . . ideas, and especially their attached values [5].

a kind of collective software or programming of the mind that distinguishes the members of one human group from another . . . It is to human collectivity what personality is to an individual [2].

For a country, its dominant values are called the **national character**, or the **modal personality** [2]. The modal personality is the degree of homogeneity and strength of the dominant personality orientations in the society. These values and beliefs begin to take shape early in life. They are the bases for individual control because an overwhelming number of the society's members accept them. Of the many different values acquired through socialization, some of the more important are those related to work, ways of responding to authority, and power orientations.

Dimensions of national culture

The modal personality of a country can be profiled on five different dimensions:

1   Uncertainty avoidance
2   Power distance
3   Individualism-collectivism
4   Masculinity-femininity
5   Long- versus short-term patterns of thought.

Societies high in **uncertainty avoidance** tend to prefer rules and to operate in predictable situations as opposed to situations where the appropriate behaviors are not specified in advance. Those with high uncertainty avoidance prefer stable jobs, a secure life, avoidance of conflict, and have lower tolerance for deviant persons and ideas. In nations low in uncertainty avoidance such as the US, there is less acceptance of rules and less conformity to the wishes of authority figures, unlike high uncertainty avoidance nations such as Germany and Japan [6]. For example, lateness and absenteeism are more serious issues in Japan than in other countries, such as Sweden, where uncertainty is more acceptable.

Japan scores higher than the USA on uncertainty avoidance while both score higher than Sweden. This means that, for instance, in Japan there is far less tolerance for deviations from accepted behavioral practices than in the USA, while Sweden is generally considered to be a very tolerant society. These differences are reflected in many educational and training programs in Japan devoted to learning the customary behaviors for all types of social situations, including how to bow, how to eat certain types of foods, how to behave at a funeral, and other social customs. This desire not to stand out in Japanese society is reflected in a proverb, "The nail that sticks up gets hammered down" [7].

Power distance is the degree to which differences in power and status are accepted in a culture. Some nations accept high differences in power and authority between members of different social classes or occupational levels; other nations do not. For example, the French are relatively high in power distance while Israel and Sweden score very low. In Israel and Sweden, worker groups demand and have a great deal of power over work assignments and conditions of work [8, 9]. French managers tend not to interact socially with subordinates and do not expect to negotiate work assignments with them.

There are some other consequences of power distance differences. For example, in low power distance countries such as the USA, powerful individuals can be forced out of their position or may be challenged by less powerful individuals or groups. You saw this happen when President Clinton was under pressure from many to step down, including members of his own political party.

Individualism-collectivism refers to whether individual or collective action is the preferred way to deal with issues. In cultures oriented toward individualism – such as the USA, the UK, and Canada – people tend to emphasize their individual needs and concerns and interests over those of their group or organization, while the opposite is true in countries which score high on collectivism, for example Asian countries such as Japan and Taiwan. In a collectivist society, you are expected to interact with members of your group. It is almost impossible to perceive a person as an individual rather than one whose identity comes from groups with which that individual is associated [6]. Certain work behaviors may also be affected. For example, in an individualistic society such as the USA, there is a tendency for persons to shirk when tasks are assigned to a group as opposed to when tasks are assigned to individuals. This tendency is not present in the collectivist country of Taiwan [10].

The **masculinity-femininity** dimension of a culture refers to the degree to which values associated with stereotypes of masculinity (such as aggressiveness and dominance) and femininity (such as compassion, empathy, and emotional openness) are emphasized. High masculinity cultures such as Japan, Germany, and the USA tend to have more sex-

Guide for Managers: WORKING IN A FOREIGN CULTURE

BE PREPARED. Being prepared for working in another culture is more a state of mind than anything else. This begins with taking a look your own culture – something we often take it for granted. You can be sure that some of your most difficult problems will occur when you expect to act as you would at home and find that something different is expected of you in the country where you are working. Of course you should also learn something about the culture of the country. This information is readily available on the Internet or through other sources. Focus on the more important local customs and habits of the locals.

differentiated occupational structures with certain jobs almost entirely assigned to women and others to men. There is also a stronger emphasis on achievement, growth, and challenge in jobs [2, 3]. In these cultures, people are also more assertive and show less concern for individual needs and feelings, a higher concern for job performance and a lower concern for the quality of the working environment. In countries high in the feminine dimension such as Sweden and Norway, working conditions, job satisfaction, and employee participation are emphasized.

Long- versus short-term patterns of thought reflects a culture's view about the future. The short-term orientation, a Western cultural characteristic, reflects values toward the present, perhaps even the past, and a concern for fulfilling social obligations. Long-term thought patterns, characteristic of Asian countries, reflect an orientation toward the future, belief in thrift and savings, and persistence. In countries with a long-term orientation, planning has a longer time horizon. Firms are willing to make substantial investments in employee training and development, there will be longer-term job security, and promotions will come slowly [11, 12]. Firms will also seek to develop long-term relationships with suppliers and customers [9].

Country clusters

There are groups of countries that share somewhat similar modal personalities, language, geography, and religion. These are called **country clusters** and they are shown in table 7.1. The Anglo

DEVELOP LONG-TERM RELATIONSHIPS WITH THE LOCALS. If you are going to be in another country for some period of time and you are like most expatriate managers, you will seek other foreign managers in the country, especially those from your own. These are good sources of local information and psychological support. However, it is useful to be able to operate not only "on the economy" but also in it, and having locals as friends to help with this makes life much easier and the experience much richer.

ABOVE ALL, BE FLEXIBLE. If you develop locals as friends you will learn about the culture very quickly. Most locals want to expose outsiders to the positive aspects of their own culture. To take advantage of this, though, you must be flexible and willing to take some risks. Trust your new friends and be willing to try new foods and experiences. We have all heard some of our international friends talk about some of the delicacies in their own cuisine that we thought wouldn't be very good. Your rule here should be, "If I don't try, I will never know what I am missing."

DON'T TRY TO FORCE YOUR WORK STYLE ONTO OTHERS IN YOUR WORK RELATIONSHIPS. Perhaps the biggest mistake that you can make when you are working with managers from another culture is to think that your approach is best and that those managers should adopt it. What is certain is that each culture has its own way to be effective and when you are in it, trust what they do and do not try to force your approach on them.

Table 7.1 Clusters of nations grouped by culture

ANGLO GROUP
  Australia, Canada, Ireland, New Zealand, South Africa, UK, USA

ARAB GROUP
  Abu-Dhabi, Bahrain, Oman, United Arab Emirates

FAR EASTERN GROUP
  Hong Kong, Indonesia, Malaysia, Philippines, Singapore, South Vietnam, Taiwan,
    Thailand

GERMANIC GROUP
  Austria, Germany, Switzerland

LATIN AMERICAN GROUP
  Argentina, Chile, Columbia, Mexico, Peru, Venezuela

LATIN EUROPEAN GROUP
  Belgium, France, Italy, Portugal, Spain

NEAR EASTERN GROUP
  Greece, Iran, Turkey

NORDIC GROUP
  Denmark, Finland, Norway, Sweden

UNIQUE CULTURES
  Brazil, India, Israel, Japan

Source: Adapted from Ronen [14].

cluster values low to medium power distances, low to medium uncertainty avoidance, and high masculinity and individualism. Both Latin clusters showed high power distance preferences, high uncertainty avoidance, and had high masculinity scores, but on individualism the Latin Americans scored lower than the Latin Europeans.

Still, there are important differences within each cluster. For example, it has been said that the English and Americans are two great peoples separated by the same language [13]. Another difference is in how they use space. In the USA, the location of one's home and office is an important cue to status; in Britain, social class is the crucial factor. Another difference is the way privacy is sought. An American who wants to be alone will move into another room and separate from others using a door; the English mostly become quiet, even in the presence of others.

ORGANIZATIONAL CONSEQUENCES OF NATIONAL CULTURAL DIFFERENCES

There are important ways in which culture affects organizations and those in them. For example, cultural differences will show up in managerial philosophies, organizational design, leadership and managerial styles, and motivation strategies.

Managerial philosophy and culture

Cultural differences will be reflected in managerial philosophies. For example, Laurent [15] conducted an analysis of managers from different countries who work for large multinational US corporations and found several differences:

- German managers, more than others, believed that creativity is essential for career success. In their mind, the successful manager is the one who has the right individual characteristics. Their outlook is rational: they view the organization as a coordinated network of individuals who make appropriate decisions based on their professional competence and knowledge.
- British managers hold a more interpersonal and subjective view of the organizational world. According to them, the ability to create the right image and to get noticed for what they do is essential for career success. They view the organization primarily as a network of relationships between individuals who get things done through influencing each other through communicating and negotiating.
- French managers look at the organization as an authority network where the power to organize and control the actors stems from their positioning in the hierarchy. They focus on the organization as a pyramid of differentiated levels of power to be acquired or dealt with. French managers perceive the ability to manage power relationships effectively and to work the systems as being particularly critical to their success.

Leadership and managerial style

There are cultural differences in the reactions to management and leadership styles [16]. For example, in Germany and France, leadership and control tend to be more centralized. German managers want to be informed about everything that is going on, and they show less interest in their subordinates. French managers see their job as an intellectual activity that requires intensely analytical work [17]. They value and excel in quantitative analysis and strategic planning. Above all, those who head large firms must be clever. The French seem to prefer managers with an analytical mind, independence, and intellectual rigor. They have a strong bias for intellect, rather than action. Unlike the Anglo-Saxon view of management, they do not place high emphasis on interpersonal skills and communications that are important managerial attributes in other countries. In the UK, managers delegate and decentralize more, they have a greater interest in their subordinates and, unlike the Germans, they only want to be informed about exceptional events. US managers tend to be hard-driving and solution-oriented, while Scandinavian managers are more consensus-oriented. Managers take different approaches to problem-solving. American managers are more direct: they will give you action plans; Europeans will take a more strategic theoretical look at problems.

Organizational design

Table 7.2 shows how the cultural dimensions might affect the organizational structure. For example, high power distance means greater acceptance of strong authority systems, high status differentials, and willingness to accept orders from superiors. Therefore, in countries such as Mexico, Venezuela, and Brazil, organizations will have more centralized authority, more organization levels, more supervisors, and a wage structure in which white-collar and professional work is disproportionately more highly valued.

The effects on motivational strategies

Motivational approaches that work in one culture may not work in others because of differences in values and preferences. For example:

- In English-speaking countries, individual achievement was more strongly emphasized than security.
- French-speaking countries tended to place greater importance on security and less on challenging work than the English-speaking countries.
- In northern European countries, leisure time was more important; there was higher concern for the needs of employees and less for the needs of the organization.
- Latin countries, Germany, and southern European countries put more emphasis on job security and fringe benefits.
- Japanese employees put a stronger emphasis on good working conditions and a friendly work environment.

Communication

Effective communication between people from different cultures is universally difficult because people have different values and, therefore, different perceptions. As a result, they do not always agree on the meaning of words and could easily have dissimilar styles of expressing themselves. Ferraro [7] gives an example:

Eastern cultures have so many nonverbal ways of saying 'no' without directly or unambiguously uttering the word. Needless to say, this practice has caused considerable misunderstanding when North Americans try to communicate with the Japanese. To illustrate, the Japanese in everyday conversation frequently use the word *hai* ('yes') to convey not agreement necessarily, but rather that they understand what is being said.

Table 7.2 Organizational characteristics and cultural values in various countries

POWER DISTANCE DIMENSION

Low	High
(*Austria, Denmark, Israel, Norway, Sweden*)	(*Brazil, India, Mexico, Philippines, Venezuela*)
• Less centralization	• Greater centralization
• Flatter organization pyramids	• Tall organization pyramids
• Fewer supervisory personnel	• More supervisory personnel
• Small wage differentials	• Larger wage differentials
• Structure in which manual and clerical work are equally valued	• Structure in which white-collar jobs are valued more than blue-collar jobs

UNCERTAINTY AVOIDANCE DIMENSION

Low	High
(*Denmark, India, Sweden, UK, USA*)	(*France, Greece, Peru, Portugal, Japan*)
• Less structuring of activities	• More structuring of activities
• Fewer written rules	• More written rules
• More generalists	• More specialists
• Variability	• Standardization
• Greater willingness to take risks	• Less willingness to take risks
• Less ritualistic behavior	• More ritualistic behavior

INDIVIDUALISM-COLLECTIVISM DIMENSION

Low	High
(*Columbia, Greece, Mexico, Taiwan, Venezuela*)	(*Australia, Canada, The Netherlands, UK, USA*)
• Organization as "family"	• Organization is more impersonal
• Organization defends employee interests	• Employees defend their own self-interests
• Practices are based on loyalty, sense of duty, and group participation	• Practices encourage individual initiative

MASCULINITY-FEMININITY DIMENSION

Low	High
(*Denmark, Finland, Sweden, Thailand*)	(*Austria, Italy, Japan, Mexico, Venezuela*)
• Sex roles are minimized	• Sex roles are clearly differentiated
• Organizations do not interfere with people's private lives	• Organizations may interfere to protect their interests
• More women in more qualified jobs	• Fewer women are in qualified jobs
• Soft, yielding, intuitive skills are rewarded	• Aggression, competition, and justice are rewarded
• Social rewards are valued	• Work is valued as a central life interest

LONG-TERM AND SHORT-TERM PATTERNS OF THOUGHT

Short	Long
(*France, Russia, USA*)	(*Hong Kong, Japan*)
• Shorter-term focus	• Strategic long-term emphasis
• Organizational socialization left to society	• Formal organizational schemes for thorough organizational socialization
• Focus on results in negotiation	• Focus on the process in negotiation

Source: Adapted from Jackofsky et al. [12] and Child [16].

122

Communication may even be a problem within a country cluster where the same language is spoken. For example, English is widely spoken around the world. This makes many Americans feel that they can cope quite well in other countries so long as they deal with individuals who can speak English. This is a mistake for reasons beyond differences in values, perceptions, word meanings, and styles of communicating. For instance, the German mode of communication is slow and ponderous compared to the French, resulting in slower decisions. The Japanese are less willing to make personal disclosures to others while the French have the greatest willingness to express conflict [18]. Studies have shown that Americans are among the most ethnocentric in their attitudes and they tend to discount what those from other countries say more than vice versa [19].

ORGANIZATIONAL CULTURE

Just as the best way to sense a national culture is when you are out of your own and in another country, you can sense differences in organizational cultures when you move from one organization to another. The reason is that, just like countries, organizations in the same society will have different organizational cultures. The **organizational culture** is the patterned way of thinking, feeling, and reacting that exists in a specific organization. It is the unique mental programming of that organization.

The most obvious and general force that shapes the organizational culture is the national character – cultural values such as individual freedom, beliefs about the goodness of humanity, orientations toward action, power distance norms, and so on. However, for the organization itself, the most direct sources of culture are organization-specific factors. Therefore, while two similar firms in a country would be subject to the same national cultural influences, their separate experiences will lead to differentiated organizational cultures.

Modal organizational personality

The organizational culture is a direct reflection of its own **modal organizational personality**, the degree of homogeneity and the strength of a particular personality orientation in that organization – and results from four factors.

1 People develop values during socialization so as to accommodate to the types of organizations in the society.
2 Selection processes screen out many who might not "fit," and organization socialization changes those who do join, so that some level of personality homogeneity develops in every organization.
3 The rewards in organizations selectively reinforce some behaviors and attitudes and not others.

123

4 Promotion decisions usually take into account both performance and personality of candidates.

There are other organization-specific factors that affect organizational culture, for example the industry in which the firm operates. Firms in the same industry share the same competitive environment, the same customer requirements, and the same legal and social expectations. For example, there is a very distinctive culture of direct-selling organizations such as Mary Kay Cosmetics, Amway, and Tupperware. These firms do not "have well-defined criteria for recruitment, they discourage competition among distributors, have few rules and managers, spawn charismatic rather than rational leadership . . . and encourage employees to involve spouses and children in their selling activities" [20].

Significant people in the organization's history are also important. We know from research about the long-term effects on the firm of founders or significant managers such as Bill Gates of Microsoft, Herb Kelleher of Southwest Airlines, and Mary Kay of Mary Kay Cosmetics. What they do is to build very strong top management groups in their early years that are able to maintain power for many years even after the founder leaves [21].

Critical events may also become part of the folklore of the organization and are a reference point for members' values and beliefs. For example, when Apple Computer was experiencing serious competitive problems with IBM and having internal organizational and technical difficulties in 1984, Steven Jobs made a powerful speech, animated, with a screen descending from the ceiling, at the annual sales conference. He challenged IBM in ways that openly excited employees and distributors. There were no changes in financial position, market position, or technology, only changes in "the organization, and how its employees (and competitors and potential customers) felt about it. That was all; that was enough" [22].

A multi-level model of organizational culture

We think the best way to understand organizational culture is to use a multidimensional and multilevel model. Figure 7.1 shows how three related levels of factors make up the organization's culture, starting with the basic values of the **dominant coalition**. The goal of that coalition is to ensure that its values are firmly embedded in the firm. Its values form the bases of the next level – the **manifestations of organizational culture** – elements such as selection and socialization, ideologies, and myths and symbols. Finally, for outsiders, the culture is obvious only in the **modes of implementation** that are apparent when they interact with the firm in different ways. To think of organizational culture in this way should help you to understand why it is so enduring, so powerful, and how it is affected by, and affects, selection, socialization, reward practices, and even the firm's products or services [23].

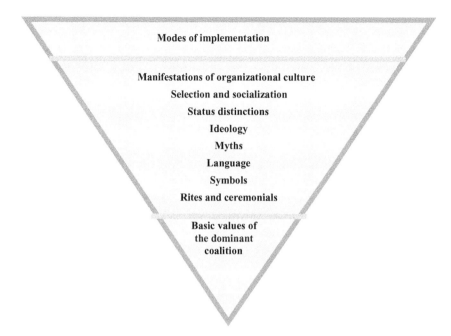

Figure 7.1 A multi-level view of organizational culture

Basic values of the dominant coalition

Organization culture has its roots in the basic values of the dominant coalition; the group that wields the most control and power. These values may have originated with the firm's founder and reflect his or her fundamental beliefs about what should be done, how it should be done, who should do it, and the way that members are treated. They could be important values like **innovation and risk-taking, stability and security, respect for people, team orientation and collaboration**, or **aggressiveness and competition** [24].

The primary interest of the dominant coalition is to maintain the cultural identity of the firm so that it is consistent with the values of the members in that coalition [23]. This permits the members of the coalition to maintain power and control because these values serve to justify crucial organizational policies, practices, and decisions such as key promotions, choices of products or services, and the selection of strategic niches. The history of several important firms in the USA is an illustration of what can happen when the top management is able to do this, even in the face of significant environmental changes. For instance, the dominant coalitions in IBM were able to remain in power for years by implementing marketing and technology strategies that protected them. As long as IBM was able to remain in the mainframe business, in spite of the technological changes in personal computers, the managerial

125

power structure remained somewhat stable and intact. After some severe losses, John Akers was replaced by Louis Gerstner. He was charged with turning IBM around. The aim literally was to change the way people in IBM think and do business, to change the values that dominated the firm because these values no longer worked.

Manifestations of organizational culture

The basic values of the dominant coalition are reflected in concepts, meanings, and messages that are embedded in their decisions and in organization practices such as selection and socialization strategies, organizational status distinctions, ideologies, myths, language, symbols, and rites and ceremonials [25]. These elements have two purposes and, likewise, convey two different types of meaning. One purpose is instrumental and rational; the other is expressive and emotional.

The **instrumental meanings** are the ways that values and beliefs are reflected in what the organization can do and how it does it. They broadly and generally define such objectives as the nature of the products or services, the markets that will be served, the philosophy of product quality levels, the orientation toward personnel within the firm, the nature of work relationships with the organization, and the general orientation of the organization to its constituencies.

The **expressive meanings** are the psychological and sociological meanings and effects of those same elements on the members. They create a "symbolic field and seek to protect stability . . . They enable the group to maintain its collective identity and offer a recognizable identity to the outside world" [23]. They often involve the creation of symbols that have important meanings to the members and are easily identified

Guide for Managers: DEALING WITH ORGANIZATIONAL CULTURE

The most important time that you will have to deal with the organizational culture will be in your early experiences of it. Here are some ways to get an idea of what the culture is like early.

DO NOT MAKE QUICK JUDGMENTS. Perhaps the biggest mistake that you can make when joining a new organization is to believe too quickly what you hear and see in your first days. Remember the importance of first impressions errors?

STUDY THE PHYSICAL SETTING FOR SYMBOLS. Look around to see how consistent the environment is from one place to another. Careful observations can give you some important clues about aspects of the organization such as how status is differentiated. You will also be able to get some idea about whether people like to work there by observing things like by others as being associated with that organization.

These instrumental and expressive meanings, and effects, can be seen in what happened when Robert Horton became the chief operating officer of British Petroleum in the early 1990s. The company was in trouble because his predecessor had made some poor major strategic decisions [26]. Horton's strategy for turning the company around was to change the corporate strategy, the culture, to reduce costs, and to reduce managerial layers. Under Horton, BP greatly expanded its US refining and marketing operations, spending more than $7.7 billion to take over Standard Oil. Later, BP began making substantial investments in the North Sea, the Gulf of Mexico, and Colombia. To reduce costs, BP eliminated 8,000 employees from the workforce. Horton attempted to foster a culture that emphasized teamwork and collaboration, empowering the workforce, reducing the bureaucracy, and increasing the focus on globalization. The instrumental effects of these changes were reduced costs and a streamlined organization – exactly the results he intended.

However, the expressive effects were not quite what Horton expected, or wanted. Rather than an empowered culture that Horton wanted, the workers were resentful because they felt

their mood, how they treat people, especially strangers and visitors. One thing to look at carefully is the company literature. For example, you can tell a lot by how the firm presents itself in words and pictures to the public when you are able to compare that with what you see to be the actual case.

LOOK FOR SIGNS OF CULTURES IN TROUBLE. Read carefully our discussion of neurotic cultures and look for those sorts of signals around you. Open expressions of strong emotions, inconsistencies in practices and policies, and other neurotic tendencies will give you some clue that something is wrong.

UNDERSTAND THAT CULTURES ARE USUALLY IMPERVIOUS TO CHANGE. Do not think you can change a culture unless you are entering the firm as its CEO. Even then, culture has developed over a significant period of time and is manifested in the characteristics of every facet of the organization including manager and employee characteristics, their behavior toward each other and toward customers, and all organizational policies and processes. The bottom line is that "the culture always wins."

that the culture changes had been unilaterally imposed. There was a feeling among many that the cultural change was more of a public relations effort than a serious attempt to change BP's values. Instead of feelings of empowerment because they had more responsibility due to the reduction of layers of management, they felt overburdened with more work and felt that BP was still a top-down-managed company.

Through **selection and socialization strategies**, organizations try to select and indoctrinate members with values consistent with the culture. When effective selecting and socializing of members results in hiring people with values congruent with the organizational culture, the results are increased job satisfaction, higher organizational commitment, and lower turnover [24].

Class distinctions, or **organizational status distinctions** – the accepted power and status relations between individuals and groups in organizations – are one basis for legitimizing influence relationships. The most obvious are hierarchical. These are consistent with the ordering of organizational levels and the delegated responsibility and authority associated with levels.

There are also other types of class distinctions. In some organizations, certain positions have higher status than others even though they are presumably at the same organizational level. In universities, there are status distinctions between professors, such as a professor of medicine and a professor of education. Another status distinction could be among occupational groups. These will occur especially when groups of trained professionals work with less trained groups or other groups with different professional training and socialization. The high-status groups will have more power and find it easier to obtain resources.

The culture of any organization is built around a shared **ideology** [20] – "the relatively coherent set of beliefs that binds some people together and explain their worlds [to them] in cause-effect relations" [17]. Ideology helps members make sense of decisions. For example, the ideology that permeates Microsoft is that any attempt by the government to constrain it will reduce innovation and competitiveness in the software industry.

A **myth** is a story of past events that is used to explain the origins or transformations of something. It leads to an unquestioned belief that certain techniques and behaviors are right. There is often no demonstrated evidence for the belief, only the acceptance of the myth [20]. Of course, myths differ in accuracy but they all represent important events or circumstances that are passed on from one organizational generation to another and become a basis for action. How much truth and how much fiction are in the myths and stories that arise from the organization's culture is not important. What matters is whether they transmit core organization values to others and that they serve as a basis of control.

A unique **language** exists for every organization. Like the mother tongue of a country, the organization's language is best used and understood by its members. Using it properly is, in fact, a way for individuals to be identified as a member. The organization's language comprises jargon, slang, gestures, signals, signs, jokes, humor, and metaphors that allow members to convey very specific and clear meaning to other members [20]. When the "right" language is used to explain an action, it is accepted because it reflects the culture. For example, when Henry Ford II personally fired Lee Iacocca after a very successful career at Ford Motor Company, Iacocca asked "Why?" Mr. Ford is reported to have said, "Because I don't like you." Ford, even though it is among the largest firms in the USA, is still under close family control, and those who work there know it – and have always known it. When this story circulated among employees, everyone there understood – because personal loyalty is very important. The language Henry Ford used was very consistent with the ideology.

Symbols – objects to which organizational meaning has become attached – can include titles, parking places, special dining-rooms, office size, location, and furnishings and other indicators of position and power [27]. In any organization, the specific symbols will be unique and related to the shared perspective of members. One plant manager attempted to convey the concept of egalitarianism in the plant by installing a round table, as a symbol, in the conference room. The idea was that there were no "heads"; everyone should expect to contribute equally. However, another symbol carried a more powerful message: there was only one reserved place in the parking lot – it belonged to the plant manager.

Symbols can also distinguish status and power differences between individuals and groups at the same level. For example, in almost every company, it is simple to know which of the vice-presidents (all presumably at the same organizational level) is most important by the location and size of office and pay differentials. In fact, it causes some consternation in an organization when a person wishes to have an office location and size that are different from others with similar status. Likewise, it can also cause problems when a lower-status person acquires symbols that are more appropriate to a higher-level position.

Rites are "relatively elaborate, dramatic, planned sets of activities that consolidate various forms of cultural expressions into one event, which are carried out through social interactions, usually for the benefit of an audience." A **ceremony** is a "system of several rites connected with an occasion or event" [20]. Like symbols and myths, rites and ceremonies convey important cultural meanings by actions and interactions. Some of the more important organizational rites are discussed below [20].

Rites of passage bring you into an organization or separate you from it. **Induction rites** that bring you into an organization convey some of its important norms and values. They can be very elaborate, like military basic training, or very simple, as when a personnel assistant explains the company rules and policies to you on the first workday. In one firm, to communicate the level of expected commitment, it was standard practice to have the spouses of married prospective employees present when the job offer was made. During this discussion, both the good points and the bad points of the job were accurately described to both.

Separation rites help you make a clean break with the organization. Retirement parties signal the end of a career, and going-away dinners separate a person from one organization on the way to another. Separation rites often involve elaborate dinners, drinking, and discussions about past life in the organization.

Degradation rites occur when someone is removed from a position or from the organization. In most organizations, these rites are less formal. At one point in the history of a large entertainment and publishing firm in the USA, releasing a top manager began with a rite of degradation. The CEO would begin to point out that a certain manager was becoming a problem because "he couldn't handle the women." The firm was noted for having many attractive women executives and workers, and it was well known that many men and women had open relationships, regardless of their marital status. However, when the president wished to remove a manager, the degradation rite started this way. Later, some "objective"

129

performance deficiency would be identified and the person would resign or be fired.

Enhancement rites elevate the status or position of a person. Awarding recognition through symbols or announcement of promotions are examples. Sometimes these are informal. In one firm, the enhancement rite that precedes promotion to the top levels begins when the CEO asks a junior executive to join him on special public occasions.

Renewal rites have the goal of strengthening and improving the current social structure [20]. Training and development programs are one form of these rites. They are usually quite conspicuous in organizations because time must be set aside during which those in the organization must attend classes and because these programs usually employ a set of new symbols and language. This was an especially important activity for a major US service company which was restructuring itself after severe economic losses. Under a new CEO, they undertook a series of management development programs which almost all managers were required to attend. While a major part of the development was directed toward improving the managers' knowledge of the latest and best business practices, a substantial effort was devoted toward ensuring that those attending were exposed to the philosophy of the new CEO and understood the type of culture he was seeking to develop.

Conflict avoidance or reduction is desired in most organizations; yet the nature of organization itself gives rise to conflict. To resolve conflict, organizations use **conflict-reduction rites** such as collective bargaining, the grievance process, the "open-door policy" where each manager's door will always be open to hear subordinates' problems, committees in which divergent views can be aired, and ombudsmen who are supposed to represent workers' interests impartially.

Integration rites facilitate and increase the interaction of the organization's members, presumably to make working together easier [20]. During integration rites, official titles and organizational differences are eliminated for a short time so that people meet others as people. An example of an integration rite is the "dining in" tradition in the US Air Force.

Modes of implementation

After you adapt to an organization and live in it for a while, you become unaware of the organizational culture and its effects. On the other hand, if you are an outsider or customer, you have no direct experience of the organizational culture; instead you experience it through the specific modes of implementation – designs for products and services, policies for dealing with customers, approaches to managing human resources, the formal structure and types of controls – all of which can be traced back to the values of the dominant coalition. They are also internally reflected in the sorts of things described above. So, one way to experience the organizational culture is through your perceptions about the company and/or the use of its products and services, how they are designed, their quality level, their price, and the level of service that is delivered. Another way of experiencing the culture is when you seek employment with a firm and are exposed to its hiring practices, promotional material and, perhaps most importantly, the way the hiring decision is transmitted to you if you are a job candidate. You also experience an organizational culture by the symbols, trademarks, and logos associated with it. The letters "GE" for General Electric and the Nike "swoosh" convey something to us about these firms. Finally, you sense some of an organization's culture from the way it deals with its social responsibility.

THE MODAL PERSONALITY OF TOP MANAGEMENT AND TYPES OF ORGANIZATIONAL CULTURES

The modal personality of the dominant coalition will determine how their values are translated into actions, policies, and behavior. This group makes the important decisions about market strategy, organization design, the nature of the reward system, and who is promoted into this group. Their visions, beliefs, and actions are translated through managerial decisions into specific policies, products, and practices that will be manifestations of the culture.

Neurotic cultures

One study that tells us a lot about how organizational culture is related to the modal personality is about how neurotic managers create **neurotic organizations** [28]. The idea of the neurotic organization is similar to the concept of the neurotic person. Neurotic people exhibit extreme psychological tendencies and behaviors, leading to problems that affect them and others. Their problems, however, are not so severe as to justify taking them out of society. Like a neurotic person, a neurotic organization is in trouble, but still able to operate, and headed by executives or groups of executives with neurotic tendencies. The result is a neurotic culture.

Of course, not all managers are neurotic nor do all organizations have neurotic cultures. Many organizations have healthy cultures that are supportive, innovative, and collaborative, creating a positive social and psychological context for their members. These healthy organizations will have a mixture of personality types, which will be neither dominant nor extreme [28]. So why study these extreme types of personalities and the resulting organizational cultures? Because it helps understand the culture of "normal" companies. Neurotic cultures are different from normal ones only by a matter of degree. Besides, the processes that lead to neurotic organizations are not qualitatively different from those that lead to healthy cultures – they are simply more extreme and intense. We now look at five types of neurotic cultures.

Charismatic cultures

A **charismatic culture** is associated with a dramatic modal managerial personality. **Dramatic managers** have feelings of grandiosity, have a strong need for attention from others, and try to draw attention to themselves. They are exhibitionists, seeking excitement and stimulation. However, they often lack self-discipline, cannot focus their attention for long periods of time, and tend to be charming but superficial. They often attract subordinates who have high dependency needs, prefer to be directed, and overlook the weaknesses of the leaders. For the subordinates, every-thing revolves around the top manager or group of top managers. The subordinates have a great deal of trust that those who lead the organization can do no wrong. This does two things: the top executive keeps close control and at the same time remains the center of attention.

Paranoid cultures

The **paranoid culture** results from a suspicious modal personality orientation. **Suspicious managers** feel persecuted by others and do not trust them and behave in guarded and secret ways toward others. They believe that subordinates are lazy, incompetent, and secretly wish to "get" them. He or she feels hostile toward others, particularly peers and subordinates, and acts aggressively toward them.

If you work in a paranoid culture, you will feel a strong sense of distrust and suspicion [28]. In the paranoid culture, people do not easily share important information with others because they fear that it could cost them some advantage. In paranoid cultures, people tend to act passively and do not actively participate in important organization matters. This results in either organization paralysis or direc-tive action by the top management to initiate events.

Depressive cultures

The **depressive modal personality** orientation leads to an **avoidant culture**. A depressive person has strong needs for affection and support from others and feels unable to act on, and change the course of, events. These feelings of inadequacy are related to very passive behavior and inaction. Depressives often seek justification of their actions from other significant actors; in the case of managers, these might be experts and consultants.

Top management seeks to avoid change in the avoidant culture. They are passive and purposeless. Change is resisted because it may threaten the current organizational values and power structure; appropriate action is avoided. The relatively low level of external changes and the desire of the management to retain control result in

132

little activity, low self-confidence, high anxiety, and an extremely conservative culture.

Bureaucratic cultures

The **bureaucratic culture** is a result of a compulsive modal organization personality. **Compulsive managers** have high needs for control. They view things in terms of domination and submission. They focus on very specific but often trivial details. Compulsive managers are devoted to their work and to showing deference toward those at levels above them, and they act autocratically toward subordinates. They have strong preferences for well-ordered systems and processes.

In the bureaucratic culture, there is more concern with how things look rather than with how things work. Managers focus more on the rules than on the purpose of those rules. There are usually specific, detailed, formalized control systems, to monitor the behavior of the members. These controls are derived from very specific objectives that have been broken down into very detailed, often trivial, plans of action [28]. These plans and the performance indicators derived from them then become the criteria against which performance is measured. The high control needs of managers are reflected in the ways that the authority structure is implemented and executed. Rank and position are important, and hierarchical deference is the norm. Ritualistic, deferential behavior toward superiors is expected from subordinates.

Politicized cultures

Politicized cultures occur in organizations when the top management has a **detached modal organizational personality**. They have a strong sense of disengagement from others and of not being connected to the environment. They believe that interaction with others will lead to harm and tend to avoid emotional relationships because they fear they will be demeaned by others. Aloofness and coldness characterize their relationships. They are socially and psychologically isolated and do not care about it.

In politicized organization cultures, there is no clear direction. The CEO is not strong, but also not psychologically connected to the organization. Lacking leadership, managers at lower levels try to influence the direction of the firm. There are often several individuals or coalitions competing for power because of the lack of leadership. Managers are involved in these divisive power struggles to enhance their own position and status, and there is only minimal concern with the success of the organization.

ORGANIZATIONAL SUBCULTURES

The fact is that most large organizations do not have a homogeneous culture. Instead they are usually a cluster of **organizational subcultures** that differ significantly from each other. There can be different types of organizational subcultures that members identify with, which include hierarchical, occupational, and culturally diverse subcultures [29].

Hierarchical subcultures

Hierarchical subcultures exist at different organizational levels and are visible in the differences in symbols, status, authority, and power between managers and workers. Hierarchical subcultures are most clearly visible and strongest in organizations where there is clear, strong stratification between levels. This occurs when the work at lower levels has been highly task-specialized so that minimal skills are required to do it. This weakens the power of lower levels and results in centralization of control and decision-making. It also is facilitated when promotion to the managerial levels requires both competence and values congruent with those of the dominant coalition. The result is a management group with strong homogeneous values that are different from those of the workforce in general.

Occupational/task subcultures

Occupational/task subcultures are those in which members have strong identification with the others who have similar skills. These skills are very important to organizational success and have been developed through intensive training during which there is strong occupational socialization. Then others who share the same occupation or task, inside and outside the organization, will be an important reference group.

Culturally diverse subcultures

Culturally diverse subcultures are those in which members identify with others with similar racial, ethnic, or gender characteristics. Many organizations are experiencing the same phenomena of multiculturalism as Digital Equipment. In one Digital plant with 350 workers, there are 44 different countries represented and 19 different languages spoken. Multiculturalism in US organizations in recent years has increased as African Americans, Hispanics, Asians, and Native Americans have entered the workforce in more significant numbers and as companies have made serious efforts to reduce discrimination in selection and promotion practices. The result has been that there are culturally diverse subcultures based on the values and beliefs of these groups that may differ in many ways from the dominant organization culture.

ORGANIZATIONAL CULTURE: SOME SPECIAL CASES

Managers are increasingly recognizing the power and effects of culture on the behavior of people in organizations. They are becoming interested in trying to manage it as a way to contribute to the effectiveness of the firm. However, while there is agreement that cultures exist in every organization and that they do change, there is disagreement over the degree to which they can be managed. We think there are some special situations in which the effects of organizational culture cause serious problems for the management of a firm.

Implementing a culture in a new organization

In new organizations, it is possible to try to shape the culture through carefully designed selection programs, socialization strategies, and the consistent use of symbols and language. Very quickly, though, the members of the organization modify the values intended by management, and the culture emerges. When starting a new organization, many managers make a conscious decision to implement a healthy culture that supports the type of high-involvement organizations (HIOs) discussed in chapter 9. This has some important advantages: costs may be lower because less direct supervision is needed, worker morale and satisfaction are higher, and absenteeism and turnover may be reduced. In one case, a firm was trying to implement an HIO culture. It failed because the cultural values were inconsistent with the personality of the plant manager. He had a dramatic personality that overpowered the attempt to create the articulated values and beliefs of empowerment and participation.

Mergers and acquisitions

Problems arise when the cultures of two firms involved in a merger are different and, more importantly, incongruent. At this writing, this appears to be the problem that the Daimler–Chrysler merger is facing. It is apparent that the more rigid, hierarchy-based culture of Daimler is not compatible with the more loose structure of the American firm. The result has been that many of the top US managers are leaving the firm.

Changes in the environment

Cultures change when there is a significant change in the firm's environment to which it must adapt if it is to survive. A good example of the problem of adapting the culture to a changing environment is in the automotive sector in the USA. The environment for Ford, Chrysler, and General Motors began changing with the advent of foreign competition beginning in the late 1960s. At that time, GM had a 50 percent share of the US market, with Ford a distant second and Chrysler barely in the picture. However, the environment did not shift sharply and severely in a short time period. Foreign manufacturers kept increasing market share gradually through a strategy of introducing high-quality and very competitively priced cars into the US market. All of the American manufacturers made some design changes, but did little to alter their processes to increase product quality. Further, many in this industry were convinced that eventually US consumers would prefer larger, traditional automobiles. Ford adapted nicely, but over some time, to the changing environment. After a long period of resistance, Ford began a serious and successful effort in the mid-1980s to improve its product quality, going through an extreme culture change. The success of this effort was finally realized ten years later in 1992, when the Ford Taurus replaced the Honda as the leader in US auto sales. GM, on the other hand, has not done so well. Its market share is hovering in the late 1990s around 30 percent, down from the 50 percent in the early 1970s. The reason is that, in our judgment, GM has not made the changes necessary in the dominant coalition; one of the major requirements for succession to top management positions has been to be from within GM.

Changing the existing culture

It is very difficult to modify the culture of an existing organization, especially when an embedded management attempts to change it by using consultants and formal change programs. Usually, attempts to modify culture center around revision of activities and practices. Imagine, for example, a compulsive chief executive who thinks that productivity might be increased through increasing employee involvement. He might decide to change the bureaucratic culture. Trainers and consultants, who use team-building development approaches that give managers experience in working together, might be retained. There might be some organization redesign to facilitate activities among groups by creating new interdependencies. However, because the basic values of the top management groups are not consistent with these practices, the change effort will fail. The more constructive culture is not consistent with the compulsive modal personality.

Changing the CEO

When a new CEO comes into a firm, a number of things usually happen that affect the culture: some members of the board of directors are usually replaced, and there is usually a change in the top management group, especially the vice-presidents. The result is a dominant coalition with values more similar to those of the new CEO that will begin to be reflected in the various procedures and processes that manifest the culture that we have described earlier in this chapter.

Whether the effect on the culture will be strong or weak depends upon the extent to which the values of the new dominant coalition are similar to those of the previous group in power. If the new dominant coalition has values similar to the previous group, there will be little change and things will continue not much different from in the past. This most often occurs when the new CEO comes from within the firm.

Then you would expect that he or she has been socialized and then been selected based on the existing culture. Internal succession is a reasonable strategy when the firm has been attaining profitability and performance objectives that are acceptable to its stakeholders, especially the stockholders and the board of directors, and if there is no evidence of a significant change in the environment that would warrant a move to a different culture. The reason for this is that an insider will be already accustomed to the existing culture that is supporting the current acceptable firm performance.

SUMMARY

The fundamental values in a society are strong forces that affect the behavior of those in organizations. Culture is the patterned way of thinking, feeling, and reacting that is characteristic of human groups and that accounts for important differences between them. Values are ideas about what is right or wrong, and good or bad, that are the basis of much human action. Culture is transmitted through socialization.

The culture of an organization is, of course, significantly affected by the broader society in which the organization exists. However, decisions by key managers, particularly the CEO, give it a more specific form in that organizational culture reflects their dominant values. Each organizational culture is unique and is reflected in the distinctive pattern of top management activity and a particular set of policies that emerge in the organization. The culture of an organization contributes to its identity and to its success (or failure). There is often an effort to maintain the culture since it supports the current power structure in the organization. Likewise, socialization strategies, ideologies, and so on will strengthen the current organization value orientations and systems. Those in organizations may do many things to ensure that the sources of culture do not change in such a way as to require changes in the organizational value systems.

REFERENCES

1 Gannon, M. J. 1993. *Cultural Metaphors: Capturing Essential Characteristics of 17 Diverse Societies*. Chicago: Sage Publishing.

2 Hofstede, G. 1980. *Culture's Consequences: International Differences in Work-Related Values*. Beverly Hills, CA: Sage Publications.

3 Hofstede, G. 1980. Motivation, Leadership and Organization: Do American Theories Apply Abroad? *Organizational Dynamics*, 2: 42–63.

4 Hofstede, G. 1992. Cultural Constraints in Management Theories. *Academy of Management Executive*, 7(1): 81–94.

5 Kluckholn, F. and F. Strodtbeck. 1961. *Variations in Value Orientations*. Evanston, IL: Row, Peterson.

6 Brislin, R. 1993. *Understanding Culture's Influence on Behavior.* Fort Worth: Harcourt Brace Jovanovich.

7 Ferraro, G. 1998. *The Cultural Dimension of International Business.* Englewood Cliffs, NJ: Prentice-Hall.

8 Cole, R. E. 1989. *Strategies for Learning: Small Group Activities in American, Japanese, and Swedish Industry.* Berkeley: University of California Press.

9 Adler, N. J. 1991. *International Dimensions of Organizational Behavior.* Boston: PWS-KENT Publishing Company.

10 Grabrenya, W., Y. J. Wang, and B. Latane. 1985. Social Loafing in an Optimizing Task: Cross Cultural Differences Among Chinese and Americans. *Journal of Cross Cultural Psychology*, **16**: 223–42.

11 Ouchi, W. 1981. *Theory Z: How American Business Can Meet the Japanese Challenge.* Reading, MA: Addison-Wesley.

12 Jackofsky, E. F., J. W. Slocum, and S. J. McQuaid. 1988. Cultural Values and the CEO: Alluring Companions. *Academy of Management Executive*, **2**(1): 39–49.

13 Hall, E. T. 1969. *The Hidden Dimension.* New York: Doubleday.

14 Ronen, S.a.S., O. 1985. Clustering Countries on Attitudinal Dimensions: A Review and Synthesis. *Academy of Management Review*, **10**(3): 435–54.

15 Laurent, A. 1986. The Cross-Cultural Puzzle of International Human Resource Management. *Human Resource Management*, **25**(1): 91–102.

16 Child, J. C. 1981. Culture Contingency and Capitalism in the Cross-National Study of Organizations. In L. L. Cummings and B. M. Staw, eds., *Research in Organizational Behavior*, 303–56. Greenwich, CT: JAI Press.

17 Beyer, J. M. 1981. Ideologies, Values and Decision Making in Organizations. In P. N. A. W. Starbuck, ed., *Handbook of Organizational Design*, 166–97. London: Oxford University Press.

18 Ting-Toomey, S. 1991. Intimacy Expressions in Three Cultures: France, Japan, and the United States. *International Journal of Intercultural Relations*, **15**: 29–46.

19 Hall, E. T. and M. R. Hall. 1990. *Understanding Cultural Differences: Germans, French, and Americans.* Yarmouth, ME: Intercultural Press.

20 Trice, H. M. and J. M. Beyer. 1984. Studying Organization Culture through Rites and Ceremonials. *Academy of Management Review*, **9**: 635–69.

21 Boeker, W. 1990. The Development and Institutionalization of Subunit Power in Organizations. *Administrative Science Quarterly*, **34**: 388–410.

22 Pfeffer, J. 1992. *Managing with Power.* Boston, MA: Harvard Business School Press.

23 Gagliardi, P. 1986. The Creation and Change of Organizations: A Conceptual Framework. *Organization Studies*, 118–33.

24 O'Reilly, C. A., J. Chatman, and D. F. Caldwell. 1991. People and Organizational Culture: A Profile Comparison Approach to Assessing Person – Organization Fit. *Academy of Management Journal*, 487–516.

25 Trice, H. M. and J. M. Beyer. 1993. *The Cultures of Work Organizations.* Englewood Cliffs, NJ: Prentice-Hall.

26 *Economist.* 1992. BP after Horton. July 4, 324: 59.

27 Pfeffer, J. 1981. *Power in Organizations.* Boston, MA: Pitman Publishing.

28 Kets de Vries, M. F. R. and D. Miller. 1984. *The Neurotic Organization.* San Francisco: Jossey-Bass.

29 Sackmann, S. A. 1992. Culture and Subcultures: An Analysis of Organizational Knowledge. *Administrative Science Quarterly*, **37**: 140–61.

CHAPTER 8

Organizational Structure and Design

THE FUNDAMENTALS OF ORGANIZATIONAL STRUCTURE

ORGANIZATIONS: THE EFFECTS OF TECHNOLOGY AND MARKETS

FORMAL ORGANIZATIONS: DESIGN AND STRUCTURE

ORGANIZATIONAL DESIGN ALTERNATIVES

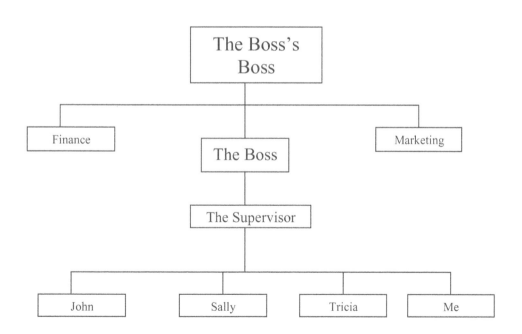

When Lucent spun off from AT&T in 1996 it was anticipated that it would be one of the more successful new hi-tech firms. Lucent's stock ran up during the hi-tech bull market, then like other stocks dropped dramatically. Lucent's performance also was less than most anticipated it would be and it became necessary to move in a different direction. One thing that Lucent did was to lay off a large number of its employees. Another approach was to reorganize. In 2001, Lucent tried to streamline itself by planning to reduce its managerial staff significantly and to restructure itself. Prior to reorganizing, Lucent comprised five major business units, the head of each reporting to the CEO [1]. It implemented a new plan, splitting its product and marketing units into two main groups. One unit, Network Solutions, would have the responsibility for the "land line" business (optical networking, switching, data, and software). The other unit, Mobility Solutions, would manage the company's wireless products. This reorganization streamlined Lucent: now there were only two vice-presidents reporting to the CEO. What the reorganization did was to change how people and work would relate to each other. But does this reorganization mean that it will become more profitable? Unfortunately not, at least as this book is being written. As you read this chapter, you will begin to understand how this reorganizing process works, and whether it can be effective. But there is always a word of caution to be heeded: organizations can be designed to improve effectiveness, but this is only the case when other things (e.g., products, services, and the financial structures) are right.

THE FUNDAMENTALS OF ORGANIZATIONAL STRUCTURE

In this chapter, we explain why organizations are different. Some differences are obvious, as when we observe organizations that are not in the same or similar fields. Hospitals are not organized like department stores, and for more reasons beyond the fact that there are doctors and nurses in hospitals while there are sales clerks and managers in department stores. However, there are also important differences between companies in the same industry – one day's observation of the women's departments at Sears and a high-fashion boutique will reveal many dissimilarities.

The reason for these differences lies in the fact that organizations are dependent upon their environments. The idea is straightforward.

1 Organizations must accommodate to the environments within which they exist.
2 For survival, differences in the environments require different activities and different relationships among those activities.

3 Managements have some discretion about how to design and coordinate these activities. These design decisions will have an impact on the effectiveness of the organization.

Some properties of organizations

An organization is a group of people, working toward objectives, which develops and maintains relatively stable and predictable behavior patterns, even though the individuals in the organization may change. There are three dimensions that contribute to the patterns of behavior that we observe in organizations: Complexity, formalization, and centralization. The patterns of complexity, formalization, and centralization are reflected in the organizational structure and the organizational culture. **Organizational structure** refers to the relationship between the tasks performed by the members of the organization and can be seen in the forms of division of labor, departments, hierarchy, policies and rules, and coordination and control mechanisms. The organizational culture is the set of dominant values, beliefs, attitudes, and norms that is the basis for justifying decisions and behavior as discussed in chapter 7.

The **complexity** of an organization is the number of its different activities, functions, and jobs, and of the number of levels in it. There are more coordination and control problems in more complex organizations because there are more task activities to perform, and there are more numerous interpersonal relationships. Complexity is usually greater in larger organizations.

The degree of **formalization** refers to the number of formal, written policies, procedures, and rules that constrain the choices of members. In a highly formalized organization, members' discretion and freedom of action are limited by the boundaries defined by these organizational devices. In less formalized organizations, there is more freedom of action and choice.

Centralization refers to the distribution of power and authority [2]. **Decentralization** refers to the degree to which authority and power are distributed vertically in an organization [2]. Organizations are decentralized when most decisions are made by those at lower levels of the organization, guided by policies and procedures. They are highly centralized when decisions are made near the top of the organization's hierarchy and the discretion of those at lower levels is constrained by formal rules and procedures.

Authority is the right of decision and control a person has to perform tasks and to meet assigned responsibilities. To have authority means that you can make decisions without having them approved by others. For workers, it means the control over the work itself. For managers, authority is the right of decision and command about the use of organizational resources by themselves and by others for whom they have responsibility. It is necessary because tasks and the responsibility for their performance are dispersed throughout the organization by the process of division of labor. It is one mechanism for coordination and **integration** of the work of those in the organization.

Authority is distributed both horizontally and vertically in organizations. The **horizontal distribution of authority** is a function of the span of control and occurs through decisions that are made in the departmentalization process, a process that we discuss later. The **span of control** is the number of subordinates who report to a manager. It is affected by the subordinates' competence, the decision-maker's philosophy about control, the nature of the work to be supervised, and organizational size and complexity. For given size organizations, the span of control will determine some critical things about the structure and the number of organizational levels. When the span of control is large, there is more horizontal dispersion of authority, resulting in **flat organizations**. In other words, it will have fewer organization levels. When the span of control is smaller, there will be less horizontal distribution of authority, leading to "tall" organizations with more organization levels.

ORGANIZATIONS: THE EFFECTS OF TECHNOLOGY AND MARKETS

In this book we think of **organizations as systems** of related activities that import resources from their external environment which are then transformed, or changed, by these activities into products or services. These products or services may be exchanged with other organizations or groups in the organization's environment, usually for revenues that are then used to maintain the organization itself.

Those groups, institutions, or other organizations outside the focal organization that provide immediate inputs, exert significant pressures on the way organizational decisions are made, or make use of the organization's output are called the **relevant environment**. At any one time, some of these are closer and have a more significant effect on what goes on in a firm than do others.

The relevant environment may be relatively simple or very complex [3]. A **simple environment** contains just a few relatively homogeneous sectors. For example, the technological environment for companies that sell long-distance service is relatively simple. A **complex environment** contains many different sectors, such as would be the case for an engineering firm that specializes in the installation of different types of manufacturing plants in different countries.

Events and circumstances can change the composition of external groups that are in the relevant environment. When this causes sufficient pressure, the organization must adapt to it. For example, when federal and state equal opportunity laws were initially passed, many firms had to change their hiring procedures as well as the criteria used for promotion. Now that some states have changed these laws, firms are changing these internal processes again.

Environmental sectors

While the relevant environment for most large organizations may be relatively complex, it is possible to understand how organizations are affected by taking a more straightforward approach and focusing on just two environmental sectors: the **technological environment** and the **market environment**. These two sectors are very important to understanding the problems of managing most business organizations and are of traditional importance in the management of economic organizations.

Markets

The **market environment** is composed of individuals, groups, or institutions that use what the organization produces, giving value to that output. It could be commodities, products, or services. For business organizations, this means products such as autos, computers, steel, television sets, bread, or the ideas and services that might be provided by advertising agencies, consulting firms, or travel agencies. The market provides the organization with some sort of exchange in return for its output.

Technology

The **technological environment** has two components. One is the set of processes that the organization uses to create the product or service. Used in this way, **technology** refers to available methods and hardware from which the organization selects some subset for its own use. Which technology is selected and used and how it is organized defines the form of the production activities in an organization. The production activities in an organization cannot be any more advanced than the technology available, but it is possible that a firm does not use all available technology. For example, computers might handle customer credit accounts in a large department store, while the same

Guide for Managers: DESIGNING ORGANIZATIONS

One of the most important tasks for a manager is to make choices about the design of the organization. There are three critical aspects to this:

1 Understanding what work has to be done.
2 How to differentiate these functions, and then group the more specific task into subunits or assign it to individuals.
3 To set up mechanisms, both structural and interpersonal, that coordinate and integrate those activities that you have just separated.

For each of these, there are important choices to be made. The guides in this chapter will provide some things that you have to consider in making these choices.

Understanding what has to be done

RECOGNIZE THAT YOUR ORGANIZATION IS DEPENDENT UPON ITS EXTERNAL ENVIRONMENT. You have to be aware of what permits the function in a small specialty store might be performed manually, using a card file.

A second facet of the technological environment is the ideas or knowledge underlying the production or the distribution of the product or service; that is, the way science is translated into useful applications.

Characteristics of the environment

What complicates the problem of the organization adapting to the environment is the degree of uncertainty, or environmental change [4, 5]. This has major implications for the internal structure of the organization, the types of individual who are likely to join it, and the perceptions, attitudes, and values of those in the organization. The most important effect of the environment is whether the activities and processes within the organizational structure take on highly routine or non-routine characteristics.

The degree of change is a continuum: at the opposite ends are stability and volatility. In the **stable environment**, changes are relatively small, occurring in small increments, with a small impact on the structure, processes, and output of the organization. In stable environments, it is possible to make fairly accurate market predictions based on some relatively common indexes. For instance, the level of automobile sales may be predicted reasonably well if you have generally accurate data available about changes in population, income, and the average age of cars on the road.

organization to exist. There are customers for your product or service. Your fundamental concern is to ensure that you provide them with the value that they want in your product or service, at the right time, at the right place, and at the right cost. If you fail at that, you will also fail to (1) obtain the revenues that are necessary to support the organization's activities and (2) make the profit that you want as a manager and/or owner.

This requires an obvious sensitivity to the environment and being willing to adapt to it. In some cases that adaptation will mean that you need to develop new products. In other cases, if you wish to keep doing what you are now doing, you will have to decide to operate at a reduced level.

KNOW WHAT WORK ACTIVITIES THE CUSTOMER IS WILLING TO PAY FOR. Customers are willing to pay for production activities that actually create the product, distribution and marketing for getting it to them, and costs of acquiring materials. They are not so interested in supporting staff activities, like human resources or even quality control. These make your job easier and they often make the product itself better. However, they are not the core work of the firm. Focus first on those core activities, and worry about organizing them most effectively. Let the support activities flow to the part of the organization where they most naturally fall.

In the **volatile environment** changes are more rapid, customers may change, and the level of demand may vary widely. The women's high-fashion market is a good

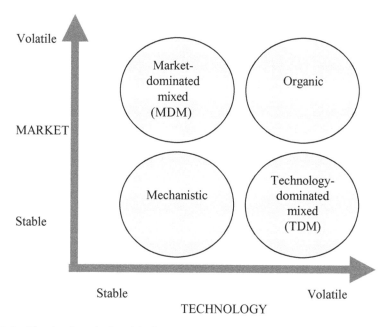

Figure 8.1   The basic relationship between environment and types of organizations

example. Product decisions of designers and manufacturers are based on predictions of customer tastes and preferences, and these are highly changeable. Who knows for instance, if the designs of Norma Kamali, Giorgio Armani, Gianfranco Ferre, or Elizabeta Yanigasawa will be the most successful in any one year?

When the technology is volatile, new concepts and ideas are being rapidly generated, and these new ideas affect either the way the production processes are carried out or the nature of the processes themselves. The electronics industry, with breakthroughs in integrated circuits, transistors, and miniaturization is a good illustration of how technology changes could affect the nature of a product as well as marketing strategies. You can see this by simply observing what is happening to camcorders. The price is dropping, the technology is rapidly changing, and they are becoming much smaller than products introduced even a few years ago.

Technology, markets, and basic types of organization

Figure 8.1 shows how the dynamics of the environment and the organization that accommodates to it are related to the basic types of organization. On one axis is the technological environment and on the other axis is the market environment. Both of these environments may range from stability to volatility. For simplicity, we have described four basic organization types that fall near the ends of both continua, but

145

if you think about it, you will correctly conclude that organizations can fall at any point in the figure [5]. These are the four basic organizational types:

1 The mechanistic organization
2 The organic organization
3 The technology-dominated mixed (TDM) organization
4 The market-dominated mixed (MDM) organization.

These **basic organizational types** reflect something different and important about the nature of power and control, how authority is distributed, and the degree of flexibility required to accommodate to the environment. The reason is that in each of the different types, parts of the organization will have different types of interaction with the environment and with each other. For example, functions such as marketing and R&D are always in direct contact with the environment, while the production activities tend to be more deeply embedded and buffered from it. Further, these activities will be affected by the nature of the environment. When it is stable, the activities will take on routine characteristics. When it is volatile, the activities will have to be more flexible.

Mechanistic organizations

Figure 8.1 shows that when the market environment and the technological environment are both stable and predictable, there will be a **mechanistic organization**. Examples of mechanistic organization types are automobile manufacturers, steel producers, and fast-food restaurants such as McDonalds, Wendy's, and Burger King. The reason that they are mechanistic is because when the market and the technology are stable, the mechanistic form is efficient, and efficiency is required for survival. In its production activities, tasks are likely to be highly repetitive. The division of labor will be extreme; the work activities will be standard, relatively limited, and simple. You can see this when you observe workers on a manufacturing assembly line or the work in fast-food restaurants. When the work is so narrowly specialized, those who perform these jobs will not see clear links between what they specifically do and the rest of the work done in the organization because of the separated, specialized nature of tasks.

In the mechanistic organization, you will find a very clear definition of responsibility and authority. The management structure will be more rigid and hierarchical. Much of the communication is vertical, flowing from the top to the bottom. This occurs, in part, because it is possible to use historically developed information that has achieved organizational acceptance and legitimacy for control purposes. The focus of these control activities will be on measuring performance outcomes.

Decision-making in mechanistic organizations tends to be highly centralized toward the top of the organization. Information can be quickly and easily collected and transmitted to the higher levels so that decisions can be made about operations at lower levels without requiring a great deal of involvement of managers at lower levels. This, of course, will put limits on lower-level discretion.

Organic organizations

Figure 8.1 also shows the **organic organization** in volatile market and volatile technological sectors [5]. Organic organizations are likely to be relatively small compared with mechanistic organizations. This small size makes it easier to adapt to the environment. Examples of organic organizations are specialized consulting firms, advertising firms, and some new Internet firms. These Internet firms often have a wide variety of clients who come to them in search of new solutions to problems. Their professional staff also have a very wide range of technical competence that can be applied to these problems.

In an organic organization, relationships and jobs are more loosely defined to permit an easier process of adapting to the changing environment. The result is a continuing shifting and redefinition of tasks as the environment changes, making it difficult, if not impossible, to have a well-defined hierarchical structure as found in the mechanistic organization. This has a number of effects. One is that those who work in these organizations must have a broader range of skills so that they can perform the more varied range of functions. Another is that information is not as easily centralized at the top, making communication more horizontal and less vertical. A person's status and importance are more based on competence than on being in a high organizational position.

The management structure in an organic organization has to be more flexible. Few policy guidelines will be used in the decision-making process because the variability of the environment will make well-defined set policies less useful over time. Performance control and appraisal will be more "subjective" and not so much based on "objective" performance measures.

In organic organizations, individuals may move from project to project as the need for their skills arises, with a different authority structure for each one, depending on what needs to be done. They may work for more than one manager. Teams will be created to work on particular projects; when the project is completed, team members may move to different teams. This can cause problems unless the individual has a high tolerance for ambiguity and change.

Technology-dominated organizations

The **technology-dominated mixed (TDM) organization** is a mixed organization type that has both mechanistic and organic elements. Examples of TDM organizations are firms that produce and sell personal computers such as Compaq, Dell, and Gateway. The underlying technology used in computers changes dramatically in short periods of time, following Moore's Law, which states that the amount of data that can be stored on a silicon chip doubles every year. This allows them to build to order and configure to process. Yet the marketing of personal computers especially is a relatively routine process, with firms like Gateway using mail-order distribution.

147

In TDM organizations, the organic part of the organization interacts with the technological environment because its major threat to survival and effectiveness stems from the uncertainty and volatility there, as we have discussed in the computer industry and as has also occurred in photography over the last 30 years. Instant cameras by Polaroid started a technological revolution in the 1960s. Later, Nikon and Canon are examples of companies that developed camera systems with automatic focus and shutter speed mechanisms. Now there are even disposable cameras that produce photos of very respectable quality and at a reasonable price, not to mention the developing revolution in digital photography.

The management structure of a TDM organization will be different in the major organization sub-units. For instance, in the marketing sector, you can expect to find fairly well-defined job responsibilities, accountability to specific superiors for work, and limited discretion for decisions. On the other hand, those in the technological functions will have more freedom of action. The production units are likely to be caught in the middle, between pressures from research and engineering to adopt newer production methods and the marketing unit's desire to maintain the product relatively as it is.

Market-dominated organizations

Another mixed organization type is the **market-dominated mixed (MDM) organization**. These organizations exist in environments that have a stable technological sector, but a volatile market sector. In MDM organizations, the major strategic and policy influence will be from the marketing unit because of the need to stay in close touch with a constantly changing consumer or client group. Examples of MDM organizations are firms in the music industry, the film industry, and high fashion. Understanding the volatile market is accomplished more through experience, intuition, and the judgment of those responsible for marketing and product development than through the analysis of standard market information such as population data, income estimates, or traditional buying patterns. For instance, in the fashion or recording industry, the clinical judgment of a designer or a record promoter is more crucial than a judgment made from more systematic market information. What is not a particularly difficult problem to manage in TDM organizations is the way the product is produced. The production of music and films, for example, requires recording equipment or cameras and setups that are readily available to anyone. What makes a difference in the success of the firm is not how the CD, cassette, or film is produced, but whether the producer has been able to find a good song or a good story that the market will accept.

The management structure will be relatively hierarchical and rigid in the technical parts of the market-dominated firm. A looser authority structure will exist in the marketing and distribution sectors, which will have more individual discretion and freedom in decision-making. Systems to monitor changes in and adapt to the environment will be developed in such a way as to be triggered by decisions made in the marketing sector. The head of an MDM organization will be someone with a marketing or sales background and the organizational culture and tone will be set by those in marketing, since they are the ones with the knowledge and skill to deal with the volatile environment.

As in a TDM, there will be problems in coordinating the organic and mechanistic segments of the organization. The well-defined structure of the technical sector may not only pose adjustment problems for the professionals who work in it but also present difficulties when it interacts with the more organic organization structure in the marketing sector.

FORMAL ORGANIZATIONS: DESIGN AND STRUCTURE

When we observe an organization chart, we do not really see whether a firm is an MDM type or an organic type. Instead, what we see is the **formal organization**, a configuration of major sub-units usually called divisions or departments, terms that we use interchangeably in this book. **Departments** engage in a distinct, defined set of activities over which a manager has authority and responsibility for specific outcomes. You can see in the discussion of Lucent at the beginning of this chapter how the major divisions will be different from what they were in the past.

Divisions or departments are created by managers who make decisions about how the basic organizational types become formal organizations. This is called **organizational design,** or the process of creating the internal conditions that facilitate strategic accommodation to the environment and the implementation of the organization's strategy by arranging the complete range of work activities into organizational sub-units and hierarchies. First, there are strategic decisions about where to locate the organization in the environment and the tactics for operating in that environment. For example, the market for women's clothes ranges from high fashion to conventional styles, and a firm may select a niche within that range. A firm such as The Limited sells somewhat expensive but more conventional women's clothing, whereas firms such as Armani and Gianni Versace focus most of their efforts in the high-fashion sector. The selection of a niche minimizes adaptation problems in the sense that management can focus on that particular environment but not on the more broad context. It allows the firm to develop a narrow rather than a broad set of competencies.

Second, three decisions have to be made which result in the formal organization structure:

1 How the work that must be done will be divided – the **division of labor.**
2 How the work is then grouped into organizational sub-units – the selection of **the form of departmentalization**.
3 The relationships between the sub-units are defined by the **distribution of authority**.

149

Division of labor and task interdependence

The **division of labor** is the way in which work in organizations is subdivided and assigned to individuals [6]. There are two different philosophies that can be used deciding how others will work, and they have different implications for what a person does in a task and how it is managed. One philosophy – the **scientific management approach** – is to make jobs simple, have few tasks assigned to a person, have the job supervised by someone other than the person doing it, give the worker little autonomy, and limit the amount of responsibility for the tasks. The other philosophy – the **job enrichment approach** – is to create more complex jobs. They consist of several tasks. The person controls the work more than in scientific management and has higher autonomy and more responsibility.

When work is divided and several different tasks, performed by different people, are required to complete a project, product, or sub-assembly, there is **task interdependence**. When tasks are highly interdependent, a person cannot complete a job until the work of someone else is finished. There are three types of task interdependence [3]:

1 An assembly line is an example of **sequential task interdependence**. This is when there are several tasks to be performed and they must be done in a linear sequence.
2 **Reciprocal task interdependence** is when the tasks of two or more people are mutually dependent. An example is when the work must go back and forth between the two workers, and each depends on the other to complete the job successfully.
3 **Pooled task interdependence** occurs when you work in a more autonomous fashion; what you do is not entirely dependent on the others, but organization success or failure depends on the unique contribution of each. Law firms and medical clinics, for example, are set up so that each lawyer or physician works with a great degree of autonomy, yet the success of the law firm or the medical practice depends upon each individual contribution.

ORGANIZATIONAL DESIGN ALTERNATIVES

Understanding the ideas we have presented so far is useful to a manager for deciding how to design the organizational structure, or the grouping of the differentiated tasks into departments and departments into units. For example, there are several bases for grouping activities:

1 Whether they are related to the same product.
2 Whether they have similar skill requirements.
3 Whether they serve particular customers or clients.
4 Whether they are performed in a particular geographic area.

We believe that some organizational designs are better suited to certain basic organizational types. For example, the mechanistic organization is likely to be more effective if the product or functional organizational design is used; mixed-type organizations seem better suited to the matrix structure, while the organic type is likely to use the project organizational structure.

Product organizations and functional organizations

For mechanistic organizations, the organization will probably take either the product form or the functional form. In the **functional organization**, the major divisions are grouped around similar work functions and responsibilities such as accounting, purchasing, production, and personnel. Managers and workers are assigned to units that are responsible for similar tasks. Figure 8.2 shows a functional organization for the hypothetical Eagle Brewing Company, a producer of beer with two brands, American Eagle Beer and Ben Jefferson Brew. In a functional organization, the brewing division produces both brands of beer that the company sells. A single brewery might produce American Eagle Beer for a period and then shift its production to Ben Jefferson Brew. The marketing unit is responsible for selling both products. All the brewing work is the responsibility of one unit and all the marketing work is the function of another one.

Most of the personnel in the units of a functional organization will have similar training and work experience. In Eagle Brewing, this means that all of those in the brewing division are specialists at making beer, while those in the marketing division are specialists in marketing.

Guide for Managers: DIFFERENTIATING AMONG FUNCTIONS

The organizing function requires disaggregating the work necessary to do the job and assigning it to different units and/or people. The two primary choices of differentiation are the product form or the functional form, and other designs are variations of these two:

- In the **product design**, you group most of the major activities for differentiated products into units that are separated from other product units.
- In the **functional design**, you group similar work functions into the same unit (e.g., production unit, marketing unit, or the human resources area).

MAKING A DESIGN CHOICE SOLVES SOME PROBLEMS, BUT LEAVES OTHERS TO BE MANAGED. For example, product organizational design, may maximize customer service but leaves problems of efficiency and effectiveness that you must manage. If your firm is a mixed type,

Because the work of each major organizational unit is so specialized, the functional form offers great opportunity for increasing operating efficiency, particularly of the production unit. Economies of scale can be more easily achieved because all the production activities are in one department. This similarity of background should also lead to easier communication within the functional departments because the individuals will have a common frame of reference. For instance, the department members will more easily understand the "jargon." On the other hand, there may be communication problems between groups because of the differences in their orientations.

One of the main problems of the functional organization is coordinating the work of these units. For instance, the marketing division would like to have a ready supply of both brands on hand at all times to meet customer demand. However, the manufacturing unit may wish to produce only one brand at a time and have very long production runs to minimize production costs. Each department's interest is best served by different goals (either long production runs or high inventories of both beers).

In the **product organization** form, divisions are formed around different products or services. Figure 8.3 shows the Eagle Brewing Company as a product organization. Each division has its own manufacturing operation, marketing, and so on. Each division is responsible for manufacturing and selling its own product, and each may be very autonomous. Note that within each product division there is considerable functional departmentation. The head of the American Eagle Division will have a production executive, a marketing executive, and other executives in charge of

then your most difficult problem will be to manage the interdependence of the various product and functional elements of the matrix organization.

IF YOU HAVE A SET OF HIGHLY DIFFERENTIATED PRODUCTS, THE PRODUCT ORGANIZATION IS THE BETTER CHOICE. This should be pretty obvious, because these differentiated products will likely require different production, marketing, and staff support. This makes each product unit the relative equivalent of a freestanding firm. With this design, however, there are some problems to be managed:

1 Communication difficulties between product units
2 There will be duplication of some staff activities
3 Units will have less concern with overall firm effectiveness and greater focus on their success.

UNDERSTAND THE POLITICAL IMPLICATIONS OF RATIONAL ORGANIZATIONAL DESIGN. In general, the choices that are made about the differentiation of activities can be justified in terms of some logical organizational objective such as profitability or efficiency. Oftentimes these choices will put some units in positions where their activities will control others. This gives the heads of those units the opportunity to engage in political behaviors that may be in their own interest.

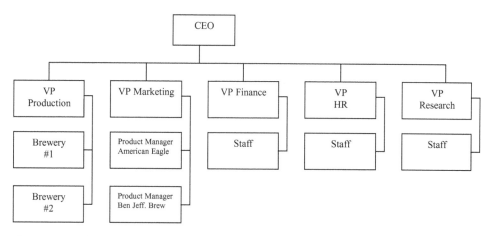

Figure 8.2 The Eagle Brewing Company as a functional organization

functional units within the product division. It is unlikely that any of them will inter-act frequently with his or her counterpart departments in the Ben Jefferson Brewing Division.

The product organization simplifies some managerial problems, but it creates others. For example, it is easier to develop accountability systems, reducing internal transaction costs, because production and selling costs can be allocated to the different products, which are almost completely the responsibility of a single unit. However, it is generally believed that some costs are higher for a product organization because it does not offer the same economies of scale associated with grouping similar activities into functional units.

The matrix organization

The **matrix organization** works well for mixed organizations (TDM and MDM). The matrix organization integrates the activities of different specialists while at the same time maintaining specialized organizational units. In the matrix organization, technicians from specialized organizational units are assigned to one or more project teams to work together with other personnel.

Figure 8.4 illustrates a matrix organization that is used in the military aircraft division of a major aerospace firm in a technologically volatile environment (a TDM organization) and a fairly stable government market. There are three functional units: production, engineering, and design. The functional departments have a "project manager" from each project who works with them. There are three project managers, each assigned to a different space project, as you can see. You can see that the specialists in the TDM organization come from the engineering side, the units

153

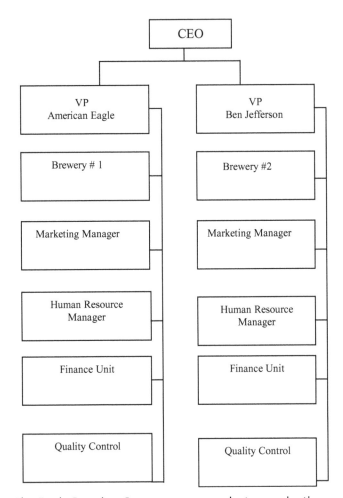

Figure 8.3 The Eagle Brewing Company as a product organization

interacting with the more volatile technological sector. However, in an MDM organization, such as a record company, the specialists would come from the marketing sectors. These specialists would be responsible for different areas of music such as classical, rock and roll, and country and western.

The project organization

When the nature of the work changes rapidly due to changes in the environment, a **project organization** is appropriate. A project is a series of related activities required

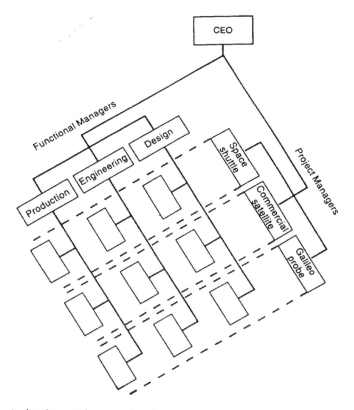

Figure 8.4 A classic matrix organization

to achieve an outcome, such as a new product or a plan for constructing a new building. Projects are generally unique; no two are the same. In a project organization, individuals are assigned to one or more temporary teams that exist for the life of the project. The specific composition of the team is determined by the project needs. When different skills are needed for different projects, the composition of the team will change.

The Construction Real Estate Development Company, shown in figure 8.5, is an example of a project organization. Each house and each commercial building is a unique project, taking a different time to complete. Workers may be assigned to more than one project or moved among the different projects as needed. Each project will have a supervisor who is responsible for the execution of the project plan and must coordinate the construction and manage its capital and human resources. When a building project is completed, a new one will be in and it will have a different configuration of people and resources.

155

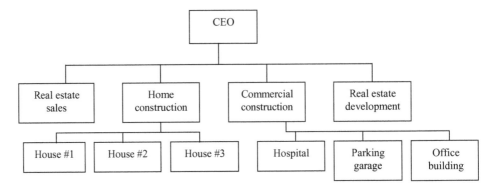

Figure 8.5 Project organization of a construction and real estate development company

The network (or virtual) organization

A relatively new approach called the network or **virtual organization** is a way to adapt to today's fast-paced economies and global competitiveness, and to meet management's desire for more effectiveness. **Network organizations** are not quite the type of organization that we have been discussing in this chapter so far. We have described, more or less, an organization that includes all of the relevant sub-systems within its boundaries. The network organization, instead, should be thought of as a group of firms in the relevant environment with which a focal organization does business. These organizations may be suppliers, customers, or even banks or other sources of capital. What distinguishes the traditional organization in its relevant environment from the network concept is the way that relationships between it and other organizations are governed, or managed. Traditionally we think of these relationships, such as how the firm deals with its customers or suppliers, to be based on economic relationships so that markets are the mechanisms that are important regulating devices for inter-organizational relationships.

What makes the concept of networks different is that, in addition to economic factors, these relationships are based on complementary strengths, reciprocity, mutual strengths, and trust between the organizations [7, 8]. When, for instance, different firms are engaged in the typical long-term buyer–seller relationships, there is usually a contractual agreement between them. There is a different kind of relationship among network organizations, one in which trust is very important. One example of these network organizations is found in the Prato region around Florence, the center of Italian textile production [9]. The organization of this textile industry is unique because there are no large, vertically integrated plants that perform the production function from beginning to end. Instead nearly 20,000 firms, most of them very small, perform very specific, specialized functions. Some process new wool, others reclaim old wool. Some spin, others dye; some clean and others cut. All in all, the industry is highly fragmented, but these firms have developed close working relationships. This results in such effective coordination that the wool-production process is quite efficient. In large part, this effective coordination stems from basic cultural values. It is based as much on social linkages as on the conventional types of inter-organizational linkages common in the USA. Many of the small firms in the Prato region are owned and managed by relatives from an extended family.

You can imagine that this type of network organization might work in Italy because of the values of close family relationships that permit trust to develop more easily. However, similar network structures exist elsewhere. For example, carpet manufacturing around Dalton, Georgia has many of the same characteristics as the wool industry near Florence. So does the consortium of firms called Sematech that was organized to cooperate in the design and manufacturing of semiconductors to enhance the competitiveness of this industry in the USA.

The organizational model that we discussed earlier in this chapter can help you to understand the network organization. As the work is differentiated into sub-units, it is useful to ask whether or not it might be more cost-effective to perform those tasks internally or have them done by some outside group. This is the "buy or make" decision that firms have always faced. In the case of the network organization, the decision is made to externalize some of the work and be dependent upon the supplier to provide what the firm needs. Whether some activity is externalized depends on several factors:

1 The costs of performing internally compared to the external costs.
2 Whether the activity is critical to the core competence of the firm.
3 The criticality of the activity to the organization itself.
4 Difficulties of coordinating that externalized activity with internal processes.

The focal firm in the network is called the **strategic center** [8]. This firm is the one that must scan and monitor the environment, make critical strategic choices about product design, distribution, and internal coordination, and facilitate the collaboration and cooperation of other firms in the network.

Guide for Managers:
DESIGNING COORDINATING AND INTEGRATING MECHANISMS

The primary coordinating and integrating device used to pull together the differentiated functions is the organizational hierarchy, especially the distribution of authority. Here are some things to keep in mind when you are making decisions about where and who should have organizational authority:

DELEGATE AUTHORITY TO THE LOWEST LEVEL IN THE ORGANIZATION POSSIBLE, CONSISTENT WITH THE CAPACITY OF THE PERSON IN THE POSITION TO HAVE THE INFORMATION NECESSARY TO MAKE DECISIONS. Too often managers are reluctant to let go of control and are unwilling to delegate authority to lower levels. This is especially a problem as organizations become more lean, with fewer organizational levels. You should keep this thought in mind, "The person who is doing the work and knows the problems is most likely to be the one who can make the best decision about it."

THE PERSON WHO HAS THE RESPONSIBILITY FOR A UNIT SHOULD HAVE THE AUTHOR-ITY TO MAKE DECISIONS ABOUT IT. This is an old principle of management, the princi-ple of the parity of authority and responsibility. It simply means that you shouldn't hold anyone accountable for those things that they can't control.

There are, of course, many other issues that are critical in the design of organization. Many of these will be revealed to you when you begin thinking seriously about the problem and view organizational design in terms of the concepts that we have discussed in this book.

SUMMARY

Organizations interact with the environments within which they exist. They take inputs from the environment; they transform those inputs into products or serv-ices, and then export these as a form of output. As a result of this interaction, the organization takes on different forms or types of organization depending upon the character of the environment. If market and technological environments are stable, organizations take on mechanistic characteristics; they are more routine and bureau-cratic. Organic organizations are found in volatile market and technological environments; they are more flexible and adaptable, and less bureaucratic. An organ-ization in an environment with both stable and volatile sectors has an internal structure with both mechanistic and organic dimensions. When the technological environment is volatile and markets are stable it is called a technology-dominated mixed (TDM) organization. Market-dominated mixed (MDM) organ-izations are in stable technological and volatile market environments.

To create the structures that we see when we observe organizations, the activi-ties of these basic organizational types are differentiated and integrated in the process of organizational design. First the activities are divided into organizational tasks. This is called the division of labor. These tasks are then grouped together into organizational sub-units, This process is called organizational design and may lead to product-based structures, function-based structures, and matrix structures or project structures. Then an authority structure is created to coordinate and control the activities. There are several organizational design alternatives, and we have dis-cussed the most common forms.

REFERENCES

1 Berman, D. K. 2001. Lucent's Latest Revamp to Split Five Businesses into Two Units. *Wall Street Journal*, B1.

2 Hall, R. H. 1991. *Organizations: Structures, Processes and Outcomes*. Englewood Cliffs, NJ: Prentice-Hall.

3 Thompson, J. D. 1967. *Organizations in Action*. New York: McGraw-Hill.

4 Burns, T. G. and G. M. Stalker. 1961. *The Management of Innovation*. London: Tavistock Institute.

5 Tosi, H. L. 1992. *The Environment/Organization/Person Contingency Model: A Meso Approach to the Study of Organizations*. Greenwich, CT: JAI Press.

6 Thompson, V. 1967. *Modern Organization*. New York: Knopf.

7 Powell, W. 1990. Neither Market Nor Hierarchy: Network Forms of Organization. In L. L. Cummings and B. J. Staw, eds., *Research in Organizational Behavior*, 295–335. Greenwich, CT: JAI Press.

8 Lorenzoni, G. and A. Lipparini. 1996. *Leveraging Internal and External Competencies in Boundary Shifting Strategies*. Faculty of Economics, University of Bologna, Italy.

9 Voss, H. 1996. Virtual Organization: The Future is Now. *Strategy and Leadership*, **24**(4): 12.

Block IV: Integrating Behavioral Theory into Effective Management and Leadership

BLOCK I INTRODUCTION

BLOCK II A FOCUS ON THE INDIVIDUAL

BLOCK III THE CONTEXT OF ORGANIZATIONAL BEHAVIOR

BLOCK IV **INTEGRATING BEHAVIORAL THEORY INTO EFFECTIVE MANAGEMENT AND LEADERSHIP** Chapter 9 Managing Performance: The Influence of Technology and Knowledge Chapter 10 Conflict Chapter 11 Decision-Making Chapter 12 Power and Politics in Organizations Chapter 13 Leadership Chapter 14 Organizational Change

Managing Performance: The Influence of Technology and Knowledge

THE CONTEXT OF PERFORMANCE MANAGEMENT

TASK SPECIALISTS: MANAGING THEIR PERFORMANCE

MANAGING KNOWLEDGE WORKERS

Trixy Merflo is a production line manager at a company that produces frozen french fries. She supervises the second shift, and every aspect of the process from washing and inspecting the potatoes that come in from the field to final packaging and preparation of the fries is part of her responsibility. Her major challenges are minimizing employee absences, ensuring safe operation of all of the sophisticated technology used in the process, and managing the production process in a way that maintains high product quality.

Bob Robinson is the senior partner in a prestigious southern law firm. His firm handles employment law-related matters. His major challenges are managing the conflict between other partners and junior members of the firm, retaining highly qualified legal assistants, and managing the effective and efficient use of the firm's administrative staff to support the widely varying needs of the firm's attorneys.

Dwight Frank is a construction supervisor who currently supervises the construction of custom homes. His major challenge is managing the construction schedule, a job made tougher because he works in an industry where absenteeism, tardiness, and leaving the job site early are a significant problem. He also has to manage subcontractors such as electricians and plumbers who don't fall directly under his supervision but who are critical to accomplishing his mission.

Each of these managers faces some similar and some extremely different challenges. Those challenges are not only a function of the context within which their organizations operate, but more are also due to the type of employees that they manage. It should be obvious that managing a worker on an assembly line making french fries is quite different than managing an attorney in a law practice. Just as managing attorneys provides different challenges than managing a construction crew. In this chapter we will consider the differences in organization context and type of employee that impact a manager's strategy in managing performance.

In blocks II and III we focused on theories about important individual and contextual influences on performance and their practical application. In this block (block IV) we address the implementation of these theories. We build on the background from earlier chapters and describe specific managerial strategies for improving your effectiveness at performance management, conflict management, decision-making, power and politics, leadership, and organizational change. In this chapter, we focus on managing individual performance within an organizational context where

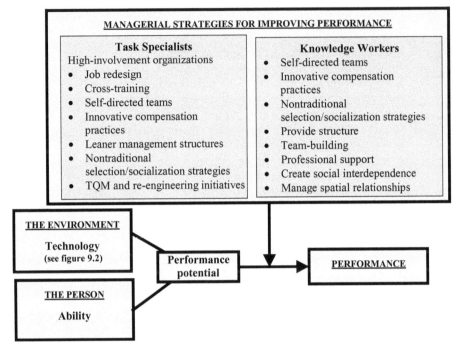

Figure 9.1 Performance management

technological innovation and knowledge are critical elements of the larger context that managers must deal with.

THE CONTEXT OF PERFORMANCE MANAGEMENT

Performance management refers to those things that managers do to influence the effectiveness of individual and group performance. These include the effective use of motivation, effective use of groups and teams, and the design of effective organizational structures. In this chapter we consider how performance is affected by two important factors that are key parts of the challenges of managing in the twenty-first-century organizational context, technology and knowledge. We also consider how these differences lead to workforces that are primarily task specialists, knowledge workers, or a combination of the two. Figure 9.1 illustrates how the concepts from the previous chapters can help managers think about how to improve the performance of individuals, groups, and organizations. Managers must be able to work with the technologies that they have at their disposal and the knowledge and ability of the people in the organization. They must develop managerial strategies that enhance individual ability and motivation and incorporate these with the organization's technology.

Technology Complexity and Stability		
	Simple/Stable	Complex/Volatile
Long-linked	McDonald's	Digital camera manufacturer
Mediating	Local farmers' market	E-Bay
Intensive	Home construction	Dell Computers

(left side label: **Structural**)

Figure 9.2 Types of technology and technological complexity

Technology

Technology refers to the tools, machines, facilities, and equipment a person uses in performing a task. If you think a bit about technology, there are two aspects that are important. These are (1) that technology can vary in its stability and complexity and (2) that it can be arranged, or structured in different ways, depending on the work to be done. Figure 9.2 illustrates some examples of organizations with different configurations of these two dimensions.

The stability/complexity dimension

Technology can vary in its complexity and its stability. Technology can be very simple and stable, for example, the technology that a great chef uses comprises pots, stoves, and recipes and, properly used, produces an exceptional meal. The technology that an artist uses such as a drawing board, paint, and a brush is also simple. Technology can also be advanced, complex, and volatile. For example, autoworkers use a complex but relatively stable technology, the assembly line, with highly interdependent activities to manufacture a car. Animation artists use highly advanced computers and software to produce technologically sophisticated graphics in animated video games and films such as *Shrek* or *Star Wars*.

The structural dimension

How a technology is arranged, or the type of work interdependence, has an important effect on how that technology is used. It also affects the types of people who you will need to use it effectively. James Thompson (1967) characterized organizational

165

work systems as long-linked, mediating, and intensive forms. A **long-linked work system** that uses very simple technology can be seen at any fast-food restaurant such as McDonalds. Hamburgers, as well as other foods, are prepared in assembly-line fashion, in much the same way as the long-linked, highly automated assembly production process is used in automobile manufacturing. An example of a long-linked work system that uses advanced technology is the process of manufacturing computer chips. These machines must perform very intricate and delicate actions at very high speeds.

The primary feature of a **mediating** work system is that several different users and several different customers are linked together through the organization and its technology. Think about how, for example, a local farmers' market and E-Bay are very much alike. Both bring many different buyers and sellers together at the same location. The local farmers' market attracts buyers from all over to purchase fresh vegetables. Many farmers come to market and set up stands. E-Bay does the same thing, bringing many buyers and sellers together. The major difference is that the local farmers' market is an example of a mediating work system that uses, at best, very simple technology while E-Bay makes use of advanced electronic technology to bring buyers and sellers in very disparate and distant locations together for transactions on the Internet.

Work can also be arranged into **intensive** work systems. In intensive work systems, the arrangement and sequencing of work must wait until the customer's needs are known. Home construction is an example of an intensive work system that makes use of simple technology. The particular subcontractors and workers for each home are determined by what the homebuyer wants. For instance, if a homebuyer wants solar heating, then a different heating system and a different subcontractor will do the work than one who might install gas or electric heating systems. Another example of an intensive work system is a hospital emergency room [1]. These have complex equipment for analysis and treatment. The technical personnel and the type of emergency being treated determine how this technology is configured and used. Think about the differences in emergency treatment for a gunshot wound and a heart attack. Finally, Dell Computers illustrates a highly advanced technological intensive work system. The different configuration of features and software that goes into each computer depends upon exactly what the buyer wants.

Ability

As you can see from Figure 9.1, technology is a key factor in determining the environment within which an individual performs their work tasks. The person component is represented by the overall ability that a person has to do the job. Ability is the capacity that a person has to accomplish a task. For our discussion, we consider a person's skills and knowledge as factors in their overall ability. Managers consider the range of a person's knowledge, skills, and abilities as a critical aspect of selecting individuals who will be successful in performing the job.

People vary significantly in their abilities and in chapter 2 we discussed several key abilities, including cognitive ability, emotional intelligence, perceptual ability, and psychomotor ability.

Performance potential: the technology/ability mix

Consider how the person component, ability, combines with technology to lead to performance potential. Effectively managing performance requires that managers optimize the performance potential of those who work for them. This requires not only optimizing the technology used in the work, and the skills and abilities of individuals, but also selecting appropriate managerial strategies consistent with the mix of technology and ability that is appropriate for their organization.

Performance potential is affected by the extent to which overall performance is based on predominantly technology, predominantly ability, or a combination of the two. This mix also may determine the strategies a manager should choose in motivating his or her employees to the highest level of effective performance. Looking back at the three managers we considered at the beginning of the chapter, Trixy Merflo, the shift supervisor in a frozen french fry plant, manages in a context where the technology is most important and individual abilities are less a factor in performance. Bob Robinson, who manages attorneys, works in a context where the ability of the attorney, measured in their knowledge of the law, is the most critical factor. Dwight Frank manages in a context where there is a mixture of technology and ability requirements. Some members of his crew may have limited skills but manage the technology used in home construction to achieve major portions of the work. Others, such as electricians, may require greater skills, and those abilities may be the key factor in their performance potential. As you can see from these three situations, the work context can vary from being dominated extensively by technology or significantly by individual ability.

Technology, in the form of tools and equipment, can have several effects on the skills and abilities required to perform work.

In **technology-dominated work**, one only needs enough skill, for instance, to start the machine and from there on perform a limited range of tasks. For example, technology can reduce the range and importance of skills that one must use at work – it can substitute for strength, dexterity, or physical coordination skills. In assembly-line work, for instance, only limited human skills are required in the job; the production technology is the most important factor.

In other work, ability may be the most important factor in determining the performance potential. This would be considered **skill-dominated work**. For example, the performance potential of a clothing designer job is much more a function of their individual abilities – giving a designer better technology or equipment is likely to have only a marginal effect on performance, just as giving a professional golfer better clubs and balls will probably not improve their game very much because golf, like most sports, is a skill-dominated task. In other instances, the skill and/or knowledge of the person is required to use advanced technology, as is the case for sophisticated equipment in hospitals or research laboratories.

Technology, skill, and the specialization of work

In chapter 8, we said that among the important decisions that affect organizational design is the decision about how work can be differentiated, or the **division of labor**. These choices result in **specialization**, which means that a person does only some part, or subset, of all the tasks needed to produce the output of the organization. Based on the discussion above, two types of specialization are especially relevant to a choice of managerial strategy, task specialization and knowledge specialization.

In task specialization, work is broken down into smaller components, or task elements, which are then grouped into jobs and generally assigned to different people [1]. In the case of knowledge specialization, the person, not the task, is specialized. The term "knowledge workers" has become common to describe knowledge specialists. Knowledge workers can and do perform a wide range of the different activities to do the work, instead of the few narrowly specified activities when tasks are highly specialized. Knowledge workers are in high-technology occupations such as engineering, software development, and advanced computer design and development. They are also in fields such as law and medicine. In the next two sections, we consider how different performance management approaches are appropriate for managing the performance of task specialists and then knowledge workers.

If you think back to our discussion of organizational form in chapter 8, we discussed the four basic types of organizations (i.e., mechanistic, organic, technology-dominated, and market-dominated) and their implications for the different types of specialization explained above. We expected that mechanistic organizations would have more task specialization and organic organizations would have more knowledge specialization. Mixed-type organizations will typically have both task specialists and knowledge workers in different areas of their operation.

TASK SPECIALISTS: MANAGING THEIR PERFORMANCE

The work of task specialists tends to be relatively repetitive: the person is doing only a small part of the complete task, and the work cycle, the time that elapses between the start of a task and when it begins again, is usually short. When there is high task specialization, it is possible to use highly automated technologies such as equipment used in heavy manufacturing to simplify the worker's job. The automotive assembly line is the prime example of this.

Task specialization may have some positive economic effects, such as increased efficiency, but it does have the effect of separating the person from the more intrinsic aspects of work. The effects of this are low intrinsic motivation, boredom, fatigue, low job satisfaction, and a tendency to withdraw from both the work and the organization [2, 3]. The problem of managing in this situation is to find ways to increase the intrinsic motivation of those in highly task-specialized work. Because tasks are more simple and repetitive, they are easier to learn and to do. Therefore face-to-face supervision is not necessary to ensure that the job is done right. Generally, it is possible to tell if the work is done correctly by inspecting the output rather than through the time-consuming task of direct personal supervision. The workers tend to be less involved with their job. High morale and motivation are especially difficult to maintain when the work is routine, repetitive, or highly programmed – a quick review of Job Characteristics Theory presented in chapter 5 will help you understand why.

High-involvement organizations

We think that most of the work done in most mechanistic organizations, with the exception of management and staff work, is characterized by high task specialization, with the attendant problems of low intrinsic motivation, boredom, low job satisfaction, and job withdrawal. To combat these, many organizations in today's competitive global environment are trying to create a **high-involvement organization** (HIO). The HIO is an organization that promotes employee motivation in the workplace; it improves the effectiveness of the organization by changing the adversarial relationship between workers and managers that dominates many firms and replacing it with a cooperative approach.

HIOs may use a number of different management practices. These include, but are not limited to, participative decision-making, self-directed work groups, job design programs to enrich work, total quality management (TQM), improved safety and working conditions, innovative compensation plans to emphasize gainsharing and skill development, the elimination of organization levels, and minimization of bureaucratic processes and practices. In this section, we discuss some of the more common and more important aspects of HIOs: redesigning jobs, cross training, self-directed work teams, new compensation practices, lean organization structures, non-traditional selection, and TQM and process redesign.

Job redesign

One managerial strategy for improving the intrinsic motivation of individuals in highly task-specialized jobs is to redesign jobs. Redesigning jobs is usually based on the Job Characteristics Model [4] (see chapter 5). Job redesign is aimed at increasing skill variety, task identity, task significance, autonomy, and feedback so that workers will have more meaningful jobs, a greater sense of responsibility, and more feedback. There are five basic ways to redesign jobs, as shown in figure 9.3, to increase their motivating potential and affect the core job dimensions, critical psychological states, and personal and work outcomes [4].

169

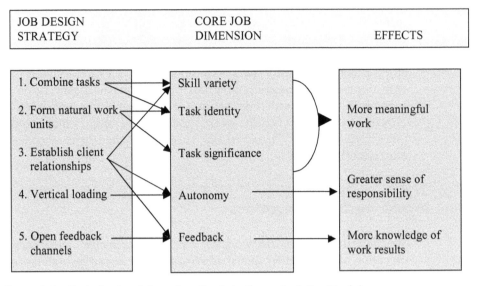

JOB DESIGN STRATEGY	CORE JOB DIMENSION	EFFECTS

Figure 9.3 Redesigning jobs using the Job Characteristics Model

1 **Combining tasks**. Narrow tasks, especially those that are "fractionalized," should be combined into larger, more complex tasks. If the new task is too large for one person, it may be assigned to a team. Combining tasks increases skill variety and task identity.

2 **Forming natural work units**. Tasks should be grouped into work units so that as much of the work as possible can be performed in the same organizational group. This leads to a sense of ownership of the job, increasing task identity and task significance.

3 **Establishing client relationships**. It is a good idea, when possible, to link the worker with the purchaser of the product or the service. Since the worker cannot often interact directly with a customer, it may be possible to devise ways that the customer can give the worker feedback. If client relationships can be established, skill variety, autonomy, and feedback should improve.

4 **Vertical loading**. The job should be enriched by vertical loading (adding responsibilities from higher organization levels) as opposed to horizontal job loading (adding more tasks from the same level). Vertical loading gives the person more responsibility and control at work that should lead to an increase in the level of perceived job autonomy.

5 **Opening feedback channels**. There are two ways to provide feedback: job-provided feedback occurs when the person knows how to judge performance from the job itself; management feedback comes from the supervisor or from reports such as budgets and quality reports. Removing obstacles to increase job-related feedback will improve performance.

Cross training

HIOs invest heavily in training to achieve workforce flexibility because job rotation is often preferred to permanent work assignments. In **cross training**, workers learn the various skills necessary to perform the required tasks of the group. Training also becomes an instrument of worker socialization, an important element in the screening process to be discussed below. For example, the initial group of employees at the GM Saturn Plant received as much as 700 hours of training in the early stages of the Saturn startup [5].

Self-directed teams

Self-directed teams place even more responsibility on the individual team members, and usually have responsibility for some decisions once reserved for management. The teams may be headed by a person from the managerial ranks or may have a member of the team designated as "team leader," but are usually headed by one of the more highly skilled members, and leadership may rotate from person to person. The members of teams are encouraged to work together as a unit, to identify problems and look for solutions to them, to help and train each other while maintaining high-quality production. Often they have responsibility for controlling other team members through self-regulating activities such as recommending disciplinary action if necessary, making individual work assignments, and sometimes deciding on member pay increases [6]. These self-regulating activities are sometimes very difficult for the team members to perform since they threaten interpersonal relationships at work.

Innovative compensation practices

Several compensation practices have been developed to provide opportunities and incentives for increased worker involvement.

One is **gainsharing**. The objective of gainsharing is to make better use of the firm's human capital, whether it is managerial employees, operative workers, or knowledge workers. There are several gainsharing approaches that are incentive plans to provide bonuses to employees based on profit improvement, cost savings, or productivity increases achieved as a result of the employees' contribution of ideas or more productive work effort [7]. Gainsharing approaches have very positive effects on firm performance regardless of how big the firm is, whether there is a union, technology differences, or the firm's environment [8].

One of the more widely used, as well as one of the oldest, gainsharing approaches is the **Scanlon Plan**. This is a way to integrate the interests of the workforce with the interests of the company to create a strong spirit of cooperation between labor and management. It involves a pay incentive system and process of worker

171

involvement [9]. For the Scanlon Plan to be effective, the workforce must be involved in many different ways. It requires not only a commitment to participative decision-making and joint problem-solving but also an organizational structure and management style that is congruent with participative decision-making and joint problem-solving [10]. The organizational culture must be based on a high level of trust between the workers and management. Both groups must be willing to take responsibility for their actions and to share the responsibility of decision-making. Together, they seek ways to improve the operation so that productivity increases. Productivity increases result in a bonus to the workers when the workers are responsible for them.

Skill-based pay is another innovative pay strategy used by many HIOs. In a **skill-based pay system** – workers are paid for the skills they possess, not for the job on which they are working, as in more traditional pay systems. The idea is that a more versatile worker is more valuable to the organization [11]. For example, Anheiser-Busch opened a new plant in which one of the key elements was skill-based pay. At first, many managers were skeptical whether skill-based pay would work and felt that it would be even more difficult in an industry characterized by "hard-nosed" union relationships. Instead, they found that the workers accepted the skill-based pay system, and that productivity and profitability were very high. Surprisingly, there was much more management flexibility since workers were willing to move to different jobs as needed since they would not suffer any wage rate change that might occur under a more traditional wage system. A study of a skill-based pay approach in a manufacturing plant found that there were improvements in productivity quality and labor costs, despite the fact that the workers actually earned more. This earning increase was offset by the productivity increases [12].

Team-based incentives are often used instead of individual-based incentives. Team-based incentives provide similar pay increases to the whole team instead of the more traditional approach of providing differential individual incentives. The purpose of the team-based incentive is to reinforce the team concept. Devising a team-based incentive approach is not simple. The main problem is trying to ensure that each member contributes equitably to team performance and does not become a "free rider," someone who fails to carry his or her load yet receives the same incentive increases as everyone else.

Leaner management structures

When redesigned compensation systems and jobs increase motivation, then responsibility and self-direction increase, and less supervision is required. To put it another way, if workers are able to monitor their own job performance because accurate task feedback is available about a challenging job for which there are performance incentives, there is less need to have a supervisor looking over the workers' shoulders. After successful implementation of HIO philosophy and practice, it is often possible to eliminate at least one level of management. In the Anheiser-Busch plant described above, the use of the self-directed work teams, skill-based pay, and higher worker participation resulted in one less layer of management than similar plants in the industry. This meant that there were three to five fewer managers, a saving of between $400,000 and $450,000 each year.

The lean management structure, along with the use of self-directed work groups, has another implication for managers. They must give up hierarchical control and must necessarily act as team leaders, coaches, and facilitators; they must take more facilitating roles, place more trust in the workers, and take a hands-off approach. At the same time, workers must believe that managers will not violate the integrity of those areas in which the group has been delegated the responsibility for self-direction. Some companies refer to employees as "stakeholders" or "associates" to reinforce the more cooperative and trusting culture that they are trying to develop. This trust relationship can only develop when the workforce is well informed and feels secure that management is not hiding anything, and after some history develops that management does, in fact, trust the work groups.

Nontraditional selection and socialization strategies

It should be obvious by now that the HIO requires an organizational culture that is different from the more hierarchical, traditional models of management to which many employees are accustomed. This means that the selection process may be of a different type than in traditional firms. Often, bringing people into HIOs is done with an approach that is specifically designed to bring "a 'whole' person who will fit well into the organization's culture" [13].

HIOs tend to use relatively "thick" screening procedures and carefully designed socialization processes, especially when the HIO is a startup organization. This thick screening process, for example, will include the assessment of technical knowledge, skills, and abilities, as well as using written tests or performance tests. Personality tests, which assess the capacity to work in teams, to act independently, to accept responsibility, and to tolerate ambiguity can also be used. Usually applicants face a series of interviews both with managers and members of the team on which they might work. Finally, there are strong socialization processes such as training or other "rites of passage" for successful applicants [13].

The thickness of the screening process may vary, depending upon the desire to ensure that members fit well with the culture. For example, in one startup organization, the selection screen was very thick. First, every applicant for non-managerial jobs was required to attend, without pay, a pre-employment course in which basic manufacturing skills were taught. The course was designed by the company and covered such areas as blueprint reading, mathematics, safety, and mechanical design and repair. There was competence testing during the course, and individual scores on the tests were among the factors used in selection. Second, the applicants were interviewed by at least seven managers, including team leaders. The goal of these interviews was to assess technical skills, interpersonal skills, and potential for working within the HIO culture. Interviewers looked for initiative, good communication skills, the ability to work without supervision, and a high achievement orientation. Third, employment offers were made by the plant manager to the successful applicants in the presence of spouses or significant others so as to impress them about the level of commitment that was desired.

TQM and re-engineering initiatives

A sharply focused effort on improved product or service quality may be a part of the HIO philosophy and process, often with some sort of **total quality management** (TQM) program. The guiding principle of TQM is to create a system of organizational processes and values that are totally dedicated to the customer. The goals are to create highly loyal customers, to minimize the time required to respond to problems, to develop a culture that supports teamwork, to design work systems that increase motivation and lead to more satisfying and meaningful work, and to maintain a focus on continuous improvement.

There is no single method for organizations to achieve these quality goals, though there seem to be some techniques common to most approaches to TQM. Common to most quality initiatives are recognition of the importance of leadership and leadership commitment, training and education, the use of teams, and development of an organizational culture that recognizes the importance of quality initiatives. These combine in ways difficult for other organizations to imitate and as a result could form a competitive advantage for the organization [14].

Statistical quality control methods are also used as part of TQM processes to identify causes of quality problems and to measure improvements, close relationships are developed with suppliers (such as just-in-time inventory systems) to minimize inventory expenses, and benchmarking is used to identify other organizations to be used as a base for comparison to the firm's activities. TQM also uses approaches from goal-setting and positive reinforcement programs (recording quality levels and giving recognition for attaining high-quality performance).

Research support for HIOs

There are many well-documented instances of firms, large and small, which have successfully created HIOs, among them General Foods, Volvo, and the General Motors Saturn Plant. Three analyses of several research studies show that enriched jobs are associated with higher performance and higher job satisfaction and had stronger effects than other types of motivational interventions [15, 16, 17]. However, the effects were not large. One reason for the modest effects is something that happens to many programs that organizations adopt to raise motivation levels – they lose their impact because, over time, managers begin to take them for granted and fail to continue to support and use the concepts [18, 19].

Perhaps the strongest evidence supporting the HIO concept is from a study of human resource practices in over 700 firms [20]. This research identified a cluster of firms that implemented high-performance work systems. These firms were able to create complementary and supportive relationships among such practices as rigorous recruiting and selection, performance management and incentive systems, and employee development and training activities. Other groups of firms tended to use more narrow approaches, relying primarily on compensation or other human resource strategies to manage their personnel. It was estimated that, on average, the HIO firms that used the elements of the high-performance approach produced very substantial increases in shareholder value per employee.

MANAGING KNOWLEDGE WORKERS

The number and importance of knowledge workers have been increasing since the 1960s [21]. Knowledge workers may use advanced or simple technology but all must have the advanced knowledge and information to use whatever sorts of tools and equipment are required for success. For example, lawyers do not use advanced technology; technologically they must know how to use computer-based reference systems to research cases and this task can easily be delegated to someone else. On the other hand, a radiologist must be capable of using the latest scanning equipment to assess the patient's health.

Three occupational types of knowledge workers are (1) professions, (2) crafts, and (3) those in technical occupations [21]. While all are all knowledge workers, these occupations differ in some important ways. For example, in the professions (e.g., law, medicine):

1 The knowledge is esoteric and well guarded.
2 The work is very heavily mental and analytical.
3 Advanced academic degrees are usually required.
4 There is usually formal certification.
5 Entrance to the profession is tightly controlled.

Crafts (e.g., electricians, plumbers, and tile-setters), like professions, also require very specific knowledge. However, in the crafts:

1 Persons outside the craft area often possess the skills and knowledge.
2 The work is largely manual.
3 Learning is often accomplished through apprenticeships.
4 Formal certification is less important.
5 Entrance to the craft is usually controlled by a union.

Technical occupations fall somewhere between "crafts" and "professions" [21]. "Science technicians, engineering technicians, medical technicians, and computer technicians all blur the attributes of crafts and professions" [21: 33]. In technical occupations:

1 Knowledge and skills are often esoteric, as in the professions.
2 The work is analytical and mental.
3 Usually some university training, and often a bachelor's degree, is necessary.
4 Sometimes technical certification is required, sometimes not.
5 Entrance to the occupation is not usually highly controlled, only the training or certification is necessary.

Issues in managing knowledge workers

There are a number of difficulties that those who manage knowledge workers face. These generally flow from the characteristics of the workers themselves (e.g., personality) and the nature of the organizations in which they work.

The professional orientation of knowledge workers

Our intuition is that many knowledge workers have the professional work orientation that we discussed in chapter 2. This means that they have very high intrinsic work motivation and their self-concept is linked more to the work itself. They are likely to be frustrated when they are in a situation in which they cannot effectively utilize all their skills. They feel under-utilized and their self-esteem may be threatened because they do not have the opportunity to do the things that they have been trained to do best. Also, it is very likely that the knowledge worker has made a relatively heavy personal investment in his or her choice of work, in that he or she has had to spend a long time training in a university or as an apprentice.

The inherent conflict between the knowledge worker and organizational authority

The conventional concept of organizational authority is that the manager has the final responsibility for decisions. The knowledge workers possess the technical expertise (a form of power) and are usually more capable of making decisions within their sphere of competence than their managers. Yet the manager is still responsible to higher organizational levels for the operation of the unit [1]. This is a common problem in both organic as well as mixed organizations, both of which make heavy use of knowledge workers. The way that this happens is that either technological advances and/or changes in the market make it difficult for a manager who was a knowledge worker but has been promoted to higher-level management to maintain their high skill levels in those fields. Still, these managers have the responsibility for decisions, as well as for the evaluation of those who work for them. But the up-to-date knowledge worker has both the knowledge and skill to do the work, and the manager does not. This puts both the manager and the knowledge worker in a position of potential conflict.

Role conflict and role ambiguity

While knowledge workers are highly trained, they know how to do just certain things well. Thus, even though they know their own specialty, there may be a great deal of ambiguity about how their jobs relate to other jobs. For example, a research scientist may be extremely skillful in scanning the physical properties of electrons, but may not be able to understand how her work ties in with an entire project. In short, ambiguity may develop because knowledge workers do not know the goals to which their activities should be directed.

In other instances, knowledge workers may not be clear about how they are evaluated. The reason is that their work assignments may not correspond to organizationally specified review periods. If, for instance, a project is completed in mid-February, but the performance review is set for mid-June, months may pass before a manager makes a determination about the success or failure of a project for which he or she is responsible. This makes it difficult to link rewards to performance, since they are separated so far in time.

Time, space, and work relationships

Time and distance can be important issues for knowledge workers. The conventional workday (i.e., 8 a.m.–5 p.m. from Monday through Friday) isn't the time that knowledge specialists do their best work. The reason is that the creativity necessary to solve the kinds of problems that they face does not operate on such a fixed schedule. Knowledge workers also often have different spatial patterns than other types of workers. Some of the best work that they do occurs away from the "office" and outside "official" working hours. Not only do telecommuters work at remote sites, but so do auditors who are on assignment, and engineering/technical staff who work at client sites. Many knowledge specialists have "virtual" work arrangements or work on virtual teams (see chapter 6) that often involve telecommuting or telenetworking – the use of electronic communications. A virtual team has members working in different locations, different buildings, or even different countries.

When they are on site at the place of work, much of the knowledge worker's task can be described as a "solo" performance. Some of their most productive time is spent working alone, free from distractions of others, though their final work product has to be integrated with those of others. In addition, though working alone, they will seek others to discuss technical problems, other work problems, or simply for some social diversion to get away from the task.

177

This poses at least two problems. First, there is usually not regular, predictable interaction with others at work, whether those others are on the same project or they are simply colleagues with other responsibilities. This means that knowledge workers are likely to often (1) work alone, (2) work in groups, and (3) move around a good bit. Second, since there is limited face-to-face conventional supervision, other methods are necessary. They must be managed using "substitutes for leadership approaches", which we discuss in chapter 13. The idea is that mechanisms such as training, policies, indoctrination, and socialization are ways of ensuring that knowledge workers meet their responsibilities.

Approaches to managing knowledge workers

Some of the approaches that we have discussed earlier in this chapter are also effective ways of managing knowledge workers. For example, **self-directed teams, innovative compensation practices**, and **nontraditional selection and socialization approaches** are widely used in organizations populated by knowledge specialists. There are some other approaches, however, which we believe can contribute to better individual and organizational performance.

Provide structure for knowledge workers

Knowledge workers, by definition, know how to perform in their areas of expertise. However, they may not be clear about how their work links with the work of other knowledge workers. This is not unusual, so much of what must be done to manage knowledge workers involves strategies to provide some structure to the work context. This can be achieved by clarifying, in expectancy theory terms, the path–goal relationship. Since the knowledge expert knows how to perform the work, the manager must do his or her best to ensure that they understand the expected goals as clearly as possible. If this is done the knowledge expert can assess whether or not, with the competencies he or she possesses, there is a reasonable likelihood of reaching a goal.

Team-building

Team-building is also a useful managerial approach. We discussed the process of team-building in chapter 6. It is the process of involving team members in a series of activities designed to improve the effectiveness of the group. This works when individual knowledge workers on the same team cannot work together effectively or when different groups of knowledge workers, who must work together, have negative perceptions or stereotypes of each other. Team-building may increase the accuracy of perceptions of others. It can help to motivate individuals to change, especially when problems that hinder group effectiveness are identified.

Professional support activities

If a person is an active professional whose external relationships represent legitimate time demands, time should be allowed to maintain these external relationships. Work can often be scheduled around these, and the organization may even pay for part of the expenses connected with attending professional meetings. Physicians, Certified Public Accountants, attorneys, HR managers, and many other knowledge-intensive professions often have significant professional organizations and intensive recurring training requirements to maintain specialties or levels of certification. Organizations that support these activities not only insure that key abilities are maintained, but also can enhance the motivation of knowledge workers if they see that the organization is instrumental in helping them develop and maintain their skills.

Create social interdependence and facilitate interaction of virtual teams

One of the major disadvantages of virtual teams is the lack of physical interaction, preventing face-to-face communication. As a result, virtual teams may have difficulty developing the level of trust necessary to become a high-performing team. To facilitate the teamwork and performance of virtual teams, we should use approaches that compensate for the lack of physical proximity [22]. For instance, it is necessary (see chapter 6) that (1) training in the use of the technologies that support team activities be given priority and (2) training be focused on three skill areas necessary for effective performance: collaboration, socialization, and communication [23]. It is also important to build trust among members, allow social and working time together, create common space, and communicate often about both work and non-work issues of interest to team members.

Manage spatial relationships

For knowledge specialists who are not organized as virtual teams, spatial relationships are also very important. Unless their job assignment is completely independent, there must be some task interaction. Think about the work of a university software programmer designing a distance-learning course to be offered on the Internet. The programmer cannot simply appear and direct the instructor to "fit" the course to the technological platform. He or she must meet with the instructor to determine exactly the content of the course, how it is to be presented, and how evaluation will be conducted before writing the specific software.

179

There is an abundance of research that demonstrates that people interact more frequently when they work in proximity. For example, the efficiency of software development is affected by the physical proximity and the level of interaction of those involved in the process [24]. People who know each other reasonably well and work near each other, as opposed to in distant locations, are more likely to interact. This means that useful information is more likely to be shared, and the work should go better.

Another spatial issue revolves around the work setting that promotes effective performance for knowledge workers. The trend toward open offices with work cubicles has taken hold as a way to increase communication and efficiency in work groups. However, there is a downside for those knowledge specialists involved in creative activities: these open offices with cubicles make it very easy to be interrupted by colleagues. Should these interruptions occur in the middle of the creative process, the effectiveness of the knowledge worker will be hampered.

One solution is to make private workspace for the knowledge specialists that they may use during the creative phases, but still provide open spaces to which they may move for the more routine parts of their job. This allows the best of both worlds; we can facilitate the effective utilization of the knowledge workers' special skills and at the same time make it easy to disseminate this information in the open office space.

SUMMARY

Perhaps the most significant challenge of managing performance is to understand that different organizational contexts require different managerial strategies to optimize performance. Two important variables to consider are the nature of the technology used and the individual skills and abilities that are required. The processes required to perform the job can often be classified as technology-dominated or skill-dominated. In organizations where technology is the dominant part of the process, the skills and abilities required are less complex and employees can be classified as task workers. Conversely, in organizations where an individual's overall abilities, including their knowledge and skills, are dominant, employees can be classified as knowledge workers.

Both task workers and knowledge workers provide different challenges and we have discussed strategies that are useful for managing the performance of both of these groups as well as strategies that are uniquely tailored to one or the other. Understanding the implications of both the technology used and the abilities required is a critical input in to determining a managerial strategy that optimizes performance.

REFERENCES

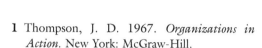

1 Thompson, J. D. 1967. *Organizations in Action*. New York: McGraw-Hill.

2 Blauner, R. 1964. *Alienation and Freedom*. Chicago: University of Chicago Press.

3 Hall, R. H. 1984. *Dimensions of Work*. Beverly Hills: Sage Publications.

4 Hackman, J. R. et al. 1975. A New Strategy for Job Enrichment. *California Management Review*, 17: 57–71.

5 Woodruff, D. 1993. Saturn: Labor's Love Lost? *Business Week*.

6 Tosi, H. L., J. H. Zahrly, and K. A. Vaverek. 1990. *The Relationship of Worker Adaptation and Productivity to New Technology and Management Practices: A Study of the Emergence of a Sociotechnical System*. Organization Studies Center, Graduate School of Business Administration, University of Florida.

7 Gomez-Mejia, L. R., T. M. Welbourne, and R. M. Wiseman. 2000. The Role of Risk Sharing and Risk Taking under Gainsharing. *Academy of Management Review*, 25(3): 492–507.

8 Bullock, R. J. and M. E. Tubbs. 1990. A Case Meta-Analysis of Gainsharing Plans as Organization Development Interventions. *Journal of Applied Behavioral Science*, 26(3): 383–404.

9 Milkovich, G. T. and J. M. Newman. 1999. *Compensation*. 6th edn. Boston: Irwin/McGraw Hill.

10 Lawler, E. E. 1976. New Approaches to Pay: Innovations that Work. *Personnel*, 53: 11–24.

11 Tosi, H. L. and L. A. Tosi. 1986. What Managers Need to Know about Knowledge-Based Pay. *Organizational Dynamics*, 52–64.

12 Murray, B. and B. A. Gerhart. 1998. An Empirical Analysis of a Skill-Based Pay Program and Plant Performance Outcomes. *Academy of Management Journal*, 41(1): 68–78.

13 Bowen, D. E., G. E. Ledford, and B. R. Nathan. 1991. Hiring for the Organization, Not the Job. *Academy of Management Executive*, 5(4): 35–51.

14 Reed, R., D. J. Lemak, and N. P. Mero. 2000. Total Quality Management and Sustainable Competitive Advantage. *Journal of Quality Management*, 5: 5–26.

15 Guzzo, R. A., R. D. Jenne, and R. A. Katzell. 1985. The Effects of Psychologically Based Intervention Programs on Worker Productivity: A Meta-Analysis. *Personnel Psychology*, 38: 275–91.

16 Stone, E. F. 1986. Job Scope–Job Satisfaction and Job Scope–Job Performance Relationships. In E. A. Locke, ed., *Generalizing from Laboratory to Field Settings*. Lexington, MA: Lexington Book Company.

17 Fried, Y. and G. Farris. 1987. The Validity of the Job Characteristics Approach: A Review and Meta-Analysis. *Personnel Psychology*, 40: 287–322.

18 Marks, M. L. et al. 1986. Employee Participation in a Quality Circle Program: Impact on Quality of Work Life, Productivity and Absenteeism. *Journal of Applied Psychology*, 71(1): 61–9.

19 Griffin, R. 1988. Consequences of Quality Circles in an Industrial Setting: A Longitudinal Assessment. *Academy of Management Journal*, 30(2): 338–58.

20 Becker, B. E. and M. A. Huselid. 1997. The Impact of High Performance Work Systems and Implementation Alignment on Shareholder Wealth. Paper presented at the Annual Conference of the Academy of Management.

21 Barley, S. R. 1996. *The New World of Work*. London: British North American Committee.

22 Kezsbom, D. S. 1999. Creating Teamwork in Virtual Teams. *Transactions of the American Association of Cost Engineers*, **PM011**(4).

23 Jarvenpaa, S. L., K. Knoll, and D. E. Leidner. 1998. Is Anybody Out There? Antecedents of Trust in Global Virtual Teams. *Journal of Management Information Systems*, **14**(4): 29–64.

24 Seaman, C. B. and V. R. Basili. 1997. Communication and Organization in Software Development: An Empirical Study. *IBM Systems Journal*, **36**(4): 550–63.

CHAPTER 10
Conflict

THE NATURE OF CONFLICT

DIAGNOSING CONFLICT

INDIVIDUAL RESPONSES TO CONFLICT

IMPROVING ORGANIZATIONAL RESPONSE TO CONFLICT

Sue Robinson, the hospital administrator, watched as her nursing supervisor quickly packed up her briefcase and walked out of the room, slamming the door behind her. This was a result of a heated verbal exchange between the head nurse, Ann Costa, and the HR manager Pete Jones. Ann had been the nursing supervisor for several years and Sue appreciated her service to the hospital, as Ann and her staff had always been a group she could count on when things became difficult. Sue had seen a problem coming for some time, though, as the external pressures on the hospital had led to so many changes so quickly. Many of the required organizational changes that had occurred has not been received well by several employee groups – perhaps the nurses most of all. In the age of spiraling heath-care costs hospitals were forced to look for opportunities to cut costs in all areas. The nurses unfortunately had borne the brunt of many these changes and had seen an increase in their working hours with minimal increase in pay, an expansion of their role to include duties that had previously been accomplished by nursing assistants, and a reduction in staff so that fewer nurses were covering a greater number of patients. Pete and Ann were co-chairs of a committee charged with looking for ways to increase the customer service ratings the hospital received from surveys sent to patients after their discharge as well as those sent to physicians who contracted with the hospital for the care of their patients. Ann had reacted to a comment from Pete that "Some of the members of the committee seem reluctant to consider new ideas for improving service to patients. If everyone is not willing to compromise a little, we just won't make any progress in improving service."

After the meeting, Pete approached Sue and said, "I didn't intend to hurt Ann's feelings, I was just trying to point out that we have reached an impasse that has kept our committee from making progress. I didn't realize Ann was sensitive to this or would take my comments personally. There must be something going on that I was unaware of but I certainly didn't want to start a conflict with the nursing staff." Sue quickly reassured Pete that there was probably more to Sue's reaction than just his comment in the meeting. She knew from experience that understanding and resolving conflict required more than analyzing the situation where the conflict became obvious. There is always a history of events that she also needed to better understand.

One of the most difficult skills of managing organizational behavior is to manage conflict. In the situation described above, Sue Robinson observed the situation where one of her staff members angrily walked out of a meeting because of a comment from another staff member. On the surface, it seemed hard to justify Ann's behavior based simply on the comment made by Pete. But as an experienced manager, Sue knew that conflict was a complex process that often had causes that were not immediately obvious to an observer. She also wasn't surprised that Pete was unaware that a conflict existed. That, she knew, was the nature of many of the conflicts she had dealt with in her career.

Conflict is a natural part of life and exists in politics, in our organizations, and within our personal lives. While some level of conflict is healthy – even necessary – in organizations, it can also increase stress and have dysfunctional consequences as people take sides on issues such as budget allocation, goal priorities, or over how fairly they are being treated. Labor unions and management conflict over compensation and work conditions. Sometimes, the problems are minor and settled easily. Others go unresolved or break out into conflicts of varying intensity from minor arguments to "organizational warfare." Not all of the effects of conflict, however, are bad. Key to successful management of conflict is how we view conflict and what we do to deal with it. In this chapter, we discuss the conflict process and how conflicts arise. We explore various styles of reacting to conflict and ways to manage and resolve conflict more effectively.

THE NATURE OF CONFLICT

Conflict includes disagreements, the presence of tension, or some other difficulty between two or more parties. It may occur between individuals or between groups. Conflict is caused when individuals or groups of individuals perceive that their goals are blocked. It can be public or private, formal or informal, or be approached rationally or irrationally.

Conflict as a process

Conflict is not a static condition; it is a dynamic process that involves several stages. Parties can go through the process in many different ways, and do so more than once. Figure 10.1 presents a model integrating different approaches to conflict [1, 2, 3, 4, 5, 6]. This is the model that will form the basis for our discussion throughout this chapter.

Antecedent conditions of conflict are the conditions that cause or precede a conflict episode. Sometimes an aggressive act can start the conflict process. For instance, in the opening case example in this chapter, perhaps Ann Costa felt that her nursing staff had already compromised enough on previous issues and that it was unfair for them to give up any more. Antecedents of conflict can also be subtle. Pressures on a production department to keep costs down may frustrate your sales manager who wants to fill rush orders on short notice. At this stage, conflict may remain below the surface because neither party presses its position.

Perceived conflict is necessary for the conflict to progress. The parties must become aware of a threat. Any person might act to the disadvantage of another, but without awareness of the act, little else will happen. Even without an action, people

185

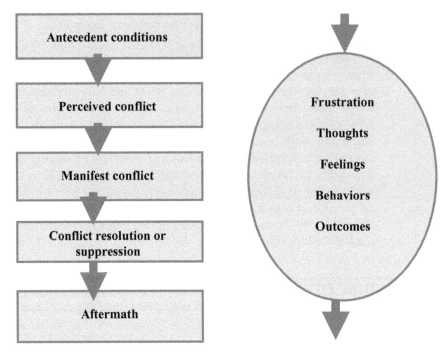

Figure 10.1 The conflict process

might perceive a threat when none is there. When conflict, real or imaginary, is perceived, it may trigger frustration, anger, fear, or anxiety. Those involved start to question how much they can trust each other, and worry about their ability to cope with the difficulty. This stage of conflict is critical because this is when the parties tend to define the issues and start looking for ways to resolve their differences.

Perceived conflict develops into **manifest conflict** when people react to the perception. One of your employees might threaten to file a grievance, prompting you to take defensive steps. Other behaviors that signal manifest conflict include: arguments, aggressive acts, appeal to goodwill, or constructive problem-solving. Ann Costa's "slamming the door" was a clear indication that the conflict in the opening case had moved to the manifest level.

Conflict resolution can come about in several ways. Parties may agree about how to solve their difficulties and even take steps to prevent conflict in the future. Conflict can also be resolved when one party defeats another. Sometimes conflict is **suppressed** rather than resolved. This happens when the parties avoid strong reactions or try to ignore each other when they disagree.

Whether conflict is resolved or suppressed, feelings remain. Behaviors during the **conflict aftermath** can be just as varied as the ways in which conflict is manifested or resolved. Sometimes good feelings and harmony result; a new procedure may be developed that clarifies the relationships between the parties. For example, one of your employees might decide not to file a grievance because you were willing to agree with the union on a new rule that solves the original problem.

Unfortunately, the conflict aftermath can also result in poorer working relationships. In the opening case, the nurses' reaction to an attempt to improve customer service may have been the result of residual feelings that still existed from earlier conflicts that led to increased work duties or a reduction in staff. If hard feelings and resentment persist, these can trigger the next conflict episode. The key question is whether the resolution draws parties into cooperation or drives them further apart.

The role of history in conflicts

Linkages between people and units of an organization persist over long periods of time. As a consequence, the parties develop a history of perceptions, attitudes, and behaviors toward each other. If one party has historically been cooperative in its relationships toward others, a single incident of non-cooperation is likely to have no significant effect. On the other hand, a history of conflict can cause the parties to mistrust each other continually, making opportunities for cooperation very difficult. In evaluating past behaviors, the parties are likely to put greatest weight on the most recent behaviors of the other.

Ignoring history is a common problem for managers who look for and react to what appears to be the most obvious cause of a conflict. If you were to see someone trying to diagnose the history of the conflict in the Middle East by looking back at the incidents of the early part of the twenty-first century, you would certainly think they would not be able to understand the issues that are the source of this conflict. Likewise, managers who take a short-term perspective on conflict without considering history often fail to understand the true cause of conflict that occurs in their organizations.

Viewpoints on conflict

There are three different viewpoints on conflict, and a manager's viewpoint may determine how they react to conflict. Those viewpoints are: conflict is preventable; conflict is inevitable; and conflict is healthy.

You may assume that conflict can be avoided simply by making employees adopt a cooperative attitude. You may also assume that conflict is preventable if managers can create positive working relationships through good planning, and with policies and procedures that ensure mutual efforts toward common goals. This perspective has merit, of course, and is part of how managers should view their role. Some conflict in organizations is preventable, and some of it is a sign that something is wrong and can be corrected.

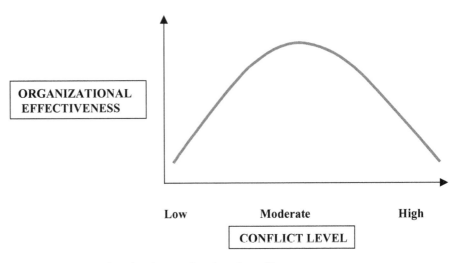

ORGANIZATIONAL
EFFECTIVENESS

Low   Moderate   High

CONFLICT LEVEL

Figure 10.2 Optimum levels of organizational conflict

The second point of view – conflict is inevitable and so there is no way to eliminate it entirely – may be true for many reasons. For example, not all organizational goals are compatible. The goal of reducing costs may be in conflict with a goal that calls for improved customer service. Organizational design also leads to conflict. Employees are grouped into departments of specialists, each with its own point of view. Conflicts may arise between the sales manager and the production manager because the required work for each group actually creates problems for the other. Conflict also arises because plans and policies are rarely perfect enough to cover all situations that might arise.

The third point of view is that some degree of conflict is healthy for an organization [7]. When would this be the case? Suppose that in a software firm the software designers and the marketing department never experienced tensions or disagreements with each other. The relative peace between the departments might mean that each department is not doing its job effectively. For example, the marketers may not be responding to new product or market opportunities, so they rarely suggest changes that would create tensions for the designers.

Healthy benefits of conflict include creative approaches to resolving problems and making decisions. In the chapters on groups and decision-making, we discuss some dysfunctional aspects of group dynamics such as groupthink. Groupthink occurs when groups attempt to achieve consensus and eliminate conflict. While this is useful for groups to make progress, it has its dysfunctional side-effects.

There is probably some optimal level of conflict as shown in figure 10.2. Too little conflict in an organization can be a threat to effectiveness. Individuals may avoid each other instead of interacting to work on generating new ideas and developing creative approaches to solving problems.

Too much conflict can also hamper effectiveness. With constant disagreement over too many issues, or through failure to appreciate the needs and problems of others, innovations may never come about, customers may be lost, and key issues may go unresolved. The organization will suffer if members are consumed with defending themselves or with winning internal organizational battles.

At the optimum level of conflict, quite different things happen. There are active attempts to improve quality and to introduce changes that might make the organization more competitive and more effective or efficient. Employees are stimulated; they are not bored and withdrawn. Individuals with different perspectives are willing to present their ideas and this may lead to improved performance. Tensions and frustrations are accepted and channeled into productive, rather than destructive, effort [8].

What triggers conflict?

To manage conflict, its causes must be understood and, if possible, changed. The causes of conflict are grouped into three major categories: the characteristics of individuals, situational conditions, and organizational conditions.

Difference in individual characteristics

Individual differences make some people more likely to engage in conflict than others. While you have been introduced to these characteristics in earlier chapters, we want to focus on how they influence conflict.

Differences in individual values, beliefs and attitudes can be a source of conflict. A worker who values autonomy and independence will probably react negatively when supervised too closely. Values also can create tensions between individuals and key groups in organizations. For example, union leaders are likely to have different values than managers. In one study, union leaders valued employee welfare and equality highly, but rated company profit maximization low. Managers' views were quite the opposite [9].

Another difference that can lead to conflict is when individuals differ in their needs and personalities. Consider the case of a chemical company that had several plants making different products [10]. Some of the plants produced products for other divisions in the company. The plant managers cooperated for a time with little difficulty. When some of the older plant managers retired, their replacements from the outside had a different psychological makeup. They were much more concerned about individual achievement and much less prone to cooperate. Disagreements between the old and new managers arose, and performance in some of the plants deteriorated.

If we perceive another person as a threat, we may act toward them in a way that also increases the potential for conflict. Perceived differences in power and status

189

are often the cause of conflict in organizations, as some individuals feel threatened by the power of others. This type of conflict is more likely when situations are ambiguous because ambiguity contributes to misperceptions and incorrect judgments.

Situational conditions

A second set of factors that can contribute to conflicts is the conditions found in different situations. The model of behavior presented in chapter 1 shows that behavior is a function of individual characteristics and the environment. Conflict, as a behavior, also has environmental causes.

Conflict is more likely when people are physically close, and when they need to interact. With frequent interactions such as occur in complex projects, conflict potential increases even more. Interactions are the stuff of life in organizations, but they need not result in conflict. It has been shown that the more productive work groups are ones that actively interact with each other by asking questions, working jointly on projects, and by sharing information and achievements [11].

Conflict may also be a function of whether agreements are needed between the parties. For example, many organizational purchases are routine and require little interaction or agreement among departments, but consensus might be needed when purchasing items such as computers or office equipment that may be shared by many users. Conflicts over quality, cost, or location could occur when pressure for consensus exists.

A classic analysis of status conflict was done in the restaurant industry, focusing on status differences as a source of conflict [12]. For a variety of reasons, cooks believed they had higher status than waitresses. When waitresses communicated their customers' orders to cooks, the cooks often reacted as if people of lower status were personally ordering them around. They often responded to the waitresses by delaying meals.

When there is ambiguity about roles and responsibilities, conflict can arise when individuals or groups posture for position. In one organization, the advertising department took the initiative to locate and order various supplies on their own. The purchasing group accused them of overstepping their authority and violating procedures. This led to continuous conflict and the distractions this caused eventually affected the quality and success of advertising.

Organizational conditions

When large numbers of people come together in an organization, many things can lead to conflict. These are rooted in roles and responsibilities, interdependencies, goals, policies, and reward systems.

Organizations often create expectations that make cooperation difficult. The classic relationships between production, sales, and research units provide a good case in point. Each unit has its own responsibilities and concerns. Sales may concern itself with customers and competition. Production seeks cost reduction and efficiency. Research focuses on technical improvements with emphasis on scientific objectives. These factors sharply differentiate these units and can be the basis for many disagreements. Organizational goals are often used to enhance cooperation but they can also increase conflict. Even when goals are clear, the method for achieving those goals may be a source of conflict. Managers all pursuing the same goals can seriously disagree over new products or services or whether to withdraw from certain markets. Nevertheless, it is very appropriate for these units to have different priorities and goals. As we said, some conflict is inevitable and healthy, even though it may be difficult to resolve.

The distinction between line and staff departments is also a basis for conflict. Line departments are those that are directly part of the organization mission, such as production departments. Staff units, such as human resources or legal departments, are indirectly involved and exist primarily to support and assist the line units. They often evaluate other units in the organization and develop new programs and procedures for them. Staff units also impose policies and procedures that line units may not understand or cannot accept.

Resources are almost always scarce in an organization, meaning that not enough exist to satisfy all the desires people might have. When resources are scarce, this may lead to conflict over the few resources that do exist. This engenders sharing of, and competition for, resources, either of which can create disagreements.

An increasingly common source of conflict is a direct result of the leaner and flatter organization structures discussed in chapter 1. These structures often mean that an employee fills many functions and, as a result, may be accountable to more than one supervisor. This violates a fundamental management theory known as the principle of **unity of command** – where each employee is to have only one superior. Conflict is often the result of a situation where employees are in a position where they receive conflicting demands from higher-level managers.

DIAGNOSING CONFLICT

When we attempt to understand the issues involved in a particular conflict situation, there are many dimensions of conflict that we should consider [13]:

- The issue in question
- The size of the stakes
- The interdependence of parties
- The continuity of the interaction
- The leadership

191

- The involvement of third parties
- The perceived progress of conflict.

An understanding of these issues allows managers to better diagnose a particular conflict. Considering each of these conflict dimensions requires you to consider some of the conflict process issues introduced earlier in this chapter. For example, considering the "perceived progress of the conflict" requires you to acknowledge that there is a history to each conflict that include a set of specific antecedent conditions that must be understood to adequately diagnose the situation. Below we discuss each of the dimensions.

The issue in question

Issues that are viewed by participants as matters of principle are the most difficult to resolve. In this case, participants have made the issue one where a possible conflict of values and belief systems is involved. Occasionally, participants in conflict make winning the focus, and saving face becomes more important than the original issue. This significantly complicates conflict resolution. The easiest conflicts to resolve are those that are easily divided. This allows for compromises in positions so that both parties can view the outcome as a partial victory at least. For example, if the issue is over a sum of money, compromise is possible because money can be divided.

The size of the stakes

When the stakes in the outcome are large, conflict is more difficult to resolve than when smaller stakes are involved. As discussed earlier, organizations often experience conflict over budget allocations. The difficulty in resolving this type of conflict is often directly correlated with the proportion of budget that is being debated. If the proportion is considered by participants as large, it is likely that a great deal of debate will occur because the parties are more likely to view the large sums of money involved as important for achievement of their individual unit's goals.

The interdependence of parties

The interdependence of the parties is also an important dimension for diagnosing conflict. In **zero-sum interdependence**, a gain by one side means a loss by the other side. These conflicts are more difficult to resolve than where there is **positive-sum interdependence**. This is where compromise settlements can lead to gains for both sides of the conflict. Continuing the example of budget negotiations, when finite budget amounts are available and sub-units are conflicting over their unit's share of the budget, it would be a zero-sum negotiation. An increase given to one unit would be at the expense of another.

The continuity of the interaction

A fourth dimension in diagnosing conflict is the continuity of the interaction among the parties in conflict. This considers the relationship among the parties. If we are talking about a conflict that has arisen between a firm and one of its long-term customers, it is likely that the conflict will be easier to resolve because both parties have an interest in protecting the long-term relationship. As a result, they may be more willing to seek compromise and may be interested in protecting the other side. When negotiations are between parties that have no previous relationship and have no plans for a future relationship, negotiation is likely to be more difficult.

The leadership

The leadership of conflicting parties is another dimension to consider. When there is a clear leader who has the authority to negotiate and make decisions, conflict should be easier to resolve than when there is a lack of a clear leader. This issue is often evident in labor relations negotiations. If the chief negotiator for management is not viewed as a party who can make decisions independently, and who may be second-guessed by the board of directors or other senior members of the organization, it complicates negotiations. The same can be said for the labor side. When both sides in a conflict have strong leadership who can decisively negotiate an agreement, it increases the confidence of all parties that promises made will be kept and supported, and thus makes the conflict easier to resolve.

The involvement of third parties

Using third parties such as mediators or arbitrators increases the ease of negotiating a resolution to the conflict. The role of third parties is discussed in more detail in the next section, but their primary contribution is an objective view of the issues. Third parties may be able to see potential compromises that are not considered by parties who have a strong interest in the outcomes of the conflict negotiations.

The perceived progress of the conflict

Finally, the perception of parties in conflict about the progress of the conflict is important in its resolution. When parties believe that both sides are compromising and giving up something of value, conflict is easier to resolve. When the perceptions of

193

one party are that they have suffered more harm than the other party, they are likely to resist additional compromises until they feel things are more in balance.

INDIVIDUAL RESPONSES TO CONFLICT

Conflict reaction style

Each of us deals with conflict in different ways. Some of us have an initial tendency to escape, and others of us are more prone to become involved. Once involved, people also vary in how they behave. There are five different styles of reacting to conflict, drawn from several important conflict theories [14, 15, 16, 4]:

1 Avoiding
2 Accommodating
3 Competing
4 Compromising
5 Collaborating.

Each style has different characteristics and different uses [16, 17].

Avoiding

Some of us become emotionally upset by conflict. Painful memories of past conflicts may make us want to withdraw from disagreement. Avoiding conflict can be based on a belief that conflict is evil, unnecessary, or undignified. You can withdraw by simply leaving the scene of a conflict. You can refuse to become involved by using silence or changing the topic of conversation. Psychologically, avoiders can also deny the existence of conflict or ignore it when it arises.

Avoiding conflict can be wise when issues are insignificant or when the costs of challenging someone outweigh the benefits. It may also be useful when there is little chance of success. Why pursue a lost cause? Avoiding also buys time. It gives others a chance to cool down or to seek more information. Finally, it might be better to avoid conflict when others can resolve it more effectively or when it concerns the wrong issue.

Accommodating

Accommodating means you give in to the wishes of another person. Accommodators feel it is better to give up their own goals rather than risk alienating or upsetting others. Like avoiders, the value system of accommodators is a perspective that conflict is bad, but rather than avoid it, they give in so as to keep or strengthen a

194

relationship. This style can reflect generosity, humility, or obedience. An accommodator may also feel that selfishness, an undesirable trait, is what causes most conflict.

Accommodation may be a very good strategy when you are in the wrong; it permits the correct position to win and is a sign of reasonableness. It can be taken as a gesture of goodwill and helps to maintain a relationship. Giving in may be a good thing to do when the issue is much more important to the other party. Fighting is not very productive when the other party has much to lose and you have little to gain.

Competing

If your style is to compete, you pursue your own wishes at the expense of the other party. The competitor defines conflict as a game to be won; he or she is not about to become the loser. Competitors are both assertive and uncooperative. Winning means success and accomplishment; losing means failure, weakness, and a loss of status. Competitors will use many different tactics such as threats, arguments, persuasion or direct orders.

A forceful position may be the best style in crises, when there is no time for disagreement and discussion. If the issue is simply not debatable, the manager may have to deal with opposition in a directive manner. As a manager, you may wish to use this style when unpopular but necessary decisions must be made, such as ordering that overtime work is necessary to meet a deadline for an important customer. Competition may also be a style to use when the other party has a tendency to take advantage of you, as it is a way to protect yourself.

Compromising

If you use a compromising style, you give and take based on the belief that people cannot always have their way; you think you should try to find a middle ground you can live with. As a compromiser, you would look for feasible solutions and will use techniques such as trading, bargaining, smoothing over differences, or voting. You value willingness to set aside personal wishes and show sensitivity to the other person's position. Through compromise, relationships can endure if people hear each other's point of view and if they try to arrive at a fair agreement.

Compromise is a common way of dealing with conflict. It may be a particularly useful technique when two parties have relatively equal power and mutually exclusive goals. Situations like this are zero-sum: what one party gains, the other loses. Compromise can also be useful when there are time constraints. Time may not be available for problems that require a great deal of effort to resolve all the issues. Compromise can allow for a temporary solution until more time can be devoted to unravel and analyze the complexities. Finally, compromise may be useful when collaboration or competition fail to lead to a solution between the parties.

Collaborating

Collaborating is a willingness to accept the other party's needs while asserting your own. If you collaborate you believe that there is some reasonable chance a solution can be found to satisfy both parties in the conflict. Such a solution might not be possible, but a collaborator believes that it is worth trying to find one. Collaboration requires that both the parties express their needs and goals, and work diligently and creatively to generate all kinds of solutions.

Collaboration, therefore, requires openness and trust, as well as hard work. It follows the principles of good problem-solving and decision-making. Collaboration is useful when each party is strongly committed to different goals and when compromise is potentially very costly. It is also useful when people agree on goals, but disagree on the means to achieve them. Collaboration can lead to an appreciation of other people's point of view. Therefore, it can strengthen relationships if mutual respect is maintained. When collaboration is successful, the commitment to the solution is high.

Conflict management through confrontation

By conflict management, we mean that a manager takes an active role in addressing conflict situations and intervenes if needed. A variety of actions are possible, ranging from preventing conflict to resolving it [18, 19]. Although avoiding conflict is a useful alternative, excessive avoidance can be very damaging to an organization [20].

Many people have a dominant style of dealing with conflict and rarely or never use more than one or two other styles. A manager would benefit by appreciating and learning to use all styles. This would broaden the manager's repertoire in coping with disagreements, and help to prevent the costs of overuse and underuse of styles.

We are not naturally disposed toward cooperating in the face of disagreement. It takes a special effort on our part to overcome past habits and attempt collaborative approaches. These are often referred to as **confrontation techniques**, and require that parties in conflict decide to face each other on the issues, and do so constructively. The parties must be willing to work together to arrive at a consensus decision, one that both parties can accept. They do not avoid or give in. They may compete or compromise somewhat, but the major emphasis of confrontation techniques is to collaborate to find mutually acceptable and longer-lasting solutions. The aim is for both parties to satisfy their needs and goals to the greatest extent possible. Effective confrontation requires skill and experience and, above all, a positive and constructive attitude in which the parties are open to ideas and information.

In confrontation methods, third parties such as outside consultants or mediators from government agencies that offer such services are frequently used.

Sometimes they come from within an organization, usually from the personnel department. Sometimes a specially trained manager can act as a third party in conflict resolution. As discussed earlier, the presence of a third party increases the chances of resolution. A third party can see to it that certain steps are followed, be a source of advice, make sure all opinions are heard, and assist in many decisions about process, such as when to have the parties work separately. In some instances, the third party may even make critical decisions that are binding on the parties. Bargaining, mediation/arbitration, and principled negotiation are all techniques for conflict management.

Bargaining

Bargaining is primarily a compromising style, but effective bargainers use a variety of techniques. They will occasionally act competitively and use force or threats. They will use accommodation, hoping that a concession on their part will stimulate the other party to concede a point in return. It is also possible for two parties to collaborate on some issues, jointly searching for a solution that is useful to both. One common use of bargaining in work organizations is when labor unions negotiate contracts.

In many bargaining situations, the goal of each party is to obtain the most it can, often at the expense of the other party. As discussed earlier, one factor that influences this behavior is the continuity of interaction. If the relationship is not a long-term one, people may drive a very hard bargain. You may bargain hard when buying a car, assuming you can buy elsewhere if the bargaining fails. In a labor-management negotiation, though, bargaining is tempered by the fact that the parties must work together when it is over.

Mediation/arbitration

Mediation is often used in labor-management negotiations, as well as in many other social settings, such as an alternative to going to court [21, 22, 23]. The parties can use third-party assistance to arrive at a solution. The Federal Mediation and Conciliation Service provides experienced mediators to help with labor-management negotiations. If both parties agree, a mediator is called in. Mediators are not empowered to make decisions or impose a solution, but they use many techniques to resolve differences. They may make suggestions and monitor the interaction of the parties. They can ease tensions with their methods and add objectivity to the process.

Arbitration is another third-party approach to conflict resolution. Unlike mediators, arbitrators actually make decisions that bind both parties. Arbitrators are used predominantly in labor-management situations, such as when contract negotiations have reached an impasse. Another use is for grievances. The arbitrator hears

197

both sides and may even follow a courtroom model. The points of view of both parties are presented. When the arbitrator feels he or she has heard enough, the arbitrator takes ample time to study the issues then makes a decision, binding on both parties.

Principled negotiation

Principled negotiation is based on a collaborative approach to problem-solving. Principled negotiation is compared to "soft" and "hard" approaches to conflict resolution. The soft approach is similar to accommodating and emphasizes giving in as a way to maintain a good relationship. The hard approach is similar to competing and emphasizes one party winning over the other. Principled negotiation emphasizes the problem and tries to make the parties in conflict collaborate toward mutual gain. There are four important elements in principled negotiation and these elements provide some extremely useful approaches for all conflict management strategies.

1 Separate the people from the problem.
2 Focus on interests, not positions.
3 Invent options for mutual gain.
4 Insist on objective criteria.

IMPROVING ORGANIZATIONAL RESPONSE TO CONFLICT

As suggested in our model of behavior presented in chapter 1, context is an important factor that influences many relevant behaviors and therefore has important consequences for organizations. As you might expect, the organizational context is often a cause of conflict that managers must deal with. Goal-setting, organization structure, and resource allocation are among the many contextual influences that lead to conflict. In addition to understanding the organizational causes of conflict, managers need to know the steps that can be taken to effectively manage conflict.

Set superordinate goals

Superordinate goals should be set that draw units into collaborative efforts. These would be goals that benefit individual sub-units and are strongly linked to overall organizational effectiveness. For example, the dean of a college of business can unite the accounting, finance, management, and marketing departments to work together in a fundraising campaign that benefits the entire school. If administrators, faculty, alumni, and students meet together to plan the campaign, they can decide on how to approach different donors. Goals can also be set concerning how the campaign money will be used. The needs of the college can be integrated with the needs of each department to try to prevent conflict from erupting.

Reduce ambiguities and jurisdictional disputes

There are many ways to decrease ambiguities. The goal-setting process is one of these. Clear and non-conflicting goals clarify responsibilities so that each employee and unit does not interfere or compete with the work of the others. Good job descriptions can also clarify duties and expectations so there is little dispute about who is responsible for what. Preparing organization charts and discussing who has the authority to make certain decisions can clarify reporting relationships.

Improve policies, procedures, and rules

Policies, procedures, and rules can often be improved to reduce conflict potential. One such case arose in the research division of a large equipment manufacturer. The scientists and engineers in this division often attended conventions and professional meetings to keep up to date, to present papers, and to work on problems with other scientists. Conflict repeatedly arose over attendance at these meetings. Some employees attended as many as five meetings, others only one. Complaints about fairness put many departments at odds with each other. A committee was established that prepared a fair policy to cover this situation. Costs were contained and conflict over the issues reduced. Think back to the chapter on motivation and our discussion of the importance of procedural justice. Fair procedures can positively influence individual reactions to organizational decision-making.

Reallocate or add resources

When there is conflict that stems from resource-sharing, personnel assignments, inventory flow, and schedules can be reviewed to look for a creative resolution to the problem. In one factory, there was constant conflict between the maintenance department and the production supervisors over maintenance priorities. Favoritism and personalities dominated, and complaints were frequent. The production manager solved the problem by reassigning some maintenance employees to production units. Each production supervisor was given maintenance responsibility and now had the personnel resources to do it. Conflict was virtually eliminated and production delays were drastically reduced.

Modify communications

One way to improve communication is to eliminate some of it. Recall the study of the restaurant industry cited earlier [12]. Cooks were resistant to "taking orders" from the waitresses, who they felt were of lower status. The problem was greatly reduced by requiring the waitresses to submit written customer orders and requests. Their orders were clipped to a rotating spindle from which cooks could select. The face-to-face interaction with the cooks was reduced, and so was conflict between them. In many of today's restaurants, orders are transmitted electronically to the kitchen.

Rotate personnel

Rotating personnel through different departments helps them to develop a fuller understanding of each unit's responsibilities and problems. Then, when the employee returns to his or her original unit, a basis for cooperation exists. Rotation is often used with new employees. You will also recall from the job characteristics model presented in the chapter on motivation that job variety can be a positive motivational tool. In this case, there are several benefits to rotating personnel into other jobs or departments within the organization.

Change reward systems

The way rewards are administered may decrease the chances of conflict erupting. Managers can be reinforced with positive feedback and good performance appraisals when they promote harmony. Even financial rewards such as bonuses can be consistent with conflict reduction. In one factory, where heavy industrial machines were assembled, employees used to work independently on various tasks such as welding, bolting parts together, and wiring electrical circuits. They argued over assignments, space, and tools. Many saw no benefit in helping each other. Management decided to create work teams and supplied each with enough tools and workspace to eliminate the competition. To prevent further conflict between the teams, productivity and cost-savings bonuses were introduced. In a short time, teams began to help their own team members and offer assistance to other teams.

Provide training

Many organizations conduct training programs in which employees learn to prevent, anticipate, and cope with conflict. They can assess their own conflict reaction style and learn how to use more than one style. They are given the chance to practice techniques of conflict resolution, especially the demanding confrontation techniques discussed above.

Guide for Managers:
MANAGING CONFLICT CONSTRUCTIVELY

In addition to the approaches discussed above, here are a number of practical approaches for managing conflict in a way that will maintain the healthy conflict that allows organizations to maintain creative and innovative energy [24].

FOCUS ON THE FACTS. Many organizations have access to timely data from objective sources. However, it is common to allow discussions about opinions rather than fact to dominate discussions. Attempt to control discussion by challenging ideas and conclusions. Encourage managers to state up front if their comments are based on anecdotal evidence or based on factual information.

CONSIDER MULTIPLE ALTERNATIVES. Rather than narrowing the focus to a small set of alternatives, it appears teams with less conflict consider more alternatives. Individuals often suggest an alternative that they may not agree with in an attempt to increase the options available to the group and induce new ways of looking at existing alternatives [24]. Multiple alternatives also may reduce polarization influences given there are more than two positions to consider.

CREATE COMMON GOALS. As discussed in this chapter, when parties have conflict goals, other types of conflict are sure to follow. If common goals can be introduced it will more likely cause collaboration rather than competition. In the chapters on groups and teams we discussed the importance of goal clarity on team effectiveness. One reason teams that don't have clear and common goals do not perform as well is because of the conflict that occurs.

USE HUMOR. Tension and stress are common by-products of groups involved in decision-making under pressure. It was found that teams that had higher conflict lacked humor in their process. Humor is also an important element in combating the effects of stress.

BALANCE THE POWER STRUCTURE. As with many issues, fairness is a key to acceptance of decisions. When there is a mismatch of power, greater tension is felt by individuals. Creating balance prevents one party from dominating the discussion and the decision-making process. When members feel like their input has equal value and possibility for acceptance, they are more willing to present their ideas. The openness of the process that ensues leads to greater willingness to accept the final decision and less conflict in the long run.

SUMMARY

Since organizations involve so much interdependence between individuals and groups, conflict can easily arise and become a serious threat to organizational effectiveness. However, conflict – when managed properly – can be a healthy aspect of the organization. It can add to creativity, be a sign of health, and bring different points of view to the attention of decision-makers.

Conflict, like other organizational behavior, often has multiple causes. Certain individual characteristics may lead some of us to become involved in more conflicts than others. Occasionally, characteristics of the situation may make conflict more likely. In our organizations, conflict can arise as a result of many issues that just naturally occur in the workplace. When many diverse individuals work side by side in complex organizational structures with numerous goals and agendas, conflict is a natural outcome.

Resolving conflict is an important managerial role. While different managers may choose different styles of dealing with conflict, one thing is certain. Just as there are often multiple causes of individual conflict, managers should consider multiple methods to resolve that conflict. Focusing on organizational goals and structural aspects of the organization are effective means of understanding and eliminating conflict.

REFERENCES

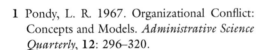

1 Pondy, L. R. 1967. Organizational Conflict: Concepts and Models. *Administrative Science Quarterly*, **12**: 296–320.

2 Pondy, L. R. 1969. Varieties of Organizational Conflict. *Administrative Science Quarterly*, **14**: 499–506.

3 Hickson, D. J. et al. 1971. A Strategic Contingency Theory of Intraorganizational Power. *Administrative Science Quarterly*, **16**: 216–29.

4 Filley, A. C. 1975. *Interpersonal Conflict Resolution*. Glenview, IL: Scott, Foresman.

5 Thomas, K. W. 1976. Conflict and Conflict Management. In M. D. Dunnette, ed., *Handbook of Industrial and Organizational Psychology*, 889–935. Chicago: Rand McNally.

6 Thomas, K. W. 1990. Conflict and Negotiation Processes in Organizations. In M. D. Dunnette, ed., *Handbook of Industrial and Organizational Psychology*, 651–717. Palo Alto, CA: Consulting Psychologists Press.

7 Cosier, R. A. and D. R. Dalton. 1990. Positive Effects of Conflict: A Field Assessment. *International Journal of Conflict Management*, **1**: 81–92.

8 Tjosvold, D. 1991. *The Conflict Positive Organization*. Reading, MA: Addison-Wesley.

9 England, G. W., N. C. Agarwal, and R. E. Trerise. 1971. Union Leaders and Managers: A Comparison of Value Systems. *Industrial Relations*, **10**: 211–26.

10 Lawrence, P. R., L. B. Barnes, and J. W. Lorsch, eds. 1976. *Organizational Behavior and Administration*. 3rd edn. Homewood, IL: Richard D. Irwin.

11 Ancona, D. G. 1990. Outward Bound Strategies for Team Survival in an Organization. *Academy of Management Journal*, **33**(2): 334–65.

12 Whyte, W. F. 1949. The Social Structure of the Restaurant. *American Journal of Sociology*, **54**: 302–10.

13 Greenlaugh, L. 1986. SMR Forum: Managing Conflict. *Sloan Management Review*.

14 Blake, R. R. and J. S. Mouton. 1969, *Building a Dynamic Corporation through Grid Organization Development*. Reading, MA: Addison-Wesley.

15 Hall, J. 1969. *Conflict Management Survey*. Houston, TX: Teleometrics.

16 Thomas, K. W. and R. H. Kilmann. 1974. *Conflict Mode Instrument*. Tuxedo, NY: Xicom.

17 Thomas, K. W. 1977. Toward Multidimensional Values in Teaching: The Example of Conflict Behaviors. *Academy of Management Review*, **2**: 484–90.

18 Tjosvold, D. 1986. *Managing Work Relationships: Cooperation, Conflict and Power*. Lexington, MA: Lexington Books.

19 Stulberg, J. B. 1987. *Taking Charge/ Managing Conflict*. Lexington, MA: Lexington Books.

20 Argyris, C. 1986. Skilled Incompetence. *Harvard Business Review*, **64**: 74–9.

21 Foldberg, J. and A. Taylor. 1985. *Mediation: A Comprehensive Guide to Resolving Conflict without Litigation*. San Francisco: Jossey-Bass.

22 Moore, C. 1986. *The Mediation Process*. San Francisco: Jossey-Bass.

23 McGillicuddy, N. B., G. L. Welton, and D. G. Pruitt. 1987. Third-Party Intervention: A Field Experiment Comparing Three Different Models. *Journal of Personality and Social Psychology*, **53**: 104–12.

24 Eisenhardt, K., J. Kahwajy, and L. J. Burgeois III. 1997. How Management Teams Can Have a Good Fight. *Harvard Business Review*, 111–21.

CHAPTER 11

Decision-Making

CHARACTERISTICS OF THE DECISION-MAKING PROCESS

MODELS OF DECISION-MAKING

IMPROVING INDIVIDUAL DECISION-MAKING

IMPROVING GROUP DECISION-MAKING

SOCIAL INFLUENCES ON GROUP DECISION-MAKING

Cindy Adams looked at the list of the three candidates being considered for the promotion. There was Bill Kearns, one of the most experienced employees in her unit. Barbara Thomas had been in the unit for two years and had brought a great deal of experience to the organization. Finally there was Felecia Armstrong, a highly capable person who had shown great promise on many of her assignments. In Cindy's opinion, each of the candidates could potentially do quite well in the new position. It would be a tough decision to make and Cindy, as she did with most major decisions, had called a meeting of her three division leaders to discuss the candidates and to reach a consensus. Cindy knew from experience that a consensus was not likely. Each candidate came from each of the three different divisions and had the strong endorsement of their respective division chief. Cindy thought back to previous meetings where equally important decisions were made and remembered how often it seemed that the group had become side-tracked by discussing criteria that seemed less relevant to the decision. It had become clear to her that, when important decision were being made, her division chiefs often had other agendas on their minds. The result was that their group often made poorer decisions, as division chiefs spent more time arguing for a particular position rather than listening to the input of others and seeking the best decision. The net effect was that Cindy often felt she had to make decisions without the input of her key staff. She knew this was a clear possibility with this decision and wondered if she could avoid the "inevitable" with this important decision.

Traditional perspectives have treated decision-making as a highly rational process and assume that decision-makers have clear criteria for decision quality and well-articulated outcomes in mind. This perspective often ignores the organizational realities faced by leaders like Cindy Adams. In reality, decision-making in organizations is a complex process of conflicting goals and criteria. Decision-makers and those who contribute to the decision-making process often have differing values and agendas that further complicate the process. This chapter looks at these different perspectives on decision-making.

Remember that in chapter 1 we said that many believe that organizational decision-making is a rational, reflective process that is a significant aspect of a manager's work – and that this is folklore and myth. The fact is that managers work at an unrelenting pace and that they are strongly oriented to action, not to reflection, and many managers cannot afford the luxury of long, involved decision-making processes. They spend more time making decisions than planning for those decisions. Modern business environments demand that managers are able to process large amounts of information – and balance the needs of multiple constituencies within a highly stressful environment. Often there is little time left for careful information-gathering, even though the decisions made can be costly in terms of lives and money.

CHARACTERISTICS OF THE DECISION-MAKING PROCESS

There are certain common characteristics to decision-making processes that are useful to consider. These are apparent when we make routine as well as critical decisions.

Decisions within decisions

Often, when analyzing the effectiveness of a decision, we incorrectly focus on the final decision. In many cases, the final decision is just one of several decisions that were made and which had a significant impact on the success of the outcome. In the recent dispute over the safety of Firestone tires mounted on Ford Motor Company SUVs, attention focused on a series of decisions that were important in both setting the stage for subsequent decisions but that also established a precedent. These were key decisions, "decisions within the decisions," made as the situation unfolded, decisions that have had a significant influence on subsequent decisions made by leaders in both companies. Some of these decisions were, for example:

- Decisions within Ford not to pass on concerns about an increasing number of accidents to members higher in the organization.
- Decisions by Firestone to delay a recall of the tires in question.
- Decisions made about the recommended tire pressure for Firestone tires mounted on Ford Explorers.

Small decisions accumulate

Many decisions we make seem trivial and so are made very quickly, yet the consequences of a series of small decisions can accumulate into a serious problem. Picture an employee who postpones a call to a customer so as to arrive home on time. Another employee overlooks a detail on that customer's order because co-workers disturbed her. Later, a shipping clerk leaves the order off a truck rather than make an extra effort to load it. Taken together, these minor decisions can add up to the loss of a major account.

Decisions are partial or temporary solutions

It is almost impossible to prevent some errors in decision-making. Most decisions, therefore, never completely solve a problem. Even if they come close, the solution often contains seeds of new problems requiring attention. Since decisions are imperfect, they are partial solutions. This means that it is necessary to follow up on important decisions and to be prepared to modify them. As a result, managers often find they have to continually address issues related to certain decisions and need to be prepared to adjust or modify those decisions.

MODELS OF DECISION-MAKING

There are different ways, or models, for thinking about decision-making: the rational (normative) model, the administrative model, and the garbage can model.

Rational or normative models of decision-making

These models are called rational because they assume that decision-makers apply a carefully designed set of criteria or rationales for their decisions. They assume the process is rational as well. The term normative is used because these models are based on observation of the actual errors that decision-makers tend to commit. Certain errors are very common, and, in normative models, an attempt is made to prevent or reduce them.

This approach follows a logical sequence of steps (see figure 11.1). It is helpful for managers who wish to improve their approach to decision-making. To optimize decision quality, the normative approach requires that you follow these steps.

1   Decision-making usually begins with a judgment that a problem exists or a change is needed. Sometimes the problem is an uncomfortable or negative condition you want to eliminate, such as a stoppage on a production line. A problem can also exist when you set a goal, because a goal also represents a desire to improve on a current condition. A manager setting a sales goal faces the problem of determining how to attain that goal.

2   Once a problem is recognized and defined, alternatives are sought that could eliminate the negative condition or achieve the goal. Alternatives are activities that you believe will lead to a better state of affairs. When you generate alternatives, you make assumptions or predictions that certain outcomes will follow. The relationship between alternatives and their outcomes is not a simple one. One alternative can result in a single outcome or several outcomes, or more than one alternative could be required to achieve a single desired outcome. Some outcomes are intended, while others are unintended side-effects of the alternative. For example, a decision to increase production to meet a certain goal may lead to lower product quality or equipment breakdown as an unintended consequence.

3   To choose among alternatives, you have to use criteria to evaluate them. Among the most common criteria used are feasibility, time, cost, and personal

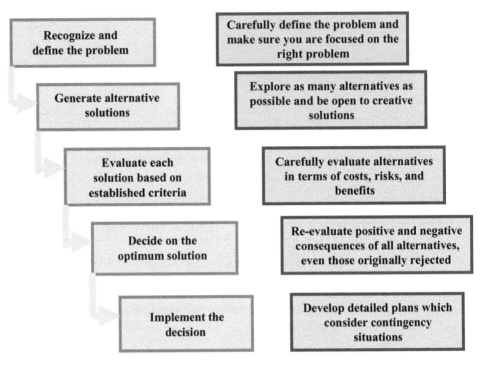

Figure 11.1 Rational model of decision-making

acceptability. Criteria will usually vary from person to person, and it is not always clear what criteria are being used.

4   Eventually choices are made among alternatives.

5   Once the choice is implemented, it becomes possible to evaluate once again. Here the evaluation can uncover faulty implementation or reveal that errors were made at an earlier stage of the decision-making process.

The administrative model of decision-making

Researchers who study what managers actually do say that the decision-making process is much less systematic than the rational process suggests [1, 2]. Two key concepts form the basis for the administrative model of decision-making: bounded rationality and satisficing.

Decisions are made with **bounded rationality**. This means that decision-makers are able to recognize only a limited number of alternatives and are aware of only a few consequences of each alternative. Human abilities are fallible and limited, information is never perfect, and money and time add limits as well. These contextual constraints place pressures on managers to circumvent the rational decision-making process by making decisions more efficiently.

A second limitation in the decision-making process often occurs in response to problems that an organization may face. When problems occur managers begin a search for "fixes" to that particular problem. This will often result in the consideration of a solution that focuses on the most easily identified (or accepted) cause of the problem. Pressures of cost and time may limit the number of options decision-makers want to consider. Instead of considering all possibilities, as alternatives are suggested, they are compared to a set of minimally acceptable criteria. The first alternative that meets those criteria is selected. This process is called **satisficing**.

The garbage can model of decision-making

Many forces in organizations complicate decision-making. For example, problems are redefined and decisions modified as different people become involved in the process over time. Even with normative approaches, organizational forces will have an effect. One approach to understanding organizational decision-making that considers these effects is the **garbage can model**, or organized anarchy [3]. The basic idea of this approach is different from those above. Where they both start with the premise that decisions will be made to solve problems, the garbage can model starts from the idea that there are decisions that are searching for a problem to which they can be applied. It is an interesting and a very political view of decision-making.

The garbage can model is most likely to operate when goals are ambiguous, methods for achieving goals are not well understood, and organizational units are scattered and loosely linked together. This model is also more likely to operate when an organization has many departments, committees, and task forces, each with vague or overlapping responsibilities. It is also likely to appear in a decision-making environment with multiple participants representing multiple sub-units with varying responsibilities and loyalties.

Here is how the garbage can approach works. First, you have to consider the participants and their priorities. The participants in complex organizations are the many decision-makers with different goals and problems. They have limited time and energy, and cannot involve themselves in all decisions. So their involvement depends on their individual needs, goals, and availability. The participation of decision-makers can be direct in that they are directly involved or responsible for resolving the problem. Alternatively they can be indirectly related to the decision and can influence outcomes. One example of this would be the role of a supervisor who provides "input" to a subordinate about a decision she or he is about to make. Decision-makers may also vary in the priority with which they view the problem. Consider what occurs within cross-functional teams, i.e., teams whose members come from different functions within the organization. While members may bring more ideas and perspectives to the discussion of the problem, they can also bring a different and perhaps competing set of priorities.

209

Second is a consideration of the problems to be solved. Within the decision-making context, various participants may view the problems differently or may, in fact, be actually working on a different set of problems. They also have ideas they would like to see adopted. Sometimes these ideas are solutions in search of a problem, rather than a problem in search of a solution. For example, a manufacturing manager might want some new equipment he saw at a trade show. He will be sensitive to decision opportunities that will allow him to buy it. Thus, goals are established to justify decisions already made rather than the reverse.

Timing is also an important element. The organization is viewed as a fluid structure in which people, problems, and solutions flow together and apart at different times. Decisions result from a disorderly convergence of these elements, heavily determined by patterns of timing and opportunities [4].

IMPROVING INDIVIDUAL DECISION-MAKING

Once we understand how people typically behave, including the errors they make, we can turn to ways to improve your individual decision-making. Here are some things that can be done.

Improve problem selection and definition

A number of steps can be taken to prevent problem selection from being dominated by our perceptions or by the order in which problems happen to arise. One of the most important things to remember is everything that you read about attribution theory in chapter 4. Next is to recognize that nothing is a problem until someone calls it that. A problem is nothing more than a personal, often very subjective conclusion that things are not the way they ought to be. It might be wise, therefore, to check out our perceptions with others before concluding that a problem exists that is worth taking action on.

Several things can improve the problem definition. The first is to work toward a thorough definition. A second is to avoid the tendency to jump prematurely into solutions before the problem is completely defined. The third comes into play if you fail to do one of the first two. That is, if you have a solution in mind, ask yourself to link that solution back to some aspect of the problem. In other words, when a solution occurs to you, ask yourself how it relates to the problem at hand. This forces you to go back to the problem definition rather than develop the solution.

One way that you can provide a better definition of a problem is to determine its causes. Investigate any events that might be related to the problem. Is there a pattern to the occurrence of the events? Does the problem occur at consistent times or within consistent situations?

210

Improving, generating, and evaluating solutions

The normative model tells us to generate, explore, and examine all possible solutions in a thorough and exhaustive manner, and to estimate the probabilities and values of all possible outcomes. Methods and criteria are established for evaluating and comparing alternative solutions. Even when extensive efforts are made to do this, errors creep in.

One important thing to remember is that you need to be aware of the mental models you use. These are assumptions and generalizations about how the world works that affect how we react to that world. These models may also affect our approach to problem resolution. Many of us tend to view problems in terms of linear relationships [5]. When looking for causes of problems, we look for the action that occurred immediately preceding the problem surfacing. We then assume causality and go about focusing on a factor that may not be the cause or that may not be at all related to the problem. The key is understanding the relationships that exist and our assumptions about those relationships.

Solution evaluation is improved if you know your personal tendencies. Some people take more risks and are more oriented toward seeking success. They are more likely to ignore what can be lost, and rather than protect themselves against losses, they will choose alternatives to maximize gain. Others will avoid the risks of maximum gain and will seek smaller but safer gains. Others may focus on losses rather than gains: their main motivation is to prevent losses, even if it means losing the chance at gaining something. This is a failure avoidance strategy and leads to conservative decision-making.

One important practice is to separate idea generation from idea evaluation. This suggestion is based on the idea that, when you evaluate an idea, you cut off the generation of other ones. A positive evaluation is more harmful than a neutral or negative evaluation. If you are neutral toward, or dislike, an alternative solution, you have an incentive to generate another one, but if you like an alternative, you might stop your search right there.

We generate and evaluate solutions better if we remember:

1 Potential solutions are often evaluated prematurely. We tend to react to an idea as soon as it arises.
2 Perceptual blocks such as old patterns of thought as well as social and cultural values put blinders on our creative thinking, keeping us in a mental rut.
3 We often fail to make our evaluation criteria explicit before using them to judge alternatives.
4 It is difficult to deal with both the value of a solution and the probabilities associated with it. Both are important, but we may ignore one or the other. In other words, if a solution is high-risk, we may ignore its value and potential.
5 Emotions can lead to self-deception. We can psychologically rationalize or justify an alternative we strongly prefer.

Improving decision implementation

Some decisions are implemented easily once we have made them. Even a complex decision can have a simple implementation. For example, a company might consider many factors in deciding whether to buy from a particular supplier. Once one is selected, an order can be easily placed. Other decisions may require more complicated implementation. Consider the case of a company that decides to expand into a new product line. The decision is just the beginning of a long process. Hundreds of new problems will have to be solved to prepare the new product. The long and detailed process from design to production, to sales and distribution of the product, will require attention.

In addition to dealing with issues directly related to decision implementation, you should be aware of some dysfunctional tendencies managers have that occur after a decision has been made. **Post-decisional dissonance** for example, can impede implementation of a solution. After a decision has been made, people may waver and hesitate. **Perceptual errors and cognitive dissonance** can also follow a decision. If people are positively disposed toward a decision, they may ignore information that suggests the decision is not working and interpret events to support their original choice. People also may make decisions and sometimes stick to them over time, even if they are bad decisions. This is called **escalation of commitment** [6]. People become trapped or locked into a course of action for several reasons. They resist admitting they made an error so as to appear competent or consistent; they can save face by holding to their original position. They may feel that changing their position will be viewed as a sign of weakness and make them more vulnerable to criticism or exploitation. Escalation of commitment may decrease or be less likely when:

1   The resources to stay with the decision are depleted.
2   The responsibility for the bad decision is shared or when people feel that more than one person was the cause.
3   The evidence is strong that negative things will continue to happen.

Summary of improving individual decision-making: a call for systems thinking

The practice of systems thinking is useful in resolving problems that occur throughout the decision-making process [5]. Systems thinking means that you look for interrelationships among other variables within the decision space. This approach is fundamentally different from that of traditional forms of analysis. Traditional analysis focuses on separating the individual pieces of what is being studied. Systems thinking, in contrast, focuses on how the issue being studied interacts with the other components of the system – in other words, what other elements are parts of the system that may be influencing the behavior or problem that interests us. This means that instead of isolating smaller and smaller parts of the system being studied, systems thinking works by expanding its view to take into account larger and larger numbers of interactions as an issue is being studied. This often results in different conclusions than those generated by traditional forms of analysis. This is especially relevant for most organizational situations because of their dynamic and complex nature and the complex way in which components of our environments influence us.

IMPROVING GROUP DECISION-MAKING

Organizations frequently use teams, committees, task forces, and other types of groups in all stages of the decision-making process. Usually this involvement or participative management philosophy is an attempt to find better decisions and more commitment by including employees in decisions that affect them, spreading responsibilities for decision-making to all employees, not just managers.

Sometimes participation works well, and sometimes it does not. To succeed, the commitment to group decision-making must be genuine. In addition, various skills are needed. First, as managers we must learn the steps and techniques of good decision-making discussed in the first part of this chapter. Knowledge of group and team dynamics is essential too. We need to know the benefits and disadvantages of group decision-making over individual decision-making. Finally, leadership is needed to guide the process so that effective decisions have a chance of emerging.

Benefits and disadvantages of groups

Using groups for decision-making has both assets and liabilities [7]. To a large degree, making them an asset depends on the skill of the leader. Compared to individuals, groups have more knowledge and information. Groups also generate a larger number of approaches to a problem, and members can knock each other out of ruts in their thinking. Group participation can increase understanding and acceptance of the decision, and the commitment to execute it. Managerial decisions often fail because of faulty communication of the decisions to those who must implement them. Employees often lack knowledge of rejected alternatives, obstacles, goals, and reasons behind the decision. These problems can be overcome when a group is involved in the entire process.

A disadvantage of group decision-making lies in social pressure for **conformity**. The majority can suppress good minority ideas, or a desire for consensus can silence disagreement. Some solutions, good and bad ones, accumulate a certain amount of support. Once support for a solution reaches a critical level, it has a high probability of being selected and other solutions are very likely to fail. Even a minority can build up support for a solution by actively asserting themselves. A final disadvantage of groups occurs when it becomes more important to avoid disagreement or win an argument than to make a good evaluation of alternatives. Avoidance of disagreement and arguments prevents open and objective discussion.

Deciding when to use a group

Not every decision that we make can – or should – be made by a group. Managers can make the decision alone or involve others in the decision-making process. They can assign the responsibility to an individual, a committee, or a task force. The question is, under what conditions is it best to use a group?

Quality and acceptance as criteria

Quality and **acceptance** are useful criteria in deciding whether to engage a group in decision-making [8]. The quality of a decision refers to the feasibility and technical aspects of a problem and calls for the use of facts, analysis of data, and objectivity. Acceptance of a decision, on the other hand, deals with feelings, needs, and emotions and is subjective in nature.

With some decisions, quality is more important than acceptance. These problems are usually technical or scientific in nature, such as how to control pressure in a valve or devising a test to select among vendors' products. When quality is the main concern, you are not likely to become emotionally involved in the outcome or decision, so, as a manager, you need only find experts with the knowledge and experience to find a quality solution. They can research, develop, and test technically feasible solutions. Facts and analysis will dominate decision-making.

Guide for Managers:
VALUE DISAGREEMENT AND CHAOS

There is more value in disagreement than in quick agreement. When group members agree, solution generation often comes to a close. If a disagreement occurs, however, solution generation is still alive. Leaders squelch disagreement when they say, "If we're going to argue, we'll never get this problem solved." Statements such as this, frustrated sighs, or other non-verbal cues soon tell group members to avoid disagreement.

Disagreements can be made to pay off. This is done when the leader accepts and probes a disagreement. The leader can say, "Phyllis, your idea really contrasts with John's. Tell us what you have in mind, and then we can get John's point of view." This tells the group that it is acceptable to disagree, and no one will be punished for doing so. It also opens the door to new ideas. Often the disagreement can be traced to different definitions of the problem, or to goals that a group had not earlier considered. Probing disagreement can prevent the rubber-stamping or the avoiding of ideas. Managers should program disagreement into discussions with the use of devil's advocate roles or by asking for counter-proposals [11].

With other problems, however, acceptance may be the most important criterion. For example, deciding who works overtime is an acceptance issue, assuming that the candidates for overtime are all able to do the work. Other changes that might involve workplace procedures or that will significantly impact a particular group and require their efforts for successful decision implementation increase the importance of the acceptance criterion.

Other problems involve both quality and acceptance: deciding how to increase productivity, introducing new methods or equipment, reducing absenteeism, or developing new safety standards. Here quality solutions are essential, and those affected by them will have strong feelings about them. The decision could fail unless employees accept it and can commit to its implementation.

The decision rule to use is, "Whenever acceptance is critical, the manager must at least consider using a group for the decision-making process. Unilateral decisions by the manager run the risk of being misunderstood or rejected." Even though shortage of time could argue against participation, group decision is a way to achieve acceptance.

The Vroom-Yetton model

A useful model for deciding whether to use a group has been developed by Vroom and Yetton [9]. They propose different types of decision-making, which vary according to the amount of subordinate influence. At one extreme is unilateral decision-making by the manager; this is a quick and efficient way to make a decision. At the other extreme is participative decision-making where the manager's role is to provide information and facilitate the group determining its own solution.

1   You make the decision with currently available data.
2   Necessary information is obtained from subordinates, but you still decide alone.
3   You discuss the problem with relevant subordinates individually. Then, without bringing them together, makes a decision that may or may not reflect their input.

Guide for Managers: AVOID LEADER SOLUTIONS

A group leader, especially one who has formal authority, should avoid offering solutions to the group. This may be difficult for you to do. You usually want to express your opinions in these situations. The problem is that a superior's idea is evaluated by group members on the basis of the source of the idea and not its worth. Objective evaluation loses out to concern over how the boss will react if the idea is supported or challenged. It is rare that a boss is treated as a peer. You will get better solutions from groups when they are given no time to prepare or think about a problem. When you prepare, you tend to think of solutions that you later find difficult to keep to yourself.

4 You share the problem with subordinates in a group meeting, gathering ideas and suggestions, then make the decision alone.

5 Problems are shared with the group. In this case, you would be using the participative management style.

The model suggests that you consider the characteristics of the situation in deciding on the extent to which you would involve the group in the decision. Those criteria include **the importance of decision quality** as discussed above. How important is it to achieve a high-quality solution? If there is no quality requirement, then any acceptable alternative will be satisfactory to management, and the group can make the decision. For example, groups can decide how to accomplish or assign routine tasks where quality is not critical.

A second criterion considers **the extent to which the decision-maker has the necessary information**. There are two kinds of information that make an effective decision: preferences of subordinates about alternatives and whether there are rational grounds to judge the quality of alternatives. When you do not know your subordinates' preferences, participation can reveal them. If you know subordinates' preferences, but the problem is such that an individual decision is likely to produce a better solution than a group decision, then clearly the situation calls for you to make the decision alone.

A third criterion considers **the extent to which the problem is structured**. In structured problems, the alternatives, or at least the means for generating them, are known. Standard procedures used in most organizations give individuals all or most of the information they need. In an ill-structured problem, the information may be widely dispersed through the organization. Different individuals will probably have to be brought together to solve the problem or to make a joint decision.

The importance of subordinates' acceptance is also an important consideration discussed earlier. Acceptance by subordinates is not critical where a decision falls in the boundaries of the psychological contract. In this case, carrying out the decision is a matter of simple compliance. The more commitment required from subordinates in the

Guide for Managers:
GAINING CONSENSUS

Eventually, group members need to evaluate their ideas and arrive at a decision they can live with. You can help in several ways.

- Summarize the group's progress to help make sure the group is ready to make the decision.
- Get members to develop criteria to evaluate the alternatives they have generated.
- Organize and present a review of the group's work in order to adequately test and gain a true consensus.

carrying out of a decision, of course, the more important subordinate acceptance becomes.

Another important factor to consider is **the probability that an autocratic decision will be accepted**. If a decision is viewed as within the legitimate authority of a manager, it will be accepted by subordinates without participation.

Two additional factors consider **the subordinates' motivation to attain organizational goals** and the level of **subordinates' disagreement over solutions**. Sometimes the objectives of superiors and their subordinates are not compatible. Then participation in decision-making may be more risky than in situations where the goals are congruent. Participative decision-making works best where there is mutual interest in the problem. Additionally, subordinates may disagree among themselves over prospective alternatives. The method used to reach a decision must facilitate resolution of the disagreement, and thus group involvement is necessary.

SOCIAL INFLUENCES ON GROUP DECISION-MAKING

No discussion of decision-making would be complete without a consideration of some specific social influences which can affect group decision-making. Those social forces can cause groups to make decisions where the most important criterion becomes group consensus, or they can lead groups or individuals to make decisions that are greater in risk.

Groupthink

Groups can make poor decisions because they fall into a pattern called **groupthink** [10]. The need for consensus and cohesiveness assumes greater importance than making the best possible decision. It happens when the group collectively becomes defensive and avoids facing issues squarely and realistically. Groupthink can occur in meetings in any organization, such as when managers meet under pressure to make an important decision. Figure 11.2 provides a model of groupthink.

Groupthink is often found in highly cohesive groups. Members' desire to remain in the group contributes to them becoming a victim to one or more of groupthink's symptoms. If the group can insulate itself and has a strong, directive leader, groupthink is more likely. Stress helps too, such as when an important decision is needed but hope is low for finding a solution other than the one desired by the leader or other influential members. Such factors can combine to create disastrous conditions. Consider a situation where an information technology manager and her subordinates are under pressure to decide on new database software that will meet the information needs of a diverse group of internal customers. They might easily convince themselves that software that requires thorough evaluation is too complex for their needs and they may overlook factors such as the amount of training that will be

217

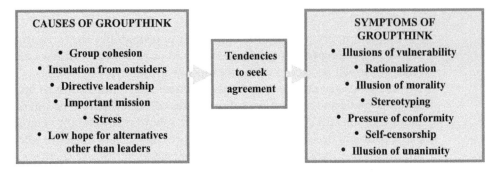

Figure 11.2   A model of groupthink

required for personnel using the software. Dissenting members of the team who see value in considering alternative vendors or who are concerned about how well the favored software meets certain criteria may feel pressure to conform and withhold their opinions.

Managers need to be aware of the symptoms of groupthink. Those symptoms include:

1   **Illusion of invulnerability**. The group acts as if it is protected from criticism. This gives members too much optimism and encourages extreme risk-taking.
2   **Rationalization**. The group tends to explain away facts or ideas that press it to reconsider its position.
3   **Illusion of morality**. This is a belief that the group is acting in the name of goodness and causes inattention to ethical consequences.
4   **Stereotyping**. Rivals or enemies outside the group are treated as evil, too stupid to negotiate with, or too weak to harm the group.
5   **Pressure for conformity**. Group members are pressured to go along with the group's illusions and stereotypes. Dissent is suppressed as contrary to group expectations.
6   **Self-censorship**. Group members become inclined to minimize their own feelings of doubt or disagreement.
7   **Illusion of unanimity**. Silence comes to imply agreement. Perceptions develop that unanimity exists.
8   **Self-appointed mind guards**. Some members act to protect the group from adverse information.

Some of the more famous examples of groupthink are found in high-level government decision-making groups.

- President Richard Nixon and his staff proceeded with the Watergate burglary of Democratic election headquarters and continued with its subsequent cover-up, despite its serious risks and implications.

- Negative information was ignored by decision-makers in deciding to launch the space shuttle Challenger in 1986.
- Enron Corporation's senior leadership failed to consider concerns from lower-level organizational members and even convinced the board to waive their own ethics rules to allow some of the financial relationships to exist that eventually led to the bankruptcy of the corporation.

The first step in overcoming groupthink is to be aware of that there is a natural tendency for groups to engage in this behavior. Other solutions include valuing disagreement, as discussed in the managerial guide boxes provided in this chapter. Sometimes just insuring that someone on the team is playing the devil's advocate role [11] is useful in insuring that the group doesn't quickly reject alternative opinions just to maintain group unity.

Riskyshift and polarization

Groupthink can be better understood in relationship to other common group phenomena. One issue related to the phenomenon of groupthink is the levels of risk group members are willing to take [12]. As an example, if the group views a decision as a choice between two positive outcomes, it should have a tendency to choose the option that has the least amount of risk associated with it. If one of those outcomes is potentially negative (such as a certain loss) as compared to a possible gain, the group will tend to choose the latter even if there is a risk of an even greater loss attached to that option [12].

A second issue concerns the widely supported concept that there is pressure within groups for **uniformity**. Traditionally, there is pressure on a minority of group members holding a position different than the majority to conform to the majority view. This conformity occurs as the result of social interaction from discussing the issues. This is coupled with **polarization**, a tendency for enhancement of the initially dominant point of view of members. As discussion and debate occur, the positions become more extreme [13].

Another phenomenon found in groups that results from social influences is the tendency for groups or teams to make riskier decisions about a course of action than individuals. This effect, known as **riskyshift**, is the opposite of the widely held belief that groups are conservative or cautious. Later studies have shown that the riskier outcome does not always occur in groups, but, together, these studies give some insight into social influences on risk behavior.

What might cause a group to shift to a riskier decision, or a less risky one, compared to individuals? The answer provides a powerful lesson in social influence. Within a group decision-making context, individuals usually have inclinations about a decision before they enter the group discussion. In general, group discussion tends to strengthen these inclinations [14]. The social process of the group discussion causes an individual who favored a particular decision before a group discussion to feel even stronger after the discussion. This process is called polarization and refers to the tendency for the average group member's position on an issue to become more extreme as the result of group discussion. It occurs as a subgroup forms of members of a group who have similar opinions on an issue. Through the decision-making process, these subgroups move further apart on the issue.

Polarization is one of the key factors in conflict, and there are several managerial solutions to minimize the problem. To reduce polarization, it may be wise to avoid premature meetings of subgroups for and against an issue. It is also helpful to mix membership within groups, or occasionally to invite outsiders or people with different ideas into meetings whenever feasible. Any action that calls for a focus on the total organization mission might reduce the tendency toward polarization. Just making members aware of this tendency may cause members to develop procedures to minimize the impact of polarization in leading their group to make a riskier decision.

SUMMARY

Decision-making is often an imperfect process that requires new decisions to compensate for prior decisions. Both evaluative and creative behaviors are important in all stages. At each step, a number of errors can be made that reduce the effectiveness of a decision. Because of such errors, many ideal models and techniques for better decision-making have been suggested. These can help decision-making significantly but rarely produce perfect, lasting solutions.

Groups that make decisions commit many of the same errors that individuals make. Group decision-making increases the opportunity to gain group acceptance and commitment to a decision, and groups can have a larger reservoir of ideas. However, it takes practice and skill to overcome the disadvantages of groups, such as pressures to conform. A skilled group leader can make a great difference in solution quality and acceptance, not only by overcoming disadvantages but by bringing out the best that the group has to offer.

REFERENCES

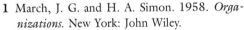

1 March, J. G. and H. A. Simon. 1958. *Organizations*. New York: John Wiley.
2 Mintzberg, H. 1975. The Manager's Job: Folklore and Fact. *Harvard Business Review*.
3 Cohen, M. D., J. G. March, and J. P. Olsen. 1972. A Garbage Can Model of Organizational Choice. *Administrative Science Quarterly*, **17**: 1–25.
4 March, J. G. and R. Weissinger-Baylon. 1986. *Ambiguity and Command: Organizational Perspectives on Military Decision Making*. Marshfield, MA: Pitman Publishing.

5 Senge, P. M. 1994. *The Fifth Discipline*. New York: Currency Doubleday.

6 Staw, B. M. 1981. The Escalation of Commitment to a Course of Action. *Academy of Management Review*, 6: 582.

7 Maier, N. R. F. 1967. Assets and Liabilities in Group Problem Solving: The Need for an Integrative Function. *Psychological Review*, 74: 239–48.

8 Maier, N. R. F. 1963. *Problem-Solving Discussions and Conferences: Leadership Methods and Skills*. New York: McGraw-Hill.

9 Vroom, V. H. and P. W. Yetton. 1973. *Leadership and Decision Making*. Pittsburgh: University of Pittsburgh Press.

10 Janis, I. L. 1972. *Victims of Groupthink*. Boston: Houghton Mifflin.

11 Cosier, R. A. and D. R. Dalton. 1990. Positive Effects of Conflict: A Field Assessment. *International Journal of Conflict Management*, 1: 81–92.

12 Kahneman, D. and A. Tversky. 1979. Prospect Theory: An Analysis of Decision Making Under Risk. *Econometrica*, 47: 263–91.

13 Myers, D. G. 1982. Polarizing Effects of Social Interactions. In J. Brandstetter, G. Davis, and G. Stocker-Kreichgauer, eds., *Group Decision Making*, 125–61. London: Academic Press.

14 Whyte, G. 1989. Groupthink Reconsidered. *Academy of Management Review*, 14: 40–56.

CHAPTER 12

Power and Politics in Organizations

A MODEL OF INFLUENCE PROCESSES IN ORGANIZATIONS

ACQUIRING AND MAINTAINING ORGANIZATIONALLY BASED INFLUENCE

ACQUIRING AND MAINTAINING PERSONAL-BASED INFLUENCE

ORGANIZATIONAL POLITICS

Opening Fig

Power in organizations can influence a variety of organization decisions. For example, over the last decade there has been a furor over the high compensation packages of CEOs in the United States [1]. The essence of the criticism is that boards of directors do not base the CEO pay decision on firm performance, but on other social or political considerations. One of the major reasons that this can happen is that, while the CEO has the legal authority to manage the firm and the board has the fiduciary responsibility to safeguard the interests of the stockholders, CEOs are able to exert a lot of influence on the board. They do it by hiring compensation consultants, by selecting board members who are similar to themselves, and by making board membership attractive for the members. This is especially possible when there are no large stockholders who can hold the CEO's feet to the fire. All of this leads to a sense of reciprocity on the part of the board and the net effect is higher CEO pay. This is how CEO power affects the level of CEO compensation.

A MODEL OF INFLUENCE PROCESSES IN ORGANIZATIONS

Influence attempts occur when legitimate authority or power is used. These relationships are shown in figure 12.1. It shows that the bases for influence in organizations are the psychological contract, legitimate authority, and power. It also shows that influence attempts lead to results intended by the influence agent or to a modification of the relationship between the influence agent and the target.

Influence is a process through which you attempt to extract compliance with your intentions from others. For there to be influence, two parties (A and B) must be in an interactive and dependent relationship. This means that the actions of A can affect the actions of B, and vice versa. Influence occurs when one of the parties (A) induces the other (B) to respond in an intended way. This is what happens in the case of CEO pay: there is a dependence relationship that is created between the board and the CEO through the sense of reciprocity that develops, and this affects the decisions that are made about CEO pay.

In an organization, there may be different reasons for **dependence** [2]. In some cases, you might want to join an organization or interact with other persons because they share important values. The basis of these relationships is **commitment**, a strong, positive involvement in the dependence relationship. There is something very important that managers must remember about commitment: do not mistake compliance for commitment [3]. Compliance can occur for other reasons, as you will see. In other cases, a dependence relationship may be **forced**, as when a person is put in a jail or a mental institution. Then the person experiences alienation and wants to

223

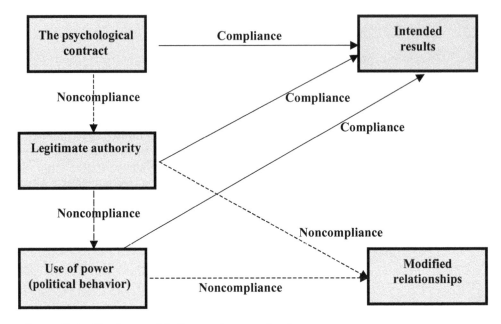

Figure 12.1 The bases of influence in organizations

escape from the relationship. These dependence relationships must usually be maintained by force. The third type of dependence relationship is **calculative involvement**, in which both parties assess the economic costs and benefits of maintaining the relationship. This is the type of dependence relationship that most often occurs in most work organizations [2].

The strength of influence one party has over another is a function of two factors. One is the need to maintain the relationship. When a person has a choice about whether to remain in a relationship, less influence can be exerted than when the relationship is necessary. The second factor is power asymmetry. Power asymmetry means that one party (B) is more dependent upon the other, giving the other (A) more capacity to influence.

Bases of influence

The psychological contract is the basis for the distinction between legitimate authority and power that we use in this chapter. The **psychological contract** is the mutual set of expectations that exist between you and an organization. These expectations cover what pay you will receive as well as "the whole pattern of rights and privileges" [4]. In return, you are expected to contribute both work and some commitment. As long as requests, commands, and directives fall within the boundaries of the psychological contract, you will comply. Take the case of the hypothetical psychological contract of a CEO with the board of directors. In general, he will do anything that falls within the boundary of the psychological contract. However, the CEO would not fix prices or make illegal political contributions. They are not only illegal; they also likely to fall outside the boundaries of her or his psychological contract.

However, there are two types of boundaries – public and real. The **public boundary** includes those activities that you want others, especially your superior, to believe are the elements of the psychological contract. Suppose, for example, the board wants the CEO to make regular reports about the return on investment of recent projects, to perform conventional CEO functions, and to represent the firm in the media. This probably falls within the real boundaries, and it will be done without question.

In some instances, the CEO may be asked to do something that falls outside the public boundary, but inside the real boundary. The **real boundary** represents the "true" limits of the psychological contract. Two activities that might fall outside the public boundaries but within the real boundaries could be (1) being involved with political parties and (2) taking an active role in the leadership of some religious organizations. For obvious reasons, the CEO will want the board to believe the psychological contract is constrained by the public boundaries. This is because compliance with requests that fall between the real and public boundaries will make it appear that the CEO is "doing a favor" for which there might be some quid pro quo – a favor in return for exceeding the requirements of the job.

These boundaries are not static; they change. Sometimes they change by mutual consent, as when a person's job changes by promotion. Sometimes they change through the use of power exercised by another person. We define all those requests from a superior that fall within the real boundary of the psychological contract and are accepted by the subordinate as legitimate authority. Power is used to extract compliance to requests that fall outside the real boundary, and sometimes it is used for directives that fall between the real and public boundaries.

Legitimate authority

Legitimate authority is the right of decision and command that a person has over others. It is sanctioned, or approved, by those in the organization. Legitimate authority is embedded in the psychological contract and, through it, a superior can expect a subordinate to comply with organizationally sanctioned requests.

Authority is legitimate when the person who is the subject of influence believes that it is right and proper for another to exert influence or attempt to exert it. The board would be exercising legitimate authority by requesting a CEO to report regularly on company activities. It might fire the CEO if he or she refuses and could do so because the legitimate authority structure may contain those decision rights for the board to use in the case of noncompliance.

Legitimate authority is reflected in the organization's structure, which defines the general distribution of legitimate authority by position location. Higher-level positions have more legitimate authority than those at lower levels. Further, it is transferable from one person to another. This means that when you leave a position, you no longer have the authority associated with it. These are now the rights of your replacement.

The **organizational culture** also reflects the legitimate authority structure. When large differences in authority exist between levels of managers, there will most likely be very significant differences in status symbols. Managers at the top level may have spacious, well-decorated offices set in very desirable locations in the headquarters building, while those at the next lower level may have smaller, less attractive offices.

Legitimate authority is accepted for several reasons. First, every culture has a concept of legitimate authority in which it is generally accepted that some forms of authority as well as relationships between superiors and subordinates are appropriate while other forms and relationships are not. For example, highly centralized authority is culturally acceptable in some Latin countries (for example, Italy and Spain) but a more even distribution of authority across different organizational levels is preferred in Anglo-Saxon countries (the UK, Canada, and the USA) [5].

Second, when you join an organization, its culture is transmitted through organizational socialization. An important theme in socialization is to rationalize the authority structure of the organization so that you accept it as legitimate.

Third, your organizational orientation, initially developed by general socialization, affects legitimacy. For example, an organizationalist usually has little trouble with most directives from higher levels.

Power

Power is a force that can be used to extract compliance, but it differs from legitimate authority. Power is not sanctioned by the psychological contract, whereas legitimate authority is [6]. The use of power, in fact, distorts the boundaries of the psychological contract. This is possible because the boundaries of the psychological contract are flexible and can be modified, even though it may take considerable pressure. The use of power in an organization is called organizational politics [6]. For example, the way that many CEOs are able to influence their boards to award them high, often excessive compensation contracts is an example of the use of power, not their legitimate authority.

Power can be used to achieve objectives that are good for the firm or it can be used to achieve the ends desired by the political actor. A person pressured to act by someone with power in an organizationally unacceptable way may comply to avoid undesirable consequences. Suppose that an organization's culture supports ethical behavior in its practice and the CEO is approached by a competitor to fix prices illegally and, at the same time, some important board members suggest this is a good idea. The CEO might act unethically, at great personal and psychological cost, if the pressure were extreme. If the result is that the firm engages in price-fixing, the board members would have exercised power, not legitimate authority.

People often respond to power even when they are not threatened with physical harm or with economic loss, even though their actions could harm others. This was shown in a classic study in which subjects were asked to assist the experimenter in a study of the effects of punishment on learning [7]. The subject was asked to be the "teacher." The experimenter's confederate acted as the "learner." The confederate was taken to a separate room where he could be heard but not seen. The experimenter then showed the "teacher" how to operate an alleged shock generator and instructed them to apply shock whenever the "learner" gave a wrong answer, and to increase it when more wrong answers were given. Although no shock was actually administered, the subject was led to believe that it was. When mildly shocked, the confederate groaned. As the shock levels increased, the confederate's reaction accelerated to shouts, screams, and cries to quit the experiment. The experimenter prodded the subject to administer stronger shocks when the subject resisted. In one experiment, 63 percent of 40 male subjects, 20–50 years old, applied the maximum 450 volts.

A person may possess different types of power [8]. The ability to reward or to coerce can extract compliance. So can being an expert or being charismatic.

Reward power exists when you have control over rewards desired by another. The more highly valued the rewards, the greater the power. Individuals in positions with high levels of legitimate authority have the right to make decisions about the allocation of rewards and promotions based on organizationally rationalized criteria. When they use organizationally sanctioned criteria, it is the use of legitimate authority – not reward power.

Coercive power in an organization exists for the same reason as reward power. The difference is that, instead of rewarding another person, punishment is threatened or applied. Those who have legitimate authority can often exercise their judgment against individuals in punitive ways. For example, in one organization, a manager was fired because her supervisor maintained that she was not performing well and was not a "team player." In several instances, she was late with reports and had experienced some problems working with other managers at her level. When the complete set of facts was analyzed, however, it was found that her unit was among the most productive, her subordinates among the best in the firm, and her customers the most satisfied. However, she had openly disagreed with her boss in meetings, and frequently she was right. Another manager who was equally effective replaced her. The decision to remove her was justified on the basis that the managerial team would be able to work better together without her.

We rely on and accept recommendations from accountants, lawyers, and physicians because we believe they have the knowledge to make correct decisions in their specific area of competence. The same thing happens in organizations: having **expert power** means that you are able to influence others because you possess some particular skill or knowledge that they do not, and that skill or knowledge is necessary for the performance of their work. Expert power usually takes time to develop; a person normally spends much time in formal training or developing skills on the job before this type of influence is acquired.

Expert power is very task- and person-specific. Because of this, it cannot easily be transferred from one person to another in the way that legitimate authority can. For instance, if you become a plant manager, you will have the same legitimate authority as the previous manager, but expert power develops from your demonstrating competence or having it "given" by others because you have the appropriate education, certification, experience, and appearance.

Charismatic power occurs when individuals are susceptible to influence because they identify with another person [8]. It is based on the feeling of oneness that a person has with another, the desire for that feeling, or the personal attraction to be like the other. The stronger the attraction, the stronger the power: "The charismatic leader, a person with charismatic power, is set apart from ordinary individuals and treated as endowed with supernatural or superhuman or, at least, specifically exceptional powers or qualities not accessible to the normal person. . . . What is important is how the individual is actually regarded by followers" [9]. Some political leaders, not all of them popular with their opposition, who have been called charismatic are Ronald Reagan, John F. Kennedy, Fidel Castro, and Saddam Hussein. Mary Kay of Mary Kay Cosmetics, Ted Turner of Turner Broadcasting, and Herb Kelleher of Southwest Airlines are business leaders who have been called charismatic.

What differentiates someone with charismatic power from those with other types of power is the reaction of the followers. "Followers of charismatic leaders do not feel pressed or oppressed. Charismatic leaders have the ability to engender unusually high trust in the correctness of their beliefs, affection for the leader, willing obedience to the leader, identification with the leader, emotional involvement of the follower in the mission, heightened goals of the follower, and the feeling on the part of the follower that he or she will be able to accomplish the mission or contribute to its accomplishment" [10].

Outcomes of influence

The use of legitimate authority or power leads to either intended results or to some modification of the relationship between the influence agent and the target; see figure 12.1.

Intended results

Intended results are the results of influence attempts that are desired by the party that exerted the influence. From an organization's perspective, compliance should lead to organizationally valued results, such as high task, contextual, and ethical performance. However, intended results may also occur because they are the wishes of a particular person, but are not necessarily part of the organizational requirements.

Usually when legitimate authority, charismatic power, or expert power is used, the target person will react in a way intended by the power agent. The psychological response of the target is called acceptance, or **compliance**. He or she will engage in the desired behavior, as well as rationalizing and justifying the compliance as being the right way to behave. Charismatic power and expert power also lead to acceptance. When charismatic power is used, the target's justification is ideological and normative. For expert power, the acceptance is rationalized by the belief that the competence of the expert is necessary to satisfy the target's needs. There can also be acceptance when reward or coercive power is used. This is particularly true when these types of power are the extension of legitimate authority.

Modification of relationships

When a target of influence resists or fails to comply with the influence attempt, there is usually some modification in the relationship between the actors. The idea is usually that the influence agent, particularly when this is a manager, can take some action such as firing or disciplining the target, usually a subordinate. There are other ways a superior could modify relationships with those subordinates who do not comply, such as assigning them to less desirable projects, not supporting them for promotion and pay increases, or changing their personal relationship at work.

Organizational and personal bases of influence

You can have influence for different reasons. One is because you are in an organizational position with legitimate authority, while, in other instances, influence is strictly due to some attribute of the influence agent.

Organizationally based influence

Obviously a person in a higher-level position has more legitimate authority than another lower in the hierarchy, making legitimate authority a type of organizationally based influence. A person may also have organizationally based power, which is the capacity to influence others beyond the range of legitimate authority, as the study by Milgram [7] shows. There are other types of position effects. Often a job description will give you control over information desired by others. Similarly, if you can control access to key people, power accrues. Executive secretaries and high-level staff assistants are likely to have influence because of this. Also, some people are in jobs where they seem to have some perceived influence over the futures of others, such as the personnel executive who handles transfers, assignments, and personnel reductions.

Personal-based influence

You acquire personal-based influence when you possess attributes or skills desired by others. These attributes are usually independent of the organization's control. There are two types of personal-based influence:

- Expert power exists when a person has competence required by others.
- Charismatic power exists when one person becomes psychologically dependent upon another.

ACQUIRING AND MAINTAINING ORGANIZATIONALLY BASED INFLUENCE

The pattern of power and influence relationships among units in an organization is called the **power structure**. For example, the marketing department may be more powerful than the HR department, and the finance group more powerful than both of them. However, the distribution of organizational power and influence is never what it appears to be on organization charts and in job descriptions. It is affected by a combination of situational factors and individual characteristics. For example, deans in a university do not have equal influence and power in the budgeting process. If they did, then budgets would be allocated to colleges on the basis of the number of students served and the cost of instruction. While these factors do count, a department's or college's power and importance also affect how much money it receives [11]. Some colleges are more important than others, and some deans have stronger predispositions to use influence and power than others.

Situational determinants of organizationally based influence

Just saying that more important organization units have more power than those that are less important is not enough. The question is: "What is it about a sub-unit that makes it more important?" The **strategic contingency theory of organizational power** explains some of these power

---

Guide for Managers:
USING POWER IN ORGANIZATIONS

There are approaches to increasing your personal power without relying on overt pressure and force. Before you begin using power and playing the game of organizational politics, there are a couple of proverbs of which we would like to remind you of. One is, "What goes around, comes around." The second, maybe a little more precise, is, "Those who live by the sword, die by the sword." This means that even if you are successful in getting others to do what you want them to do, if they have lost something there may come a time when you will have to pay for your success. Before you start, however, you should ask yourself if you have the stomach for the game. The way to know this is to review the sections of this chapter that discuss the personal attributes of those who acquire organizational and personal power. Without these, you

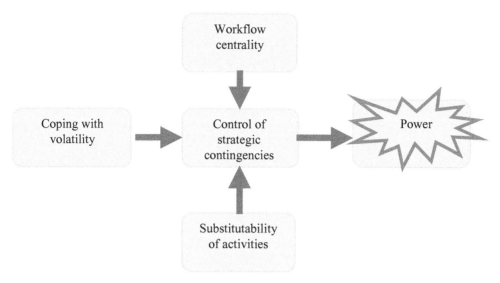

Figure 12.2 Factors affecting power from the strategic contingency theory of power

differences; see figure 12.2 [12]. A sub-unit's power depends on whether, and by how much, it controls strategic contingencies for the organization. "A contingency is a requirement of one sub-unit that is affected by the activities of another sub-unit" [12].

There are three conditions that make a sub-unit strategic:

1 Coping with volatility
2 Substitutability of activities
3 Workflow centrality.

Organization sub-units that interact with more volatile, threatening, and uncertain environments have more power than those that interact with stable ones. If the sub-unit can successfully interpret an unclear environment and help the organization to cope effectively, it will be able to influence policy and strategy. This is one of the factors might not fare well in this contest. Here are some things that you can do.

CONTROL THE CONTEXT. If you have the legitimate authority to do so, you can structure the context so that the intended behaviors are likely to occur. Your legitimate authority can be extended in political ways because a position in an organization gives you some degree of control over the allocation of resources, the distribution of rewards, and the implementation of sanctions. As a manager, you can exert influence in many ways by careful contextual control of others' behavior and decisions. Suppose that you are a vice-president of marketing and asked by the CEO to make a recommendation about which one of five new products a firm should develop. A nonpolitical evaluation that give physicians so much power in hospitals. They control three of the critical variables that affect what happens in the hospital: the admissions, the length of stay, and the demand for auxiliary services.

When there is no **substitutability for activities** of a sub-unit, that sub-unit will be very powerful. For example, physicians in hospitals also are, for the most part, not substitutable, particularly when they are specialists. Because the physician has the technical competence to solve patients' problems and other groups either do not have it or are restricted from using it, they have substantial power.

Workflow centrality has two aspects. Units with high workflow centrality are interconnected with many others. Most accounting departments have high workflow centrality because they obtain information from many units and provide it to other organization units. A unit with low workflow centrality would be a legal department, which may provide services to only a few other sub-units.

The second aspect of centrality is **workflow immediacy**. This is the speed and intensity with which the work performed in a unit affects the results of other departments. The higher the workflow immediacy then the greater the power that unit will have. Suppose a firm has a policy of maintaining very small finished goods inventories. The production unit has high workflow immediacy because if production stops, then goods do not flow on to the customer.

process would subject each product to a rigorous assessment of costs and benefits. Suppose, however, that you prefer one of the products to the others. You could influence the choice process by appointing a committee composed of people who are likely to favor the product.

DEFINE THE PROBLEM YOUR WAY. As a manager, especially with subordinates, you can often select or define the problem that is to be solved. This limits the range of solutions that can be considered. If the academic vice-president of the university asks a committee to develop a program to "enhance the reputation of the university," the committee will attack the issue differently than they would if the problem is "How can the university enhance its reputation as a graduate institution?" People will have an opportunity to exercise some influence over the different ways that the problem is solved but not over the selection of the problem, which by definition was confined to graduate emphasis.

MAKE SUBJECTIVE USE OF OBJECTIVE CRITERIA. An effective way to use political power is to influence the criteria used in decision-making [6]. For example, as the marketing vice-president involved in the product choice decision above, you could define the criteria that will be used in the product evaluation process. In other words, you can "structure" them in a way that will lead to a favorable evaluation of the preferred alternative.

Environmental changes and power

The power structure of organizations tends to be relatively stable because those who hold power are reluctant to let it change. For example, in a semiconductor firm, the longer the founding entrepreneur stayed in the firm, the less likely it was that there would be a shift in departments' power [13]. The initially dominant departments were able to institutionalize their initial, strong power position.

Power structures are more likely to change when there are significant changes in the environment that destroy the competence of the dominant managerial coalition [14]. This occurs when markets or technologies change in ways that require different managerial skills and competence.

Personal attributes of those who acquire organizationally based influence

Some people have very strong predispositions to seek, acquire, and use power and authority, and they compete with others who have similar predispositions [15]. In this section, we discuss the personal characteristics of those who seek and acquire organizationally based power, specifically legitimate authority and reward and punishment power.

Because legitimate authority depends on the position a person holds in the organization, it follows that, to increase it, a person must advance in the hierarchy, increase the amount of discretion in the current position, or move into sub-units that are more powerful.

A second, related, political strategy is to discount objective criteria so that although one of the alternatives appears better than others the rating of the alternative is lowered for political reasons. Suppose the board of directors has two candidates for the CEO position: one is from inside the firm and the second from outside. Further suppose that the outside candidate is now the president of a small but very profitable firm. Those who favor the inside candidate might argue that the success of the smaller firm is not due to the president but to other factors such as luck, lack of competition, or a special competitive advantage such as a patent. If they are successful in discounting the outside candidate's performance, then the insider will be selected. Though a little different in specifics, this is what happened when Robert Allen was stepping down as CEO of AT&T.

USE OUTSIDE EXPERTS. You can get support for your position by using outside experts to justify and rationalize decisions [18]. This combines legitimate power and expert power. At one extreme, expert opinion can be brought in through research reports and published articles to support a position. At the other extreme, consultants or members at the board of directors can be used to make recommendations, to introduce changes, and to reinforce decisions [37]. This is how it worked in the AT&T succession case of Robert Allen. He was able to use two consulting firms in ways that furthered his agenda. By letting

If you want to have legitimate authority, it is necessary to have

- Competence
- Self-confidence
- An organizational orientation
- Power needs.

Competence is necessary; a person must be good enough at his or her job to be judged capable of performing at higher-level positions. Competence is usually demonstrated by past performance and achievement. Self-confidence is your belief that you will be successful. People with high generalized self-confidence have stronger beliefs that their leadership attempts will be successful [16]. An organizational orientation is also likely to be characteristic of one seeking legitimate authority. The organizationalist finds organizational achievement and advancement reinforcing, making a high position a sought-after value for them. This orientation will also facilitate advancement because an organizationalist with an adequate level of competence usually has the right combination of factors to be successful, according to the Good Enough Theory of Promotion. **Power needs** must be very strong. Power needs are a person's desire to have an impact on others, to establish, maintain, or restore the prestige of power.

In organizations, reward and punishment power stems from the extension of legitimate authority because the person has some discretion in how it can be used. Therefore, the personal attributes already listed above are necessary because you have to be in a posi-

candidates know that the position would be "CEO in training," neither consulting firm could come up with the "Class A List" of candidates, leaving those on the list who were more likely to agree to his agenda.

CONTROL THE FLOW AND QUANTITY OF INFORMATION. A person can control when information is released, how much is released, and what others get. Suppose the board of directors, in the example above, favors an inside candidate for president, the number of outside candidates can be limited in several ways. One is by delaying the announcement of the position and setting an early date for the appointment. The board could also affect the selection by limited release of information. When prospective candidates inquire about the job, the board may provide general, not specific, information about salaries and benefits.

Controlling the agenda of meetings is another way to manage the flow and type of information [6]. Both the content of the agenda and the order in which items are considered can influence decisions. This is a common occurrence at stockholder meetings. The board of directors usually determines the agenda, with little time for shareholders interested in other matters to raise them. If such issues are raised, then the board can usually influence the decision because it controls the proxies.

tion with legitimate authority but they are sufficient to acquire reward and punishment power. In addition, the person must have a political orientation. A political orientation is the willingness or attempt to exert influence beyond the boundaries of legitimate authority [15]. The stronger the political orientation, the more reward and punishment power will be sought and acquired. People with a political orientation have these tendencies:

- Machiavellianism
- Strong personalized power motives
- Cognitive complexity
- Articulation skills.

Machiavellians have high self-confidence, high self-esteem, and behave in their own self-interest. High Machs are cool, are not distracted by emotion, and can exert control in power vacuums. They use false or exaggerated praise to manipulate others and are able to detach themselves from a situation. **Personalized power motives** will be very strong for those who acquire reward and punishment power. People with a higher personalized power orientation have strong self-interest and exercise power in an interpersonal way with an adversary. A person with **cognitive complexity** is able to find what patterns and relations exist in a situation, even though they are embedded in noise and confusion. This is a necessary skill because if you seek power you must be sensitive to subtle but complex situations in an organization so as to know when to exert influence. Accurate perceptions of the organizational power structure are related to a person's power reputation [17]. Those who are attributed higher power by others tend to have more accurate perceptions of the power network. Being **articulate** is another important skill. The articulate person will be able to present arguments logically, which should facilitate persuasion. He or she may be able to form coalitions easier and may be chosen by a group to represent them.

ACQUIRING AND MAINTAINING PERSONAL-BASED INFLUENCE

Sometimes influence is entirely a function of personal attributes. The expert attracts a following because of the skills possessed. Entrepreneurs attract loyal subordinates because they believe in the entrepreneur's message. These are examples of expert and charismatic power, both personal-based and requiring a fit between the attributes of the power actor and the follower [18]. Personal-based power is also important to managers. It can supplement legitimate power and be helpful in "motivating commitment to the tasks that require high effort, initiative, and persistence" [19]. However, it is more difficult to perpetuate and pass on to others than organizationally based influence.

Charismatic power

Charismatic power results from the identification of one person with another. It is based on personal attraction that develops in certain contextual settings that interact with the personal attributes of those involved.

Charismatic power develops in a crisis situation, when there are high levels of uncertainty and a group needs inspiration and direction. For example, US presidents engage in more charismatic behavior during political and international crises [20]. As long as the crisis continues, the charismatic leader continues to have power. For example, Fidel Castro was able to maintain his charismatic image for many years because he was able to perpetuate the perception of a crisis in Cuba because of threats from the United States. Organization start-ups are another situation in which charismatic influence can develop because members are usually seeking direction and support for their involvement in the new organization.

One reason for charisma in both crises and start-ups is that the situational context is weak and unstructured. When the situation is unstructured, those in it may not know how to respond [21]. In this weak context, the charismatic person can provide psychological boundaries and direction by creating new meanings and beliefs for the followers.

Some of the characteristics we have already discussed as personal attributes of people with the capacity to acquire legitimate authority are attributes of charismatic leaders [22]:

- Need for power
- Self-confidence
- Articulation skills.

In addition, two other attributes are present when charismatic power exists [12]:

- **Nonverbal communication skill**. The charismatic person has the capacity to convey meaning to followers easily with body language, gestures, and symbols. The manipulation of symbols is very important. Revolutions all have slogans, symbols of unity, or other signs that identify the struggle and convey meaning to those involved in them.
- **Strong convictions about beliefs**. This is transmitted to the followers both verbally and nonverbally.

For example, during the period following the world trade center disaster in New York City, mayor Rudy Giuliani was viewed as a charismatic leader during the most difficult period immediately following the incident. Despite leaving the mayor's position, Giuliani remains a powerful political force both in New York City and nationally. Perpetuating the charisma can be done in several ways:

- **Perpetuating the charismatic image**. By maintaining images of the leader during the period when charismatic power was the dominant model of influence and control, the perception of charisma can be retained. The way that the group sees the charismatic leader, after institutionalization, is usually very controlled so that the charismatic image is not destroyed. Though much older, Castro still maintains a similar appearance to that which he had during the Cuban revolution. He keeps his beard and generally appears in public in a fatigue-like uniform. Pictures of him appear everywhere in Cuba.

- **Controlling interaction with groups**. When the charismatic leader interacts with large groups, it is usually in controlled settings such as speeches, rites, or ceremonies. These can reinforce the organizational culture as well as present the charismatic leader in a very positive light. When there is a small group with more interpersonal interaction between the leader and the members, these situations are very controlled. Usually the meetings are of a short duration. Normally, those who are in the meeting are carefully selected because they are loyal to the leader or to the organization. In most cases, they also appear to be representative of the larger group of followers.

- **Evoking specific negative images of the past**. A charismatic leader can remind group member of past specific crises or times of uncertainty so that they can recall "how bad it was." Revolutionary political leaders usually refer to very specific cases of tyranny and poverty under previous regimes. The charismatic business leader can evoke the difficult times when he or she was leading the firm through the crisis. The charismatic union leader can be very specific in helping the rank and file remember the low wages, poor safety practices, and unfair working conditions of the past that gave rise to the need for a union. This response was demonstrated by the Cuban government's reaction to the Elian Gonzalez incident where a young Cuban boy was found drifting in the ocean after his mother's attempt to flee Cuba with him and others on a small boat turned into tragedy. Castro used this as an opportunity to rally public support for the return of Elian to his father in Cuba and remind Cuban citizens of past struggles with the US.

- **Speaking in general, but very positive, terms about the future** [23]. This is the counterpoint to recalling the past bad times. The charismatic leader can evoke images of "how good it will be" in the future. This is most effectively accomplished when the leader speaks in general terms. Avoiding specifics allows followers to project their own meaning into the leader's words. Because of the psychological connection between the group and the leader, this will result in a strengthened bond between them.

Expert power

Expert power results from having the ability to do things that are valued and needed by others. It exists in those situations in which specific skills are necessary in an organization and when the individuals who possess these skills are in short supply. This often happens when the organization's environment is volatile. Then firms must import the newly required skills, and often there is little incentive to try to institutionalize them. Thus, the power remains with the individual.

To acquire expert power, a person must possess the necessary physical, mental, or interpersonal skills that can help others. There is no way, however, to specify what personality factors might cluster around people with expert power because there are so many potential types of expert power. Expert power, however, can be facilitated by the organization or by other external institutions. Both of these can provide legitimacy by giving the expert the appropriate titles, licenses, or certification.

Three conditions are necessary to perpetuate expert power:

1   If you have expert power, you must be able to maintain your skill level. In one large law firm, only one partner is the environmental law "expert." He is important to the firm because he accounts for a large share of the firm's revenue. To maintain his competence, he regularly reads, studies, and attends seminars on the topic. Frequently, he teaches a class in environmental law at a nearby university.

2   It is important to ensure that the dependence relationship between the individual and the organization does not change in such a way as to weaken the expert's position. The law firm needs "environmental expertise" because it is a growing area of practice and an important share of the firm's revenue.

3   The expert must maintain personal control of the expertise. This ensures that others cannot be substituted for him. If environmental law becomes a larger part of the firm's business, it may wish to add other experts in this area, threatening the expert's power. He does this by a careful selection of clients so that new attorneys are not needed or by managing new experts who join the firm.

ORGANIZATIONAL POLITICS

Earlier in this chapter we said that the use of power in organizations was called organizational politics. At this point we will provide an expanded discussion of the role of politics in organizational settings. Discussions of organizational politics are often associated with negative connotations. Some have commented on the appropriateness of the word politics to describe the range of behaviors associated with the concept: "Only in America do we use the word 'politics' to describe the process so well; 'poli' in Latin meaning 'many' and 'tics' meaning 'blood-sucking creatures'!" [24].

The concept of organizational politics

Organizational politics refers to the intentional behaviors of individuals or groups with the goal of protecting their own self-interests [25]. Organizations rarely typify the rational and efficient mechanism that the name implies. Instead organizations are often complex, diffused and ambiguous activities typified by human interaction. The space between rationality and ambiguity is where politics takes place [26].

There are two diverse views of organizational politics. One view is that political behaviors can contribute to the function of the organization and that these behaviors can have both functional and dysfunctional elements [6]. The other view is that political behaviors are those that are not consistent with organizational norms. While these behaviors are self-serving, they are not always considered dysfunctional [27].

238

There is certainly a dark side of politics that can be seen in certain organizational practices and policies. For example, when managers are making important personnel selection decisions, they are often trying to hire someone who "fits" with the organization. While the notion of fit is an important one, it is also not well defined and this ambiguity provides room for the introduction of politics. Lacking objective and valid selection criteria, managers are prone to assessing fit by looking for characteristics in the candidate that are similar to their own. This allows potential candidates to adopt impression management tactics and to portray themselves as a person with similar beliefs and values as those of the manager [26].

Studies of political tactics have also shown that the perception of high political activity can be associated with greater stress [28], lower organizational commitment [29, 30] and higher absenteeism [31]. These negative factors associated with the perceptions of political activity have important implications for organizations. Rather than focusing on the debate as to whether politics is positive or negative in organizational contexts, we prefer to take the position that politics is an organizational reality and therefore effective managers should be skilled at political behaviors in the enactment of their duties. This skill is referred to as political savvy and is a subtle, unseen influence that occurs in most organizations [32].

The context for organizational politics

Organizational politics are likely to occur in situations where social and task conditions are ambiguous [33]. This includes situations when:

- Emotional or task involvement are low so that the individual feels self-conscious.
- Opportunities or threats create the perception that political behavior may be useful and has a chance to be successful.
- Outcomes are important.
- Others are observed successfully engaging in political behavior.

There are many organizational situations that create ambiguity and, as a result, lead to a greater presence of political behaviors. These situations are similar to the conditions when people are more likely to use power as well. One such situation is when resources are scarce. Scarce resources increase pressure on employees to try new tactics to ensure that those who allocate resources are well aware of the "importance" of his or her function. Consider the situation when, as a result of a shortage of resources, a senior manager asks supervisors to justify the budgets they had submitted for their units. Supervisors may adopt tactics such as downplaying the needs of other units or exaggerating their own needs in an attempt to influence the perceptions of the managers [25]. These tactics are called impression management, as discussed below, and have the specific purpose of managing the perceptions others have of you or your sub-unit.

Another situation where political behaviors are more likely to occur are contexts where important organizational decisions are made but the criteria for those decisions are not well established or understood by those affected by the decision. Lacking objective criteria, employees may attempt to manage the perceptions of decision-makers about individual skills and qualifications. Again, this opens the opportunity for impression management and other tactics so one can differentiate their performance relative to that of others who may be competing for a similar position. The ambiguity of the situation allows employees to redefine situations that optimize their personal positions [25].

Finally, organizational politics are likely to be prevalent when people see that they are effective. When an organization's reward system primarily focuses on individual rewards, it increases the likelihood that employees will focus on individually oriented, self-serving behavior. If self-serving behavior is seen by others to be effective for achieving those rewards, it is likely others will engage in those types of behaviors as well.

Political tactics

Numerous behaviors have been defined as political. These behaviors are often organized into sets of behaviors or tactics that are designed to achieve certain types of objectives. The tactics discussed below are not an all-inclusive list but do represent many of the most common political tactics seen in organizations.

Impression management

Impression management refers to a broad array of political behaviors that have the purpose of altering and maintaining a person's image. You are probably aware of impression management tactics that you commonly use. When you dress, speak or behave in a certain way to instill in someone a positive impression of yourself you are practicing impression management. Most of us have been involved in the process of "dating" and so are well versed in the behaviors you demonstrate to give your date a positive impression. These tactics are effective in organizations as well and include activities to increase our visibility such as attending important

Guide for Managers: POLITICAL TACTICS TO ENHANCE YOUR PERSONAL POWER

ACQUIRE A SPONSOR. A sponsor is a person at a higher organizational level or in a powerful position who represents and advances the interests of another. Sponsorship provides influence in two ways.

1 The sponsor may be an advocate for a person in a promotion

meetings where you will be seen. Volunteering for an extra assignment, making a point of showing the boss a work product that you are especially proud of, or routinely insuring you are the first person to arrive at work, are all tactics that may be intentionally done to create an impression in others.

Interestingly, recent research has suggested that individuals may intentionally try to create an unfavorable impression in the workplace. One study found that some individuals intentionally tried to look bad by reducing performance, not working to potential, or displaying a bad attitude. These individuals appeared to have motives such as a desire to avoid responsibilities, beliefs that their behavior would be rewarded (if I look overworked I may get a pay raise), or a desire to manipulate to gain additional power [34]. While this form of impression management may appear counter-intuitive, managers nonetheless must consider it as a form of political behavior.

Blaming or attacking others

This refers to the act of blaming others for your own personal failures or attacking others by attempting to minimize their accomplishments. For example, a division chief in a company that does significant business online who comes under pressure because of slumping sales in his unit may resort to blaming the IT division and its website management for the poor performance. In chapter 4 we discussed attributional processes and found that individuals tend to attribute their own poor performance to external causes

decision. This could result in advancement for the person while at the same time creating a loyal subordinate for the sponsor.

2   Second, the sponsor may advance ideas and projects that are developed by the person. If the projects and ideas are good, the sponsor may even be given some credit for bringing them to the attention of decision-makers.

The two things that you have to do to acquire a sponsor is to demonstrate competence and engage in integration. If you do well on important tasks, you will usually come to the attention of someone at a higher-level position, who may be a willing sponsor. Then, by ingratiation, you can increase your attractiveness to others [38]. It is usually accomplished through flattery and a display of commitment or potential commitment. Flattery positively reinforces the target. In one organization, a young engineer with high power needs successfully used ingratiation to acquire the sponsorship of a senior project engineer. The senior engineer had been assigned the task of improving the productivity of a plant that was having serious performance difficulties. He had very little support from the plant's staff because they feared that his changes would reduce their status. The young engineer, in a quiet and discreet way, began to let the senior engineer know that he believed the project could work. He gave the senior engineer a good deal of positive feedback about the plans that (self-serving bias). While this behavior may be to some extent human nature, at the extreme it is a political tactic that can be organizationally destructive.

Control of information

Information is a powerful organizational resource and so managers who secure access to important information and who then disseminate that information carefully can enhance their ability to influence others. This tactic obviously flourishes in situations when there is significant ambiguity. For example, during the process of organizational change, as discussed in chapter 14, employees often become desperate for information as they try to determine what the implications of the change are for them personally and for their unit. Any source of information becomes important, and information from a source viewed as "in the know" becomes highly valued. This provides a form of power and managers can use this to their political advantage by controlling with whom they share the information and what specific information they actually choose to share.

Coalition-building

Coalition-building is the tactic of collaborating with others to increase the power of the group. In our discussion in chapter 11 on decision-making, we discussed how when a group meets to consider an important decision, subgroups often form that eventually lead to polarization of the group. One common political tactic is to form alliances outside of the meeting for the

were being developed. He also made certain that the senior engineer believed that he too thought the resistance from the old staff was unwarranted. While he supported the change project, there was only one problem: because he was new to the organization, he told the senior engineer, it did not seem wise to support the proposals publicly. Because there were no other supporters, the senior engineer began to confide in the younger person. He also started to sponsor him, recommending him for special assignments and early promotion.

USE IMPRESSION MANAGEMENT. One way to develop power is by impression management to create the illusion that one has it. This is done by the control of information, or cues, imparted to others to manage their impressions. Specialists practice impression management when they use jargon unique to their profession. The doctor's white coat and use of medical terms does nothing to increase technical competence, but it conveys important meanings to patients. A top executive may try to create the impression of power by high activity levels and demonstrations of organizational loyalty. This may be done by using symbols such as large offices, deep carpets, and special furniture. The executive may also remain aloof and apart from lower-level members to maintain status distinctions.

Those at lower levels can also try to manage impressions of them by purpose of influencing an important outcome or decision. Finding other individuals who have similar beliefs or interests and joining forces with them to influence important organizational activities is a commonly used political tactic.

Networking

Networking refers to developing relationships with others both internal to the organization and externally. Throughout their career, politically astute managers develop trust-based relationships with a variety of individuals whom they meet. This includes previous bosses or mentors, co-workers, subordinates, and even customers with whom they have developed a relationship. Actively managing these relationships can be beneficial to managers by providing access to valuable sources of information, a powerful internal ally who can influence decisions to your advantage, or a key contact whom they can refer someone else to as a favor. If you have ever met someone who seems to know a trusted agent in every organization, then that is probably someone who understands the value of networking. This can be a powerful tactic, and developing a network is often a career-enhancing process.

superiors. They may seek to give the impression that they are loyal and to create the belief that they are competent in their job and always busy. Being a "good" subordinate may be a way to gain power because superiors may place trust in him or her. Then the subordinate may be able to expand the power from the current legitimate authority base.

Managerial responses to organizational politics

Perhaps the most important managerial response to the existence of organizational politics is to accept that it is organizational reality. Superiors, peers, and subordinates all behave politically and effective managers are those who successfully navigate through organizational political waters [35]. You should also realize that politics can help you achieve organizationally important outcomes. There is significant evidence that individuals need to develop political skills in order to be successful. This becomes even more important as individuals reach higher levels of the organization [36].

There are also ways for managers to address the negative implications of the perception of politics such as its negative effect on organizational commitment as mentioned earlier [29, 30]. One managerial response to these negative implications for organizational members is to ensure that subordinates have clearly established priorities. One study found that subordinates' commitment was less affected by politics when they shared goal priorities with their supervisors [30]. Insuring goal congruence reduces the ambiguity about "what is important" and so can reduce the implication of organizational politics.

243

Finally, effective mangers should appreciate political activity as a method of building social and reputational capital. Just like companies that work to enhance their reputation for the purpose of enhancing the company's value, managers are appropriately concerned about their reputation and make investments (in the form of political behaviors) to increase their reputational capital [24]. Most managers want to be viewed by their superiors, peers, and subordinates as competent and effective. Our discussion of impression management addressed the importance of managing the perceptions others have of you. As a result, even if a manager is reluctant to "intentionally" practice impression management, he or she needs to be aware that many aspects of their behavior contribute to their reputation and, as a result, their ability to have influence within the organization.

SUMMARY

This chapter has explained some of the most important and fascinating topics in organizational behavior: influence, power, and politics. They are at the heart of what managers do to achieve things with and through others. A model of influence processes showed that compliance – the degree to which a person acts in accordance with the wishes of another – can occur for several reasons. In some cases, individuals comply because of the psychological contract; in others it is because of legitimate authority, and in other instances the use of power may lead to compliance.

The characteristics of the situation and the individuals are related to the different types of influence that are acquired and exerted. The organizational context for power is related to the extent to which sub-units interact with volatile environments, perform non-substitutable activities, or are central to organizational functioning. Once power is achieved it influences a person's ability to perpetuate the settings in which power was originally developed. In many instances, legitimate authority, reward power, and punishment power can be maintained because the power holders have control of organizational processes, such as the choice of strategies, selection of personnel, and promotions.

When power is used we refer to those behaviors as organizational politics. Political behavior is a fact of life in organizations and is more likely to occur when situations are ambiguous. There are numerous political tactics, including impression management, controlling information, and developing coalitions with others. Effective managers are those that not only are aware of political activity within the organization but who also understand how political behavior can increase their effectiveness as a manager.

REFERENCES

1 Colvin, G. 2001.The Great CEO Pay Heist. *Fortune*, 64–71.

2 Etzioni, A. 1961. *A Comparative Analysis of Complex Organizations*. New York: Free Press.

3 Zaleznick, A. 1971. Power and Politics in Organizational Life. In E. C. Bursk and T. B. Blodgett, eds., *Developing Executive Leaders*, 38–57. Cambridge, MA: Harvard University Press.

4 Schein, E. A. 1970. *Organizational Psychology*. New York: Prentice-Hall.

5 Hofstede, G. 1980. *Culture's Consequences: International Differences in Work-Related Values*. Beverly Hills, CA: Sage Publications.

6 Pfeffer, J. 1981. *Power in Organizations*. Boston, MA: Pitman Publishing.

7 Milgram, S. 1974. *Obedience to Authority*. New York: Harper & Row.

8 French, J. R. P. Jr. and B. Raven. 1959. The Bases of Social Power. In D. Cartwright, ed., *Studies in Social Power*, 150–67. Ann Arbor: University of Michigan Institute for Social Research.

9 Weber, M. 1947. *The Theory of Social and Economic Organization*. New York: Free Press.

10 House, R. J. 1984. *Power in Organizations: A Social Psychological Perspective*. Toronto: University of Toronto.

11 Pfeffer, J. and G. Salancik. 1974. Organizational Decision Making as a Political Process: The Case of the University Budget. *Administrative Science Quarterly*, **19**: 135–51.

12 Hickson, D. J. et al. 1971. A Strategic Contingency Theory of Intraorganizational Power. *Administrative Science Quarterly*, **16**: 216–29.

13 Boeker, W. 1990. The Development and Institutionalization of Subunit Power in Organizations. *Administrative Science Quarterly*, **34**: 388–410.

14 Tushman, M. L. and E. Romanelli. 1985. Organizational Evolution: A Metamorphosis Model of Convergence and Reorientation. In L. L. Cummings and B. M. Staw, eds., *Research in Organizational Behavior*, 171–222. Greenwich, CT: JAI Press.

15 House, R. J. 1988. Power and Personality in Complex Organizations. In B. J. Staw and L. L. Cummings, eds., *Research in Organizational Behavior*, 305–57. Greenwich, CT: JAI Press.

16 Mowday, R. T. 1980. Leader Characteristics, Self-Confidence and Methods of Upward Influence in Organization Decision Situations. *Academy of Management Journal*, **44**: 709–24.

17 Krackhardt, D. 1990. Assessing the Political Landscape: Structure, Cognition, and Power in Organizations. *Administrative Science Quarterly*, **35**: 342–69.

18 Pfeffer, J. 1992. *Managing with Power*. Boston, MA: Harvard Business School Press.

19 Yukl, G. A. 1998. Leadership in Organizations. Upper Saddle River, NJ: Prentice-Hall.

20 House, R. J., W. D. Spangler, and J. Woycke. 1991. Personality and Charisma in the U.S. Presidency: A Psychological Theory of Leader Effectiveness. *Administrative Science Quarterly*, **36**(3): 364–96.

21 Mischel, W. 1977. The Interaction of Person and Situation. In D. Magnusson and N. S. Enders, eds., *Personality at the Crossroads: Currents Issues in Interactional Psychology*, 166–207. Hillsdale, NJ: Erlbaum.

22 McClelland, D. A. and R. E. Boyatzis. 1982. Leadership Motive Pattern and Long-Term Success in Management. *Journal of Applied Psychology*, **67**: 737–43.

23 Conger, J. A. and R. Kanungo. 1987. Toward a Behavioral Theory of Charismatic Leadership in Organizational Settings. *The Academy of Management Review*, **12**(4): 637–47.

24 Ferris, G. R. et al. 2000. Political Skill at Work. *Organizational Dynamics*, **28**(4): 25–37.

25 Kacmar, K. M. and G. R. Ferris. 1993. Politics at Work: Sharpening the Focus of Political Behaviors in Organizations. *Business Horizons*, **36**(4): 70–4.

26 Ferris, G. R. and T. R. King. 1991. Politics in Human Resources Decisions: A Walk on the Dark Side. *Organizational Dynamics*, **20**(2): 59–71.

27 Zanzi, A. and R. M. O'Neill. 2001. Sanctioned Versus Non-Sanctioned Political Tactics. *Journal of Managerial Issues*, **13**(12): 245–64.

28 Ferris, G. R. et al. 1996. Perceptions of Organizational Politics: Predictors, Stress-Related Implications and Outcomes. *Human Relations*, **49**(2): 233–66.

29 Ferris, G. R. and K. M. Kacmar. 1992. Perceptions of Organizational Politics. *Journal of Management*, **18**(1): 93–116.

30 Witt, L. A. 1998. Enhancing Goal Congruence: A Solution to Organizational Politics. *Journal of Applied Psychology*, **8**(4): 666–74.

31 Gilmore, D. C. and G. R. Ferris. 1996. Organizational Politics and Employee Attendance. *Group and Organization Management*, **21**(4): 481–94.

32 Delucca, J. 1999. *Political Savvy: Systematic Approaches to Leadership Behind the Scenes*. 2nd edn. Berwyn, PA: EBG Publications.

33 Ferris, G. R., G. S. Russ, and P. M. Fandt. 1989. Politics in Organizations. In R. A. Giacalone and P. Rosenfeld, eds., *Impression Management in the Organization*, 143–70. Hillsdale, NJ: Erlbaum.

34 Becker, T. E. and S. L. Martin. 1995. Trying to Look Bad at Work: Methods and Motives for Managing Poor Impressions in Organizations. *Academy of Management Journal*, **38**(1): 174–99.

35 Buhler, P. 1994. Navigating the Waters of Organizational Politics. *Supervision*, **55**(9): 24–6.

36 Davenport, T. H., R. G. Eccles, and L. Prusak. 1992. Information Politics. *Sloan Management Review*, Fall: 53–65.

37 Tosi, H. L. and L. Gomez-Mejia. 1989. The Decoupling of CEO Pay and Performance: An Agency Theory Perspective. *Administrative Science Quarterly*, **34**: 169–89.

38 Liden, R. C. and T. R. Mitchell. 1988. Ingratiatory Behaviors in Organizational Settings. *The Academy of Management Review*, **13**(4): 572–614.

CHAPTER 13

Leadership

TRAIT APPROACHES TO LEADERSHIP

BEHAVIORAL APPROACHES TO LEADERSHIP

CONTINGENCY THEORIES OF LEADERSHIP

PROCESS THEORIES OF LEADERSHIP

SUBSTITUTES FOR LEADERSHIP

We know from the research, as we know from common sense, that leaders do have strong effects on organizations. For instance, changing CEOs can affect the evaluation of the firm by stockholders. One of the many studies on this issue demonstrated that an announcement of a change in CEOs increased the short-term value of stocks of small firms when the new CEO is an outsider [1]. CEOs can also affect the strategy of a firm [2]. More importantly, other studies have shown that CEOs can have a marked effect on a firm's performance [3, 4]. However, there is an important caveat. Simply replacing a poor manager with another is not the answer. A competent replacement is required [5]. One study of the effects of coach replacements on team performance in the National Basketball Association showed that replacing a coach, alone, had little effect on team success. What made the difference was the competence of the new coach, as measured by experience in the NBA and success in turning around other teams.

Those who select managers and coaches are faced with the difficult problem of predicting success, a problem so difficult that millions of dollars and much time have been spent thinking, talking, and writing about leadership. This theorizing, speculation, and research about leadership have persisted for a long time, always with the same objective: to understand leadership in ways that make it possible to select persons who are likely to be effective leaders and to provide better training and development of leadership skills. Who makes use of it? Companies like Hewlett Packard, Fuji, Xerox, GE, PepsiCo, and McKinsey and Company spend large sums of money on the selection and training of their managers.

Leadership, as we define it here, is a form of organizationally based problem-solving that attempts to achieve organizational goals by influencing the action of others [6]. While this definition places leadership in the broad domain of influence, power, authority, and politics discussed in an earlier chapter, there is an important difference. In this chapter, the focus is on leadership theory – which, almost without exception, focuses on individuals in organizational positions with legitimate authority to make decisions about others. In this chapter, we focus on understanding what makes a leader effective.

The early research on leadership studied it as a collection of personal traits or characteristics of those identified as leaders. Later research emphasized leadership as a series of acts, or a behavioral repertoire, designed to help a group to achieve its objectives. Beginning in the mid-1960s, attention has been directed toward contingency theories of leadership. These theories state effective leadership is a function of the situation in which leader and followers interact. A more recent approach is to focus on the leadership process, an approach that examines not just the traits or behavior of the leader but also the critical dimensions of the relationship between the leader and the followers that lead to leader influence. These themes are the main thrusts of leadership theory and research discussed in this chapter.

TRAIT APPROACHES TO LEADERSHIP

We often hear that leaders are forceful, tend to be very outgoing, and are persuasive. These common-sense observations form the basis of the belief that personalities of effective leaders are different from those of non-leaders. **Trait theories of leadership** are based on this idea. Studies have examined factors such as age, height, intelligence, academic achievement, judgmental ability, and insight, all of which were thought to predict successful leadership. These studies were done in a wide variety of settings such as military units, business firms, student organizations, elementary schools, and universities. They led to a rather disappointing conclusion. No specific traits seem to be correlated with leadership in all situations.

There are several explanations for such a result. First, just because a person has a particular single trait is not a sufficient condition to be in a leadership position or a management job and be successful at it. The person must want the job, seek it, and want to be effective. Also, traits do not operate alone, but in consonance with other factors. Those who have such a grouping of factors, that include leadership traits, have an advantage over those who do not, and over those who have a similar constellation but do not want to be in a leadership or management position [7].

The second reason these research studies produce very divergent results is that the studies have been done in too many different situations. Traits may be related to effectiveness in certain situations but not in others.

Third, there is also the possibility that the trait research tended to focus on very specific traits instead of more general factors. After a careful review of several hundred trait studies, it appears that if specific traits were grouped into general classes of factors, there were differences between effective and

Guide for Managers:
CHOOSING A LEADERSHIP STYLE THAT IS RIGHT FOR YOU

Prior to choosing a leadership style that is right for you, you must understand your own behavioral tendencies and your own personality. The reason is, as we note in several places in this book, that these behavioral tendencies will influence your natural response to almost any situation. Knowing this natural response will help you plan in advance for those situations where a different response may be appropriate. To be an effective manager, you will sometimes have to cognitively modify your actions to ensure they are appropriate for the situation. Can you do this? The research, and common sense, say that you can, but only within a range. You obviously should avoid engaging in any ways that appear to be feigned and forced and that are inconsistent with your personality. If you try to act significantly differently than your natural style, ineffective leaders [7, 8]. The characteristics are:

- High energy and stress tolerance
- Self-confidence
- Internal locus of control
- Emotional stability and maturity
- Personal integrity
- Socialized power motivation
- Moderate achievement motivation
- Low need for affiliation.

There are two things to point out here. First, we have discussed each of these characteristics, except high energy and stress tolerance and personal integrity, in earlier chapters. High energy and stress tolerance is useful for leaders because they have to cope with the hectic, frenetic pace of the managerial job. Personal integrity, being honest, is a critical determinant of personal trust, which is necessary for long-run leader effectiveness with subordinates. Second, McClelland [9] has shown that the leader motive pattern (socialized power motivation, moderate achievement motivation, and low affiliation needs) is related to managerial effectiveness [10, 11, 12].

you will be seen as untrustworthy, something that is a problem for any manager.

Once you understand your tendencies and personality, choosing a leadership style that is right for you requires two things. First, you must have a clear understanding of the situation. Second, you should understand the repertoire of behaviors that have been shown to be effective in different situations. Third, choose a behavioral response that meets the needs of the situation and that fits with your personality and style. As a manager you should experiment some and try to find behavior that works for you with your group. What could be the biggest enemy to your effectiveness is your own rigidity and unwillingness to be flexible.

Throughout this chapter we have inserted managerial guides that describe in greater depth the different behavioral repertoires available and the situations within which they are appropriate.

BEHAVIORAL APPROACHES TO LEADERSHIP

Behavioral approaches to leadership examine how what a leader does is related to leader effectiveness, while the trait approach focuses on what a leader is. How many times does the leader discipline an employee? How often did the leader communicate with employees? There are two classes of behavior that have received much attention in the leadership literature:

1 Decision influence behaviors
2 Task and social behaviors.

Distribution of decision-making influence

Many studies have been conducted on how the distribution of decision-making influence between superiors and subordinates is related to the performance and satisfaction of individuals and work groups. One of the important studies in this area was done over 50 years ago [13]. A classification of leader behavior emerged that was based on the sharing of decision-making between a leader and a follower. Leaders were described in three ways:

1   Autocratic
2   Participative
3   Laissez-faire.

In **autocratic leadership**, the leader makes all decisions and allows the subordinates no influence in the decision-making process. These supervisors are often indifferent to the personal needs of subordinates. For example, an autocratic manager would assign a worker a task or a goal without any discussion with the subordinate. The manager simply meets with subordinates and gives them a set of goals that the superior prepared.

Participative supervisors consult with subordinates on appropriate matters and allow them some influence in the decision-making process. Participative leadership is not punitive and treats subordinates with dignity. The participative leader might set goals with subordinates after talking with them to determine preferences. For instance, a manager might communicate departmental goals to subordinates in a meeting. Using this information, subordinates would then develop their goals, or the superior might develop goals for the subordinate and later meet to arrive at some mutual agreement about the subordinate's goals.

In **laissez-faire leadership**, supervisors allow their group to have complete autonomy. They rarely supervise directly, so that group members make many on-the-job decisions themselves, such as what jobs they want to do. With such an approach, subordinates set their own goals with no managerial inputs and work toward them with no direction.

Effective groups have had autocratic leaders and participative leaders [7]. Participative leadership is associated with higher levels of subordinate satisfaction. Those who work for participative leaders are less resistant to change and show more organization identification than those who work for autocratic leaders. The laissez-faire style has not been studied as much as the autocratic and participative styles, but the results are consistent, showing that subordinate satisfaction and performance under laissez-faire are lower than under the participative approach but higher than under the autocratic approach [7].

Task and social behaviors

Two very important programs of research on leader behavior were conducted at Ohio State University and the University of Michigan. They centered on whether effective leaders emphasize task activities and assignments or tend to concentrate on trying to keep good relationships and cohesion among group members, or do both of these things. You will recall that in groups, task functions and socio-emotional functions are the two key sets of activities (see chapter 6).

The Ohio State studies

From the late 1940s through the 1950s, a group of researchers at Ohio State conducted extensive studies of leadership and effectiveness in industrial, military, and educational institutions [14]. They developed instruments to measure leadership and evaluated factors that might determine group effectiveness. Two leadership behavior dimensions consistently emerged from these studies:

1 **Consideration** is the extent to which the leader is likely to have job relationships characterized by mutual trust, respect for subordinates' ideas, and consideration of their feelings. Considerate leaders tend to have good rapport and two-way communication with subordinates.
2 **Initiating structure** is the extent to which the leader is likely to define and structure his or her role and those of subordinates toward goal achievement. High initiating structure leaders play an active role in directing group activities, communicating task information, scheduling, and trying out new ideas.

Most studies show that consideration is generally related to high employee satisfaction; it is related much less often to high performance, although it is occasionally. In some studies, initiating structure has been found to be related to job satisfaction but less often to high productivity, low absenteeism, and low turnover [7].

The Ohio State studies had a profound impact on leadership thinking and research. Perhaps their major effect is that wide use has been made of the Leader Behavior Description Questionnaire (LBDQ), for measuring consideration and initiating structure. These concepts have become part of the conventional wisdom about leadership and are the basis of many programs to train leaders [15, 16].

The Michigan studies

At about the same time, the Institute of Social Research at the University of Michigan conducted a number of studies in offices, railroad settings, and service industries. From early studies, the researchers concluded that leadership behavior could be described in terms of two styles: a supervisor may be production-centered or employee-centered.

1   In **production-centered leadership**, the supervisor was primarily concerned with high levels of production and generally used high pressure to achieve them. He or she viewed subordinates merely as instruments for achieving the desired levels of production.
2   In **employee-centered leadership**, the supervisor was concerned about sub-ordinates' feelings and attempted to create an atmosphere of mutual trust and respect.

The group at Michigan, at first, concluded that employee-centered supervisors are more likely to have highly productive work groups than production-centered super-visors. This is an important difference between the Ohio State and Michigan studies. In the early stages of the Michigan studies, leaders were described as engaging in behavior that was either production-centered or employee-centered while the Ohio State studies characterized an individual on both dimensions [14]. The Ohio State and Michigan researchers used somewhat different measures, however, which make their studies less directly comparable.

CONTINGENCY THEORIES OF LEADERSHIP

The interest in contingency theories of leadership grew out of the fact that there were some inconsistencies in the research results. For example, initiating structure might be related to performance and satisfaction in some studies, but not in others. Similar inconsistencies were found in studies for the effects of consideration. The idea developed among contingency theorists that there might be different situations in which different leadership styles would be effective. They developed **contingency theories of leadership** that systematically account for how situational factors might result in different relationships between what leaders do and their effectiveness. Contingency theories tell you how a leader's or manager's behavior is related to effectiveness in different circumstances. There are three most prominent contingency theories [17, 18, 19, 20]:

1   Fiedler's contingency theory of leadership
2   The path-goal theory
3   The Vroom–Yetton model discussed in chapter 11.

Fiedler's contingency model

In 1967, Fiedler proposed a contingency model to theorize how the leader, the group, and the task interact to affect group performance. Much research has been

253

done on this theory since it was introduced and the evidence shows fairly strong support for it [21, 22].

There are three important things about this theory. First, it was the first theory to systematically account for situational factors. Fiedler integrated situational factors such as relationships between the leader and the group, task structure, and leader power into a theory of leadership. Second, Fiedler's concept of leadership considers the leader's orientation, not leader behavior. This orientation is a function of leader needs and personality. Although this may affect a teacher's behavior, it is the leader's orientation toward those with whom he or she works that determines how effective the group is. Third, because leadership orientation is relatively stable, it is not likely that a leader will change orientations when confronted with different situations, though the leader can change his or her behavior when it is necessary and when the leader wants to. There is some evidence, for example, that a person can change behavior from directive to supportive, and vice versa, in different situations [23, 24]. For example, when a critical, stressful situation exists at work, the supervisor is likely to act in a directive way with subordinates. In a low-stress situation, the same supervisor may be much more considerate.

Situational variables

There are three important situational factors that determine leader effectiveness in this theory:

1 Leader–member relations
2 Task structure
3 Position power.

These determine the amount of **situational control** that a leader has [25]. The more these are present, the more control the leader has over the situation. The level of situational control determines whether a particular leader orientation will be effective.

Leader–member relations refer to the trust a group has in the leader and how well the leader is liked. When leader–member relations are good, there is usually high satisfaction with work, individual values are consistent with organizational values, and there is mutual trust between the leader and the group. When relations are bad, mutual trust is lacking. Group cohesiveness is low, making it difficult to make members work together. If group cohesiveness is high but leader relations are bad, the group works together to sabotage the organization and the leader.

A job with high **task structure** is spelled out in detail – you know what the goals are and how to achieve them. You have little leeway in doing the job and must follow the instructions. For example, the telephone salesperson who works at a computer terminal has very high task structure. For the whole workday, the person sits at a terminal, answers the phone, enters the order, enters the customer's name and other relevant information, then completes the sale.

Low task structure is present when the objectives of the task or the way it is to be done are somewhat ambiguous. With low task structure, you must decide how to perform a task each time it is to be done. For example, a machinist may work in the tool room of a factory and be responsible for making a wide range of different parts needed to keep equipment operating. The work of managers and many professionals is unstructured.

Position power is a critical factor. High position power exists when you have much legitimate authority, which means that you can make important decisions without having them cleared by someone at higher organization levels. Low position power means that you have only limited authority.

Leader orientation: the LPC scale

Leader orientation is one aspect of your motivational hierarchy. It is not a leader behavior, but does reflect a behavioral preference [23]. Your **leader orientation** is determined by how you view the person that you least like to work with, whether you see him or her in a positive or a negative way. Your leader orientation is measured by the **least preferred co-worker (LPC) scale**. You are asked to think about someone that you worked least well with, then indicate if you have positive or negative feelings about the least preferred co-worker. You "may produce a very negative description . . . or a relatively more positive description of the least preferred co-worker" [23].

If you are a **high LPC leader**, you have relatively favorable views of your least preferred co-worker. High LPC leaders are people-centered and more positively oriented toward the feelings and the relationships of people in the work group. These leaders are able to see some positive things in the people they least like to work with. The high LPC leader wants to be accepted by others, has strong emotional ties to people in the workplace, and has higher status and self-esteem and is more likely to act in a considerate way [26]. If you are a **low LPC leader**, you have more negative views of your least preferred co-worker. Low LPC leaders are more oriented toward the task, and personal relationships tend to have secondary importance for them. They tend to be directive and controlling and to make

Guide for Managers: DIRECTIVE BEHAVIORS

There are times when it is very critical to provide direction and guidance to subordinates. A subordinate will generally perceive your actions to be directive if you engage in work-oriented interactions – and you take the initiative in these interactions. We emphasize, though, that providing guidance is not the same thing as dominating and demeaning someone. Instead it is giving direction and subjective, rather than reasoned, judgments about those who work with them.

Leader effectiveness

Either high or low LPC leadership orientations can be effective, depending on the **situational control** that the leader has [25]. A leader has high situational control when:

- Leader–member relations are good.
- There is high task structure.
- The leader has high position power.

A leader has low situational control when:

- Leader–member relations are poor.
- There is a low task structure.
- The leader has little position power.

clarification as to how to do something or what is expected. This means you have to be careful here and not create the perception that you are overly rigid or dominating. Some ways to be directive are:

- Clearly define responsibilities.
- Provide the necessary information to do the job.
- Emphasize the policies and procedures that should be followed.
- Make regular checks of the subordinate's progress.
- Behave in ways that reinforce status differences between you and your subordinate.
- Provide constructive feedback on a regular basis.

In this case, obviously, the leadership situation is not a favorable one. Moderate situation control means the situational characteristics are mixed. Some work to the advantage of the leader (for instance, high position power) whereas others do not (poor leader–member relations).

These levels of situational control require leaders with different LPC orientations, as shown in figure 13.1. The low LPC leader, with a strong task orientation, is most effective when situational control is either very low or very high. Weak situational control is good for the low LPC leader. The group may fall apart or it may not attend to the task requirements unless the leader exerts a good deal of direction. When situational control is strong and the conditions are favorable, the low LPC leader is also more effective. The group may be willing to accept the task-oriented leader since success is assured because of their own performance and the vigilance of the leader.

The high LPC leader is most effective when there is moderate situational control. In this case, the high LPC may be more effective in motivating group members to perform better and to be cooperative toward goal achievement. The lower LPC leader does not have tendencies to do those sorts of things. The low LPC would probably exert pressures to work harder to produce more, which may counteract good performance.

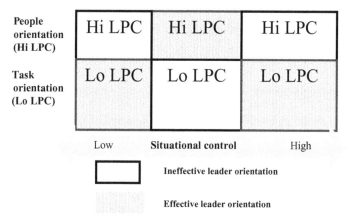

| People orientation (Hi LPC) | Hi LPC | Hi LPC | Hi LPC |
| Task orientation (Lo LPC) | Lo LPC | Lo LPC | Lo LPC |

Low   **Situational control**   High

Ineffective leader orientation

Effective leader orientation

Figure 13.1   Contingency approaches: Fiedler's contingency theory

Path-goal theory

Path-goal theory links leader behavior to performance using the expectancy theory of motivation [19, 27]. The basic idea of path-goal theory is shown in figure 13.2. To achieve the desired organizational results, certain tasks must be performed. The results are the goal; the tasks are the path. When appropriate tasks are performed, the goals are achieved. When the goals are achieved, rewards for the individual should follow. The role of the leader is to ensure that the path to the goal is clearly understood by the subordinate and that there are no barriers to the achievement of the goal [28].

Leader behaviors

In path-goal theory, there are four different styles of leader behavior which affect outcomes and reward [27].

1   **Directive leadership** is the style in which the leader gives guidance and direction to subordinates about job requirements. The leader defines the work roles of group members, determines and communicates performance standards to them, and manages using specific policies, procedures, and rules.
2   **Supportive leadership** is a style in which the leader is concerned with the needs of those who report to him or her. The supportive leader is friendly and approachable. Members are treated as equals. This set of behaviors is similar to the style called **consideration**.
3   **Participative leaders** act in a consultative style. They seek advice from subordinates about problems and consider these recommendations seriously before decisions are made.

257

Path   **Goal**   **Outcomes**

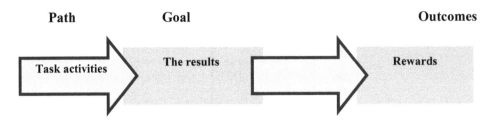

Figure 13.2 Contingency approaches: path-goal theory

4 In **achievement-oriented leadership**, leaders set challenging goals for their work groups. These leaders expect their groups to perform well and they communicate this to subordinates.

What leadership style is best?

The leader's role in path-goal theory varies, depending on the situation. Depending on the characteristics of the situation, you can make predictions about which leadership styles would be most effective. If there is a high level of task certainty because the subordinate knows how to do the job or because the task is routine, then the path to the goal is clear and the best leadership style here is supportive, not directive. Directive leadership may increase performance because there is added pressure to produce, but it may lead to decreased job satisfaction because of close supervision. More information on choice of leadership style is provided in the Guides for Managers throughout this chapter.

When there is high uncertainty about the task or the goal to be

> # Guide for Managers:
> ## CONSIDERATE/SUPPORTIVE BEHAVIORS
>
> Like the dangers of appearing too directive and dominating, the dangerous side of acting in a considerate/supportive way toward subordinates is that some might view it as a sign of weakness and lack of concern for performance. However, if you know when to act in this way and can, you will get better performance. Here are some ways that you can be considerate or supportive:
>
> - Show concern for the personal well-being of subordinates.
> - Be an active listener. Let the subordinate do most of the talking.
> - Personalize the way you deal with subordinates, minimizing organizational status differences.
> - Encourage individualism, creativity and initiative.

achieved, the leader must clarify the path. When the subordinate is uncertain about the best way to do a job, the manager should give instructions. If the goals are not clear to the subordinate, then they should be spelled out. When there is high task uncertainty, the most effective leadership style is to be directive.

Research on path-goal theory

Path-goal theory is a complex view of leadership, with four different types of leader behavior, three subordinate characteristics, and two environmental factors. Most research tests some specific proposition from path-goal theory, and the results are mixed, partly because of the difficulty in testing the theory. However, when path-goal hypotheses are tested in carefully designed studies that reflect the conditions of the theory, the results are more encouraging.

PROCESS THEORIES OF LEADERSHIP

Trait approaches, behavioral approaches, and contingency approaches focus mainly on the leader, what the leader is or what the leader does. Some recent theories, called **process theories of leadership**, explain the processes by which a relationship develops between leaders and subordinates. One theory is called transformational leadership theory. Another is called vertical dyad linkage (VDL) theory.

Transformational leadership theory

Transformational leadership theory explains how leaders develop and enhance the commitment of followers. In this approach, transformational leaders are contrasted with transactional leaders. In **transactional leadership**, the leader and subordinate are bargaining agents, negotiating to maximize their own position [29]. The subordinate's motivation to comply with the leader is self-interest, because the leader can provide payoffs, perhaps both economic and psychological, that are valued by the follower. The style of the transactional leader is [7]:

1 To use contingent rewards – rewards are associated with good performance and accomplishment.
2 To manage by exception – the leader acts when he or she anticipates that performance is likely to deviate from standards or takes action when standards are not met.
3 To take a hands-off approach – the leader acts in a laissez-faire manner, abdicating and avoiding responsibility.

Transformational leadership is based on the leader's effect on the followers' values, self-esteem, and trust, and on their confidence in the leader and motivation to perform above and beyond the call of duty [30]. The transactional leader's influence is derived from the exchange process, but it is different in an important way from transformational leadership. Transactional leadership works within the context of the followers' self-interests while transformational leadership seeks to change that context [7].

259

The transformational leader's influence is based on the leader's ability to inspire and raise the consciousness of the followers by appealing to their higher ideals and values. This occurs because the transformational leader has charisma, and engages in particular behaviors as well. Specifically, this is the style of a transformational leader [7]:

- To be charismatic – the charismatic leader creates a special bond with the followers and is able to articulate a vision with which the followers identify and for which they are willing to work.
- To be inspirational – the leader creates high expectations and effectively communicates crucial ideas with symbols and simple language.
- To practice individual consideration – the leader coaches, advises, and delegates to the followers, treating them individually.
- To stimulate followers intellectually – the leader arouses them to develop new ways to think about problems.

Transformational leaders may have strong effects. There are many corporate executives who fit the description of the transformational leader (for example, Herb Kelleher of Southwest Airlines and Mary Kay of Mary Kay Cosmetics). They were able to build or change organizations in dramatic ways and, at the same time, obtain very high levels of commitment from others in the firm. Transformational leadership effects have also been demonstrated to

Guide for Managers:
TRANSFORMATIONAL LEADER BEHAVIORS

In this chapter we have discussed the fact that managers have been successfully trained to behave in transformational ways. When you examine the content of that training, here are some of the behaviors that they learn:

- Articulate a vision that subordinates can understand and accept. Do this by providing an optimistic and attainable view of the future.
- Show self-confidence.
- Challenge subordinates, but be sure that they are capable of stretching to achieve the goals.
- Find ways to use non-verbal cues and symbols that are consistent with your message.
- Be dramatic and outgoing, but in ways that are consistent with your personality. This means that you have to sometimes take personal risks that others know about and believe are important to the success of your organization.
- Empower subordinates. This means two things. First, you must be willing to delegate important responsibilities to them to demonstrate your confidence in their ability. Second, you have to use language that lets them know that you believe they can succeed and that you will help them to succeed.

result in higher performance, member satisfaction, and higher commitment in several studies [31–39].

An important question is whether it is possible to develop a transformational style. There is some research, though it is currently rather limited, which suggests that it is possible to develop a charismatic style through training [39, 40]. In one study, actresses learned scripts that portrayed charismatic leaders, structuring leaders, and considerate leaders [40]. The emotional state, body language, facial expressions, and other symbolic cues were described and learned for the charismatic role. The charismatic leader was able to gain high productivity from the experimental group. Subjects generated more alternatives and were more satisfied with both the task and the leader.

Vertical dyad linkage theory

The **vertical dyad linkage (VDL) theory** focuses on the relationship between the leader and the subordinate [41]. The assumption is that leadership can be understood best in terms of role relationships between managers and subordinates – members of a vertical dyadic relationship – in an organization. Managers must ensure that superior–subordinate relationships are well defined since managerial success depends on subordinate performance. Therefore, managers and subordinates negotiate these role relationships through a range of formal and informal processes that occur primarily in the early stages of their relationship [42].

This negotiation results in different relationships with different subordinates. In VDL theory, the agreement between leaders and subordinates about the degree of trust in the relationship, subordinate competence, loyalty, and similar factors is measured. Leader–member relationships are classified into in-group and out-group categories depending on the level of agreement.

1 **In-group relationships** between leaders and subordinates are close, the leader spends more time and energy in them, role participants have more positive attitudes toward the job, and there are fewer problems than in out-group relationships [42]. The quality of the linkage affects some subordinate behaviors and perceptions, but has not been related to subordinate performance.
2 **Out-group subordinates** spent less time on decision-making, did not volunteer for extra assignments, and were rated lower by subordinates [43].

In-group or out-group status does not appear to be related to the subordinates' actual performance, but it is linked to several other important aspects of life in organizations [42]. It could be, for example, that the nature of the relationship is an important predictor of subordinate advancement. Further, it may better define the critical dimensions of the leader–subordinate relationship. It also emphasizes the evolution of that relationship, which has received little attention in the other leader literature.

SUBSTITUTES FOR LEADERSHIP

The very image of the leader in leadership theory is of a person who is able to influence others to act toward organizational objectives. This image is reinforced by the popular press, television, and films [44]. However, we know that other factors such as ability, intrinsic motivation, the nature of technology, and the structure of the organization also affect the performance and satisfaction of members. In fact, in some instances, these factors may be even more crucial to performance than leadership [45, 46]. They can serve as **leadership substitutes** because they, not the action of the leader, contribute to success or failure [45]. Suppose that effectiveness of a group depends on two things: performing the task and good working relationships among members. From a leadership behavior perspective, by initiating structure behavior you could provide the members with knowledge about how to perform the task. Good working relationships can also develop because you, as a leader, use a considerate style of behavior.

However, there are other ways that task knowledge and good relations can be present, and they are substitutes for the behavior of the leader. Task knowledge may be present because those who work for you know how to do the job or because there are specific procedures that are well known by them. These work in place of initiating structure. There may be good working relationships because of work group norms, because all the workers are friends, or for many other reasons. These are substitutes for consideration.

There are three types of leadership substitutes: the subordinate characteristics, the task factors, and the organizational dimensions. Specific substitutes are shown in table 13.1. This table shows that, for example, if you receive feedback because the task itself allows you to make a judgment about how well things are going, there is no need to have a manager give you feedback.

The concept of substitutes for leadership is important for two reasons. First, it suggests that contextual control is an alternative to active leadership to obtain good results. The results of several studies show that these substitutes can have significant positive effects on employee attitudes, role perceptions, and both task and contextual performance [47].

Second, there are implications about the interaction of leadership, leadership substitutes, and the nature of the organization. The various factors that may act as substitutes will differ, depending upon the type of organization that we have described in chapter 7 [48]. For example, in mechanistic organizations, the task itself will provide clarity, formalization will provide direction, and lower-level workers will be indifferent toward organization rewards. In organic organizations, however, task competence, high intrinsic task motivation, and cohesive work groups will be more powerful substitutes.

Table 13.1 Leadership substitutes

Subordinate characteristics	Task factors	Organizational dimensions
Ability	Receptiveness	Formalization
Experience	Clarity	Availability of special staff
Background and training	Task-provided feedback	Work group cohesiveness
Professional orientation		Spatial distance between the leader and the group
Indifference toward organizational rewards		

Source: Adapted from Kerr and Jermier [45].

SUMMARY

Organizations are concerned with leadership because of the need to select and promote individuals into management positions. The manager's role is to make sure the work of the organization is done through the effective use of physical and human resources. Therefore, we believe that an effective manager should be a good leader.

There is a close relationship between leadership and management, but there is more to it than simply understanding the role of the leader/manager. There are many reasons why people are willing to cooperate to achieve organization goals, and many of these are only incidentally related to the superior–subordinate relationship. For instance, the broad shape of the psychological contract is probably constructed in early socialization, before one joins an organization.

However, it is important to know how situational factors, the work setting, and the characteristics of the subordinate interact with the personality and the behavior of a manager/leader to affect the level of individual and organization performance. This chapter has discussed several theories of leadership that illustrate this. Path-goal theory and Fiedler's work explain leadership phenomena with a greater number of situational factors than had been used in earlier approaches. VDL theory contributes to understanding leadership because of its focus on the relationship between the leader and the subordinate. However, we have also shown how contextual control of members can be achieved through substitutes for leadership, showing that leadership is an aspect of power.

Guide for Managers:
DEALING WITH COMMON LEADERSHIP PROBLEMS

Regardless of your personal style, there are some common mistakes that all leaders make. In this guide, we have tried to identify of those pitfalls.

LOOK FIRST AT RESULTS, THEN THE PERSON. Before acting in any situation, you want to ensure that you avoid the fundamental attribution error; see chapter 4. Otherwise your biases, assumptions, and likes for that manager will color your evaluation. That means if you have a performance problem with a subordinate with whom you have a good relationship, you will tend to be considerate/supportive even though a directive approach might be more effective. Likewise, a performance problem with a subordinate that you do not like as well might lead to more directive actions when a considerate/supportive approach is called for.

WHEN PERFORMANCE OF A LOWER-LEVEL MANAGER IS NOT UP TO PAR, THEN REPLACE THE LEADER OR CHANGE THE SITUATION. This is one way to attain some congruence between leader behavior and the situation. For example, if it is called for, task structure can be increased or decreased. Jobs can be made more routine and simple or be enlarged and the task structure reduced. The position power of a manager can be increased by delegating more authority and responsibility, or it can be reduced by taking them away. Leader–member relationships may be improved through any number of different training and group development methods.

IDENTIFY AND REMOVE BARRIERS TO PERFORMANCE. Remember that it is not your job as a manager to make someone's job more difficult. You want to make it easier because your success depends upon their success. One of the more important things that you can do, and often one of the easiest, is to make the job of subordinates easier by eliminating difficulties that are in their performance path. Another way to make a subordinate's job easier is to make sure that they have the necessary competence to do the work and that might entail that they have some training.

KNOW WHAT THOSE IN YOUR GROUP ARE CAPABLE OF DOING. There are two facets to this, your subordinates' ability and their motivation. If those who work for you are very capable, then you should avoid, when possible, directive leader styles and emphasize the considerate/supportive style. When subordinates don't have the requisite competence, information, or resources, a directive style is probably more effective.

From the motivational side of the issue, it is helpful to know how intrinsically motivated are your subordinates. For those that are highly motivated with high ability, you will want to be considerate/supportive and get out of their way. For those who have high ability but lower motivation, a more directive style will be effective.

CONSIDER HOW MUCH STRESS YOUR SUBORDINATES ARE UNDER. The level of stress that a subordinate is experiencing should also affect your leadership style in reacting to any situation. The stress could be from organizational sources or external sources. Leaders can often deal with stress caused by organizational sources, but are often frustrated when stress from external sources impacts on workplace performance. You might prefer that employees do not bring "personal issues" to the workplace, but they will. And if they do, the effects of these stressors on their work will be the same as if they are job stressors. In this situation, your leadership behavior style should be, at least at first, considerate/supportive so that you do not make the situation even worse. At some point, if there are still performance problems, you might have to take a more directive approach. You want to be careful, though, and not switch to that style prematurely.

REFERENCES

1 Reinganum, M. R. 1985. The Effect of Executive Succession of Stockholder Wealth. *Administrative Science Quarterly*, **30**: 46–60.

2 Smith, M. and M. C. White. 1987. Strategy, CEO Specialization, and Succession. *Administrative Science Quarterly*, **32**: 263–80.

3 Weiner, N. and T. A. Mahoney. 1981. A Model of Corporate Performance as a Function of Environmental, Organizational, and Leadership Influences. *Academy of Management Journal*, **24**: 453–70.

4 Thomas, A. B. 1988. Does Leadership Make a Difference to Organizational Performance? *Administrative Science Quarterly*, **33**: 388–400.

5 Pfeffer, J. and A. Davis-Blake. 1987. Administrative Succession and Organizational Performance: How Administrator Experience Mediates the Succession Effect. *Academy of Management Journal*, **29**: 72–83.

6 Fleishman, E. A. et al. 1991. Taxonomic Efforts in the Description of Leadership Behavior: A Synthesis and Functional Interpretation. *The Leadership Quarterly*, **2**: 245–80.

7 Bass, B. M. 1990. *Bass and Stogdill's Handbook of Leadership: Theory, Research, and Managerial Applications*. New York: Free Press.

8 Yukl, G. A. 2002. *Leadership in Organizations*. Saddle River, NJ: Prentice-Hall.

9 McClelland, D. A. 1985. *Human Motivation*. Glenview, IL: Scott, Foresman.

10 McClelland, D. A. 1975. *Power: The Inner Experience*. New York: Irvington.

11 McClelland, D. A. and R. E. Boyatzis. 1982. Leadership Motive Pattern and Long-Term Success in Management. *Journal of Applied Psychology*, **67**: 737–43.

12 Cornelius, E. T. and F. B. Lane. 1984. The Power Motive and Managerial Success in a Professionally Oriented Service Industry Organization. *Journal of Applied Psychology*, **69**(1): 32–9.

13 Lewin, K., R. Lippitt, and R. K. White. 1939. Patterns of Aggressive Behavior in Experimentally Created Social Climates. *Journal of Social Psychology*, **10**: 271–99.

14 Stogdill, R. M. 1974. *Handbook of Leadership: A Survey of Theory and Research*. New York: Free Press.

15 Blake, R. R. and J. S. Mouton. 1969. *Building a Dynamic Corporation through Grid Organization Development*. Reading, MA: Addison-Wesley.

16 Hersey, P. and K. Blanchard. 1988. *Management of Organizational Behavior*. New York: Prentice-Hall.

265

17 Fiedler, F. E. 1967. *A Theory of Leadership Effectiveness*. New York: McGraw-Hill.

18 Evans, M. G. 1968. *The Effects of Supervisory Behavior on Worker Perceptions of their Path-Goal Relationships*. Yale University.

19 House, R. J. 1971. A Path-Goal Theory of Leader Effectiveness. *Administrative Science Quarterly*, 16: 334–8.

20 Vroom, V. H. and P. W. Yetton. 1973. *Leadership and Decision Making*. Pittsburgh: University of Pittsburgh Press.

21 Strube, M. J. and J. E. Garcia. 1981. A Meta-Analytic Investigation of Fiedler's Contingency Model of Leadership Effectiveness. *Psychological Bulletin*, 90: 307–21.

22 Peters, L. H., D. D. Harke, and J. T. Pohlman. 1985. Fiedler's Contingency Theory of Leadership: An Application of the Meta-Analysis Procedures of Schmidt and Hunter. *Psychological Bulletin*, 97(2): 274–85.

23 Fiedler, F. E. and M. Chemers. 1974. *Leadership and Effective Management*. Glenview, IL: Scott, Foresman.

24 Fodor, E. M. 1976. Group Stress, Authoritarian Style of Control, and the Use of Power. *Journal of Applied Psychology*, 61: 313–18.

25 Fiedler, F. E. 1978. The Contingency Model and the Dynamics of the Leadership Process. In L. Berkowitz, ed., *Advances in Experimental Social Psychology*, 59–111. New York: Academic Press.

26 Fiedler, F. E. 1992. Time Based Measures of Leadership Experience and Organizational Performance: A Review of Research and a Preliminary Model. *The Leadership Quarterly*, 3: 5–21.

27 House, R. J. and T. R. Mitchell. 1974. Path-Goal Theory of Leadership. *Journal of Contemporary Business*, 4: 81–97.

28 Filley, A. C., R. J. House, and S. Kerr. 1976. *Managerial Process and Organizational Behavior*. Glenview, IL: Scott, Foresman.

29 Downton, J. V. 1973. *Rebel Leadership: Commitment and Charisma in the Revolutionary Process*. New York: Free Press.

30 House, R. J. and J. V. Singh. 1987. Organization Behavior: Some New Directions for

I/O Psychology. *Annual Review of Psychology*, 38: 669–718.

31 Bass, B. M. 1985. *Leadership Beyond Expectations*. New York: Free Press.

32 Bass, B. M., B. J. Avolio, and L. Goodheim. 1987. Biography and Assessment of Transformational Leadership at the World Class Level. *Journal of Management*, 13(1): 7–19.

33 Avolio, B. J., D. A. Waldman, and W. O. Einstein. 1988. Transformational Leadership in a Management Game Simulation. *Group and Organization Studies*, 13(1): 59–80.

34 Deluga, R. J. 1988. Relationship of Transformational and Transactional Leadership with Employee Influencing Strategies. *Group and Organization Studies*, 13: 456–67.

35 Hater, J. J. and B. M. Bass. 1988. Superiors' Evaluations and Subordinates' Perceptions of Transformational and Transactional Leadership. *Journal of Applied Psychology*, 73: 695–702.

36 Seltzer, J. and B. M. Bass. 1990. Transformational Leadership: Beyond Initiation and Consideration. *Journal of Management*, 16: 693–703.

37 Howell, J. M. and C. A. Higgins. 1990. Champions of Technological Innovation. *Administrative Science Quarterly*, 35: 317–41.

38 Bycio, P., R. D. Hackett, and J. S. Allen. 1995. Further Assessments of Bass's Conceptualization of Transactional and Transformational Leadership. *Journal of Applied Psychology*, 80(4): 468–99.

39 Kirkpatrick, S. and E. A. Locke. 1996. Direct and Indirect Effects of Three Core Leadership Components on Performance and Attitudes. *Journal of Applied Psychology*, 81(1): 36–51.

40 Howell, J. M. and P. J. Frost. 1989. A Laboratory Study of Charismatic Leadership. *Organizational Behavior and Human Decision Processes*, 43: 243–69.

41 Dansereau, F., G. Graen, and W. J. Haga. 1975. A Vertical Dyad Linkage Approach to Leadership within Formal Organizations: A Longitudinal Investigation of the Role

Making Process. *Organizational Behavior and Human Performance*, **13**: 46–78.

42 Dienesch, R. M. and R. C. Liden. 1986. Leader–Member Exchange Model of Leadership: A Critique and Further Development. *Academy of Management Review*, **11**(3): 618–34.

43 Liden, R. C. and G. Graen. 1980. Generalizability of the Vertical Dyad Linkage Model. *Academy of Management Journal*, **23**: 451–65.

44 Meindl, J. R., S. B. Ehrlich, and J. M. Dukerich. 1985. The Romance of Leadership. *Administrative Science Quarterly*, **30**: 78–102.

45 Kerr, S. and J. Jermier. 1978. Substitutes for Leadership: Their Meaning and Measurement.

Organizational Behavior and Human Performance, **22**: 375–403.

46 Tosi, H. L. 1982. When Leadership Isn't Enough. In H. L. Tosi and W. C. Hamner, eds., *Organizational Behavior and Management: A Contingency Approach*, 403–11. New York: John Wiley.

47 Podsakoff, P., S. McKenzie, and W. Bommer. 1996. Meta-Analysis of the Relationship between Kerr and Jermier's Substitutes for Leadership and Employee Job Attitudes, Role Perceptions, and Performance. *Journal of Applied Psychology*, **81**(4): 380–400.

48 Tosi, H. L. 1992. *The Environment/Organization/Person Contingency Model: A Meso Approach to the Study of Organizations*. Greenwich, CT: JAI Press.

267

CHAPTER 14
Organizational Change

How our Work Life is Changing

Stages of Successful Change

Resistance to Change

Helping Individuals Cope with Change

Organizational Development

Amy shifted in her chair and gazed out the window in response to the interviewer's question. "Did I feel threatened when the announcement was made that we were downsizing? I'd have to say yes. In fact, I can't think of a more stressful time in my professional life than the change we have seen in the last 12 months. I went from thinking I would be with this organization until retirement, to wondering how I would make my house payments if I were among those who lost a job. I had trouble eating and sleeping and I spent a great deal of my time trying to figure out what was going to happen. Even now that the organization is telling me that there are no more changes to come, I am skeptical. I am not sure I trust them. I am certainly a different person now and I have a different view of the organization."

Amy is describing her reaction to a significant change in the organization she worked for – a change that fundamentally impacted her mental models of organizational life and subsequently impacted her attitude about the organization, impacting how she viewed herself, her future, and the organization to which she belonged. Her reaction to the change is normal. The personal stress created by the uncertainty that restructuring has created is among the top causes of that stress in the workplace.

Change affects us all in different ways but the reality is that dealing with change is a complex and stressful process. This chapter focuses on the changing nature of our work. We look at some models of change and build on those models to consider ways of achieving effective change in organizations. We begin by introducing some of the dynamics of modern organizational life that are leading to significant changes in our work lives.

HOW OUR WORK LIFE IS CHANGING

Significant change has become a common occurrence in the modern workplace. Even the largest companies are experiencing significant change in many areas. We are experiencing change in how we work, including where we work, change in the structure of our organizations, change in the nature of business to an increasingly global marketplace, and change in the increased diversification of our work colleagues. Perhaps the most common internal change pressure is dissatisfaction with performance. Increased competition, rapid change in consumer tastes, or increased emphasis on service or quality can all trigger pressure to change. Dissatisfaction with employee turnover or performance failures may also instigate change efforts. Here are some specific factors that are driving change in the workplace.

Changes in the work itself

There have been some important changes in how we work and the skills required for that work. Increases in information technology and a shift from physical activities to intellectual activities have changed the work tasks of workers.

One significant change in workplace activities is the increasing shift toward the virtual office in the Information Age. This has changed the face of the workplace so that, rather than having a specified office in a specific building, many workers nowadays work in their homes, cars, or motel rooms. It is anticipated that the number of employees who work in virtual offices will increase by 10 percent each year for the foreseeable future. Not only does this change the nature of how we work; it forces us to learn a new set of skills to cope with the increased use of technology in our work lives.

Organizations are changing structurally

Downsizing, rightsizing, mergers, and acquisitions are so commonplace that it is virtually impossible to keep up with them. Among the companies in the last ten years that have been affected by these actions are Compaq Computer, Ford, the American Stock Exchange, the Nasdaq market, AOL-Time-Warner, and Lucent. These actions have a large effect on the number of employees in the firm, the style of managing, and employee commitment. For example, in takeovers, the acquired organization must adopt the management styles, philosophies, and systems of the acquiring organization, often in a very short period of time. Changes in ownership where the new owner is a foreign company creates special change problems for organizations since here there is often a culture clash. The compromises and adjustments that have to be made are often especially severe.

Shifts to a global economy

The increased globalization of the marketplace causes several changes that we must accommodate. These changes affect organizations and individuals in many ways. First, many companies have an increased need for employees to work in foreign countries as expatriates. This requires employees to cope with extremely different cultures. Second, global competitiveness has caused organizations to constantly find ways to increase their competitiveness, changes which lead to subsequent changes in the work processes and procedures. An example of this was the competition in the automotive market that opened up opportunities in the USA for foreign automobile manufacturers that were experienced in making fuel-efficient cars. As foreign automobiles entered the market, US firms were motivated to change their existing product lines and form joint ventures with foreign manufacturers and to sell foreign-made automobiles under their own names. This required enormous modifications in company operations. Entire plants, including personnel, technical processes, and administrative procedures, had to change so as to compete more successfully against global competitors. Another result was the significant reduction in the US workforce; these were also political pressures to impose quotas against foreign automobile companies. This, in turn, encouraged foreign manufacturers to locate in the USA to avoid the quotas. New problems arose in managing plants in a new culture.

Increased diversity in the workforce

The increased diversity within the workforce has been a change that has provided challenges for many individuals and organizations. Women increasingly comprise a larger percentage of the workforce and bring with them a diverse set of skills and needs. By 2050, the US Census Bureau projects that ethnic minority groups such as African Americans, Hispanics, Asians, and Pacific Islanders will compose almost half of the US population. While the increased diversity is seen as good for the competitiveness of US businesses, it brings a different set of issues that result in organizational change.

STAGES OF SUCCESSFUL CHANGE

For an organization to be successful, it must adapt to changes in its environment to ensure survival. The approach we take here is a basic model of how change occurs that can be attributed to the work of [1]. A useful model for understanding change is the biological perspective, i.e., organisms adapt to pressures in their environment. As the environment changes, the organism must change or it will cease to exist. In many cases, there are opposing forces that affect the organism and so it simultaneously adapts to numerous powerful opposing forces. This leads to an equilibrium that allows the organism to continue to exist. Given the organism has adapted to these pressures over a significant period of time, it is resistant to any change that would upset that careful balance. To effect future change would require changes in the environment.

Adaptation as a model of change

Organizational change can be viewed from this perspective as well. Let us focus on a desired change in an organizational process or procedure – their way of doing things. These processes are often the result of competing organizational pressures caused by conflict, internal political pressures, and diverse needs. A process that evolves from these pressures usually works because it is an equilibrium of pressures. Perhaps any one constituent does not prefer the process but it is a compromise caused

271

by the pressure in the context. Subsequent attempts to change that process may face even greater resistance.

To effect change in the organization, three things must occur:

1 Unfreezing
2 Transformation
3 Refreezing.

Unfreezing requires that there be a change in the status quo before there can be a change to a new condition. Just because a change is attempted does not mean it will be effective. The members in the organization will resist the change unless significant pressure can be brought to bear to require them to recognize the need to change (unfreeze). Only after unfreezing takes place and members are willing to at least try to learn new ways can the change process continue. This is the second step in the process and is called **transformation**. It is the movement that must occur for the organism to change. Finally, the change is made permanent through the process of **refreezing** [1]. This becomes the new equilibrium point. A significant factor in the refreezing process is modifying the organizational system so as to make the changes permanent.

Organizational adaptation

Successful change depends on moving through the key stages of the change process in a systematic manner. The first stage is the development of motivation to change among those who are initiating it and those who are implementing it. This is the unfreezing stage of change. Motivation to change depends on two basic questions:

1 Is it worthwhile to change?
2 Can the change be successfully carried out?

In determining whether it is worthwhile to change, a calculation, at least in a rough sort of way, must be made of the positive and negative outcomes associated with not changing relative to the outcomes associated with changing.

The second key stage, when sufficient motivation to change exists, is use of an appropriate change method. This is the stage where transformation occurs. Not all change methods are equally effective. Techniques for knowledge change are different from those for changing skills. Methods for changing individual behavior may be completely ineffective for achieving change at the group level.

The third key stage in successful change is reinforcement of change. This is the refreezing process. New behaviors, working relationships, procedures, and so forth must result in rewarding positive, not negative, outcomes. Otherwise, the individuals, groups, or organizations will revert to previous conditions or look for new ones.

RESISTANCE TO CHANGE

There is usually some resistance to change in organizations. It may be traced to individual, group, or organizational characteristics. To take a specific example: a consultant had revised an organization's performance appraisal system several times. There was deep resistance to changing the existing system in spite of the fact that it was well known that it was not working well. A general fear of the unknown and a preference for the known appeared to be operating. Supervisors may have felt that a new system would prove even more difficult to use than the present one. They may have thought that their subordinates' performances would look worse under a new system, which might reflect back on them. They may also have feared that they would have to face new problems and decisions for which they lacked experience. Finally, changing may simply not be worth the trouble. The gain is not worth the pain. In this section, we discuss reasons for that resistance.

Structure, culture and power

The organizational structure, the organizational culture, and the power structure help to maintain stable behavior patterns in organizations. They are self-reinforcing and potentially significant barriers to change. After all, the very nature of change may put them in jeopardy. It is therefore likely that the change efforts will not work unless they are compatible with the organizational culture and the power structure. This is a very well documented reason why many change efforts fail. Quite often, for example, a top management group decides to decentralize decision-making, giving more responsibility to lower-level managers. This requires a climate of trust and willingness to

Guide for Managers: CREATING DISSATISFACTION AS A CHANGE STRATEGY

In this chapter we discussed a model of organizational change that required unfreezing by disturbing the status quo prior to an organization's attempting to cause a transformation by way of change. Another way to think of this is as a method of creating dissatisfaction among organizational members. If they are happy with the status quo, they are unlikely to be motivated to change. Creating dissatisfaction is an important aspect of managing change and here are some ideas for its creation [14].

SHARE COMPETITIVE INFORMATION. Managers often keep the organization's position relative to its competitors a secret. Employees are often unaware of important changes in the market that may affect the long-term health of the organization. As a result they may view efforts delegate. In an organization that has a political organizational culture, a lack of trust, and strong centralized decision-making, decentralizing will be very difficult.

Changing systems: the effects of interdependencies

When an organization is viewed as a complex system of interdependent parts, it is clear that a change attempted in one area may be resisted by other parts of the system. It also suggests that, for change to be effective, it must consider the interdependencies that exist because these interdependencies may interfere with effective change.

Change programs often focus on changes in tasks, people, technology, or structure. In task changes, the duties assigned to individuals are changed. In people changes, an attempt is made to alter individual knowledge, attitudes, or skills. Technological change focuses on the machinery, procedures, workflows, or materials. Structural rearrangements focus on changing how members are grouped together or on the systems and procedures that the organization employs to guide and direct interactions. However, to change any one of these means that the others are very often affected as well. These change interdependencies may cause an effort to fail eventually, even though a desired change in one of the factors had initially taken place. Change efforts directed toward one area may be resisted in another.

The McKinsey 7-S model shows that key interdependencies exist among

by management to implement new changes as unimportant.

HIGHLIGHT SHORTCOMINGS IN INDIVIDUAL ON-THE-JOB BEHAVIORS. There is a tendency in organizations to cover for or not publicly discuss the implications of ineffective behavior. For example, when a supervisor knows that her subordinates are generally dissatisfied, they may avoid any systematic attempt by management to assess employee attitudes. This was the case in the consulting effort of one of the authors of this text. He visited an organization where employee opinion surveys were only reported at the aggregate level. These results were difficult to interpret because there was wide variance in the response but it was obvious that overall employee morale and satisfaction were low despite numerous interventions. The consultant convinced the organization's senior leaders to systematically assess employee attitudes and report them by department level. These results were also made available to everyone in the organization. This helped the organization identify specific departments with lower morale. It also forced supervisors in those departments to specifically address the underlying issues.

OFFER MODELS THAT SUGGEST WHERE THE COMPANY IS HEADED AND HOW FAR IT IS FROM THAT GOAL. These models can include other successful organizations or perhaps even other successful units within the same organization. The seven factors that are major determinants of organizational success (see figure 14.1) [2, 3]. The structure of an organization, whether it is organic or mechanistic, must fit the style of management (directive versus democratic), the shared values of organization members (toward collaboration and innovation), and the staff (abilities of people). The strategy of the organization (market focus) must be congruent with the organization's skills (unique organizational abilities) if the organization is to be successful. The systems employed by the organization (reward, control) must be congruent with the type of people employed and their characteristics as well as being compatible with the way people are grouped together by the organization's structure. When one of these elements is changed, others will be affected. We discuss some of these factors more extensively in the section below on leverage points for change.

Leverage points of change

Overcoming resistance to change is the process of unfreezing the organization and causing movement. As discussed above, significant resistance to change can exist in many forms. To overcome this resistance, a solid understanding of key organizational components is needed before a manager can effect the required movement that will lead to successful change. These components can be thought of as leverage points for effecting organizational change. At the same time, they can be potential barriers to successful change if they are not appropriately managed. Archimedes is

goal is to provide a clear model of success and to demonstrate that the status quo of the organization falls short of "where they should be."

MANDATE DISSATISFACTION. One method of causing change is to inspire change from within the individual, which is the outcome of the three points listed above. Quite different is to mandate that organization members must be dissatisfied with the status quo. Remember that the equilibrium state was only achieved over an extended period of time and so significant external force may be required to initiate the transformation process. Bert Spector, who authored the article that outlines this checklist, provides an excellent example:

When Don Singer, the newly named chairman of Scranton Steel, announced at an executive meeting what changes he considered necessary, one member of his management team objected. "You're talking about participative management – about collaborating with the union, information sharing, cooperative problem solving. But it won't be easy. There's a lot of history to overcome." Singer listened while the executive finished his cautionary speech. He then pointed his finger directly the executive and said, "things are going change around here. This is a way of life. And if things don't change," he added, "I won't be the first to go."

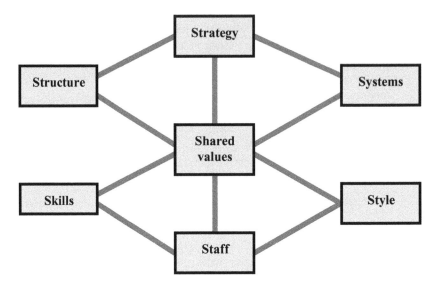

Figure 14.1 The McKinsey 7-S framework

said to have commented, "Give me a lever long enough and single-handed I can move the world."

This section explores five leverage points thought to be critical to overcoming resistance to change [4, 5, 6]:

1 The setting
2 The organization
3 Management and management skills
4 Culture
5 Teams and team-building.

The setting

The setting includes the potential external barriers of success and also levers that could be catalysts for organizational change. This includes aspects of the organization's history as well as its relationship with the marketplace. Another aspect of the setting are the external stakeholders. This may be government agencies, competitors, or members of the community that have a stake in the organization.

The organization

The organization's strategy and structure are important levers and potential barriers to change. Strategy encompasses the mission, goals, and objectives of the organization. Goals of growth are often a source of organizational change. However, the structure of the organization, its allocation of resources, rules, and policies can be formidable levers of change as well. An example includes the organization's reward system. Are the correct employee behaviors being rewarded? For example, if an organization change requires a team effort, incentives in the reward system that are tied to individual performance may be dysfunctional. On the other hand, organizations that carefully understand the employee behaviors required to effect the change may be able to facilitate those changes more quickly by directly rewarding those behaviors.

Management and management skills

Implementing change in organizations requires managerial skills. It also requires a keen knowledge of critical aspects of the organization. Managers typically control many of the other levers discussed in this section. While top managers control the strategy and structure process, just controlling this does not necessarily mean they hold the skills required to implement effective change. A key managerial ability is to have a systems perspective of the organization. The McKinsey 7-S model introduced above is an example of a systems perspective. A systems perspective allows managers to at least consider the role of each of the levers and barriers discussed in this section in implementing change.

Culture

There are many aspects of culture that influence organizational members' willingness to change. As discussed earlier, culture is the characteristic of the organization that pervades every aspect of the organization: the shared values and beliefs of organizational members. Often, those values and beliefs deal with topics like change and organizational identity. Key aspects of culture include members' trust and the quality of communications. Trust is critical in organizations undergoing change. In the opening to this chapter we introduced Amy. One of Amy's reactions to change in her organization was that she felt distrustful of the future intentions of the organization's leaders. One study of the downsizing that occurred in the US federal government in the 1980s and 1990s found that organizational members had to adjust to significant change in their beliefs about the organization. Up until the mid-1980s most employees felt that they had employment for life as part of their "psychological contract" with the government. When significant staff reductions were announced, it came as a shock to many employees because a pervasive aspect of the organization's culture was threatened. The result is that many people now view working for the federal government differently than they did before [7].

Schein has identified three management cultures that can exist within the same organization and which can impede an organization's ability to learn [8]. These cultures include the **operator culture** that focuses on how the job gets done. Often the techniques used to accomplish a job are "local" and are the result of the core technology. This culture can subvert attempts to improve productivity that often requires different methods of getting things done. A second culture is the **engineering culture**. This culture is characterized by linear thinking and simple cause-and-effect relationships [8]. The emphasis is often to design humans out of the system. A third culture is the **executive culture**. This culture has a financial focus and tends toward hierarchical structures. Like the engineering culture, the executive culture tends to see people as impersonal resources.

These different cultures have unique and important perspectives that contribute to an organization's functioning. However, they also lead to potential conflict as members of these different cultures often speak a different "language" and rely on a different set of assumptions. Schein argues that for organizations to effectively learn they must consider three things [8]:

1 Culture must be taken seriously as an issue in implementing organizational change.
2 The increased technological complexity and globalism inherent in twenty-first-century organizations requires the elimination of old assumptions and improved communication across cultural boundaries.
3 Managers need to learn how to have effective cross-cultural dialogues.

Key to successful change is recognizing the impact cultural and structural issues can have in effectively changing our organizations.

Teams and team-building

Effective change often requires members to view themselves as part of a team. As discussed earlier, team skills are not common to individuals and often need to be the focus of training. Important in the process of change is developing cooperation among team members. There is significant evidence that participative management and change implementation using groups or teams is a critical lever to achieving successful organizational change – specifically because it affects member commitment to the change [5].

HELPING INDIVIDUALS COPE WITH CHANGE

To understand individual reactions to change events it is useful to understand the concepts of trigger events and amended mindsets [9, 10]. **Trigger events** are unanticipated events in an organization's history that lead employees to take stock of their situation and interpret the short- and long-term implications of the changing context. As managers attempt to grapple with the significant but not well understood implications of employees' interpretation of events, it may be helpful to view any trigger event as unfolding over a period of time or in stages. The resulting interpretation of the change event is called the **amended mindset**. This is a well-developed perceptual interpretation of the event.

Each stage of a change process involves significant disruption of the workforce. For example, in downsizing, managers can take several actions that could positively affect the organizational members' psychological response to a change environment. In the next section, we discuss each stage and propose proactive managerial actions to assist members in dealing with the change in a personally and organizationally healthy manner.

Before the change event

Four important time frames or stages comprise trigger events. First is the **pre-event stage** that describes the time period when rumors about an impending change abound and complete information is not yet available. Within the pre-event stage is the appearance of rumors or pieces of information from various sources that can create anxiety within the workforce. An individual mentally assembles each piece of information along with other bits of information in an attempt to draw meaning and increase their ability to predict the future. It is important to remember that this process of interpretation is a social one, where meanings are discussed among those affected and then jointly constructed. Pieces of information are shared and the input of everyone is considered as each employee copes with the uncertainty created by the event [9].

Organizational leaders actively help employees to manage the assembly of these complex puzzles [9]. This can be accomplished by quickly, freely, and truthfully sharing information in a public forum and actively helping employees to interpret the surrounding events – maintaining open lines of communication throughout the organization. Managers need to be sure they are in the "communication loop" so they will hear and be able to respond to any rumor that surfaces. Carefully managing the sources of information is also critical. It seems unreasonable to ignore the fact that a rumor presented in the local media would not be the topic of discussion in the break room. Senior leaders typically have better, but often slower, access to accurate information. As a result, a more efficient use of employee time would be for them to go to the organizational leadership to receive information. However, this requires managers to be viewed as knowledgeable, reliable, and approachable sources. Even if the information gathered has negative implications for the workforce, it is critical for the long-term effectiveness of the organization for management to be viewed as a reliable and open source of information.

After the change event is confirmed

The second stage is the **event confirmation stage**, the time period immediately surrounding an official organizational announcement that a change will occur [9]. This critical stage is when employees search for explanations for the change and attempt to understand the personal implications of the action. This stage begins when an official announcement or action confirms that the change will take place. While rumors continue to occur at this stage, employees will immediately begin to consider the personal implications of the change. If the change involves organizational restructuring for example, employees will consider their personal job security and the implications of the event for their work environment (i.e. potential changes in colleagues, leadership, work rules or conditions). This is where employees draw from personal experience and the experiences of others to try to improve the predictability of the future. Making comparisons is a standard technique for dealing with the complexity of these events [9]. Individuals may contact their friends or family who have gone through similar experiences to try to understand the implications of the change. Again, the emphasis is to resolve the uncertainty caused by the change.

Managerial actions at this stage vary with the type of change and the setting or context of the change. One critical aspect is to manage the announcement of change. Again, communication is critical. Larger international organizations often include multiple work locations across the world. Management should expressly ensure that all organizational members are informed as quickly as possible about everything that is known about the change. If managers are aware that employees are looking for comparisons to reduce uncertainty, they can provide examples of positive past experiences and rationale for why negative past experiences will be avoided. In one organization that had international offices around the world, the CEO had pre-positioned a video with leaders in the field offices of him personally announcing that the organization was going to be acquired by a larger organization. Managers in the field office had been thoroughly briefed on the action and were in a good position to answer employee questions and address concerns. The announcement was well orchestrated and presented to all employees at one time.

During the change

The third stage incorporates the **time frame in which the actual events occur** and employees are forced to cope with changes in the pattern of events surrounding their work lives [9]. Depending on the significance of the change, employee responses to these events can vary significantly and include feelings from anger, cynicism, and anxiety to resentment, resignation, retribution, and hope [11].

In addition to the open communication needed, managers must manage employee perceptions of how critical decisions that relate to the change are made. Cynicism and feelings of helplessness occur and it appears that decision-making about the change is a random process or one that employees are not involved in. High employee involvement in change processes is important, not just to enhance the quality of the decision but to influence employee commitment to the change that may occur from implementation of that decision.

Another important role of managers is to focus attention on the opportunities created by any organizational change. Putting change in a positive light, such as emphasizing the opportunity to eliminate redundant tasks and redesigning jobs and workflows to increase efficiency and create more enriching jobs, is a critical orientation.

After the change

A final stage is the **aftermath**, the time period when organizational members assess the event and try to understand what they have learned based on their interpretation of the experience [9]. This is certainly the most critical time for the long-term health of the organization as people attempt to evaluate the events of the recent past. Important here is how individuals are thought to make sense of a series of events. Again, openness and honesty are critical in helping individuals to interpret these events. If employees have come to be confident that management will be open and honest with information, it is more likely that management can play a role in how these events will be interpreted.

One suggestion is to create events to help all organizational members evaluate the past. The establishment of groups chartered to study and draw conclusions is an important symbol of this process [9]. After the downsizing and restructuring within the federal government, many task forces and work groups were used to force all organizational elements to look forward to the future – after the change. As former vice-president, Al Gore realized the symbolic as well as actual value of this action: he developed the "reinventing government" theme and "Went from agency to agency celebrating reinvention success stories, giving what he admits is 'overdue positive reinforcement to the good folks who are doing a terrific job'" [12].

ORGANIZATIONAL DEVELOPMENT

Change efforts that focus on the whole organization fall into the broad category of **organizational development** (OD). They usually involve an attempt to change through an organization-wide program in which most workers, managers, and professionals participate. Organizational development is concerned with planned change. In other words, change is to be anticipated, planned, and consciously designed rather than approached in a crisis mode when a problem occurs. Often an attempt is made to produce different organizational structures and cultures to support any new systems or approaches introduced. This is because in organizational development, it is assumed that all organizational functioning involves a number of organizational components working together. To change any part of the system requires sensitivity to adjustments across the entire system as in the McKinsey 7-S model. Organizational members who collaborate with change agents usually execute the change program. Change agents seek to enhance the capacity and motivation of those in the organization to learn, improve, and change through their own efforts in the future. They emphasize development through human growth and improvement.

Organizational analysis

Organization-wide change programs often begin with some type of **action research** showing where and why a particular system is not working so well. **Survey feedback** is an action research method fairly widely used in organizational development. The survey feedback approach begins when an organization recognizes that it has problems. This provides the initial motivation to change, but organizational members still must have confidence that improvements can be realized from the program. A pilot program can provide such assurance by demonstrating in one part of the organization that a system change can be successfully implemented and can produce improvements.

An organizational needs analysis is usually done with a survey, using interviews or structured questionnaires, to identify what should be changed. The survey may reveal problems with performance, employee morale, and absenteeism, or failure to achieve unit or organizational goals. The problems identified may also be perceptual or emotional. Once specific problems are identified, different remedies may be initiated to change behaviors, perceptions, attitudes, or other unsatisfactory conditions.

Organizational development methods

Organizational development efforts may be designed using a variety of methods including mentoring, team-building, positive reinforcement programs, and goal-setting strategies. Used appropriately, each of these methods has been implemented and been found to be effective in both public and private organizations. The important aspect of any of these approaches is that they systematically involve organizational members throughout the whole change process and that they are based on action research. Here is a brief discussion of some useful methods.

Mentoring

Mentoring has become an increasingly popular method of implementing change on an individual level. A mentor is an older and more experienced organization member who helps a younger, less experienced person in the organization learn to navigate in the world of work. This older person does not have to be the direct supervisor of the younger person. Some organizations have a more formal mentoring program in which mentors are assigned to protégés. Other organizations rely on informal relationships. Mentoring can be of special value to those who are often excluded from organizational networks, such as women and minorities. Through mentoring, they can obtain valuable information that they would not normally receive in addition to having a champion who can make their talents visible to upper ranks in the organizational hierarchy.

282

Training

There are a number of different training methods that may be used individually or in combination to change knowledge, attitudes, or skills. Lectures, case studies, discussions, and business simulations are training methods you are familiar with in formal education and they are equally useful as a training method to implement organizational change.

There are a number of principles for conducting training [13]. The first is ensuring trainability. Individuals must have sufficient ability and motivation. Second, an optimum training environment is important. Participants must be able to practice the new behaviors and skills. The material must be learned well enough in training so that it can be transferred, even under adverse conditions, to the work setting. It is very important to maximize the similarity between the work setting and the training setting to ensure the transfer of training. Third, participants should be given knowledge of the results of training.

One sure way to impact negatively an organizational change is to provide the training needed to make the change but fail to remove other barriers from the work environment. These barriers may include a supervisor who is reluctant to allow the trainee to apply new skills in the workplace or the lack of available proper equipment to use.

Team-building

Team-building is the process of involving team members in a series of activities designed to improve the effectiveness of the group. In our discussion of teams in an earlier chapter we discussed the stages a team goes through to reach a point where it can perform effectively. Team-building can accelerate that process. Team-building efforts often begin with self-examination. A consultant may ask each group member: What can be done to increase the effectiveness of the operations of this team? What are the obstacles to achieving this? Answers are analyzed and then fed back to the team members. The feedback helps to motivate the group to change since problems that hinder group effectiveness are identified. These problems then can be converted into solutions by the group. Then the group sets goals to carry out these solutions. In the goal-setting approach to team-building, participation in the group's decisions enhances commitment to problem solutions.

Reinforcement of organizational changes

The final step in planned change is to follow up to ensure that the change has been effective. This follow up could take several years and many modifications may be made before a desirable level of effectiveness is achieved. Improved organizational results can also be reinforced through feedback showing that revenue costs, quality, and quantities are better than before. In the next section, we discuss specific ways to evaluate the organizational change. Once the feedback from this evaluation has been provided to the organization, change programs are modified and the change process begins anew.

Evaluation of organizational change programs

To change individuals, groups, or organizations takes time and money. There are also hidden costs, such as political issues that make change and improvement difficult when they are not resolved. For these reasons, it makes sense to try to determine whether the change program was effective.

Change programs can be evaluated in very sophisticated ways. These evaluations involve very complicated measurement techniques, statistics, and research designs. The manager can seek help from professionals when it is needed but can look at other factors as well. Managers consider a number of factors in judging the effectiveness of a change program and whether it was worthwhile. What is most critical and most important will depend on the organization's situation at the time. Those threatened with bankruptcy do not have the luxury of evaluating the effectiveness of a change by waiting to look at long-term performance improvements.

There are a number of difficult problems in evaluating change. First, it is difficult to isolate the effects of the change. Second, there is often a time lag between development and evaluation. Third, it is often difficult to specify what to measure. For instance, while the ultimate goal of much training is improved economic performance, the training itself may focus on attitudes and group relationships with the assumption that improvements in them will increase profitability. In this case, assessing changes in profitability may be the wrong measure since it is not likely to be easy to tease out the effects of the training. Finally, it is possible that several changes are introduced with several different methods. In this case, it is almost impossible to know which method, or combination of methods, produces effects when they occur.

SUMMARY

Organizational change is a pervasive aspect of modern organizational life. There are numerous pressures from both the external and internal environments that lead to organizational change. Change can be viewed as a process of unfreezing the status quo (altering the equilibrium), causing transformation, and then refreezing to make the change permanent. Using this model, we can see that factors within the organizational context need to be used to cause the organism to move from a state of equilibrium to a state of disequilibrium. Change can be implemented by considering the levers and barriers to change that exist within the organizational setting, the organization's structure and strategy, the management structure and its skills, the culture, and the group.

Change is easier if the organization has a climate or culture that is generally supportive of change. Successful changes require effective communication in which concerns and expectations flow easily up and down the organization. There should be a climate of trust in the organization, especially between workers and management, which will help them to cope with the risk, uncertainty, and fear that often accompany organizational change.

REFERENCES

1 Lewin, K. 1951. *Field Theory in Social Science.* New York: Harper & Row.

2 Pascale, R. T. and G. Athos. 1981. *The Art of Japanese Management.* Boston, MA: Little, Brown.

3 Peters, T. J. and R. H. Waterman. 1982. *In Search of Excellence.* New York: Harper & Row.

4 Kilmann, R. H. 1984. *Beyond the Quick Fix.* San Francisco: Jossey-Bass.

5 Kilmann, R. H. 1989. A Completely Integrated Program for Creating and Maintaining Organizational Success. *Organizational Dynamics,* 5–19.

6 Kilmann, R. H., T. J. Colman, and associates. 1988. *Corporate Transformation.* San Francisco: Jossey-Bass.

7 Mero, N. P. and A. R. Anna. 1998. Dealing with Angst in the Ranks: Managerial Perspectives on Downsizing within the Federal Government. Unpublished working paper.

8 Schein, E. A. 1996. Three Cultures of Management: The Key to Organizational Learning. *Sloan Management Review,* Fall: 9–20.

9 Isabella, L. A. 1990. Evolving Interpretations as a Change Unfolds: How Managers Construe Key Organizational Events. *Academy of Management Journal,* 22(1): 7–41.

10 Isabella, L. A. 1993. Managing the Challenges of Trigger Events: The Mindsets Governing Adaptation to Change. In T. D. Jick, ed., *Managing Change,* 18–29. Burr Ridge, IL: Irwin.

11 O'Neill, H. M. and D. J. Lenn. 1995. Voices of Survivors: Words that Downsizing CEOs Should Hear. *Academy of Management Executive,* 9(4): 23–34.

12 Shoop, T. 1994. True Believer. *Government Executive,* 16–23.

13 Wexley, K. N. and G. A. Yukl. 1984. *Organizational Behavior and Personnel Psychology.* Homewood, IL: Richard D. Irwin.

14 Spector, B. A. 1989. From Bogged Down to Fired Up: Inspiring Organizational Change. *Sloan Management Review,* 29–34.

Name Index

Adler, N. J., 117, 118, 138
Adler, S., 24, 36
Agarwal, N. C., 189, 202
Ajzen, I., 41, 52
Albanese, R., 110, 113
Alderfer, C., 74, 91
Allport, G. W., 23, 35
Ambrose, M. L., 63, 67
Ancona, D. G., 190, 203
Argyris, C., 13, 18, 32, 35, 196, 203
Arvey, R. D., 25, 35
Athos, G., 275, 285
Avolio, B. J., 260, 265

Bailey, D. E., 103, 112
Balkin, D. B., 101, 112
Ball, G., 89, 91
Barley, S. R., 175, 176, 182
Barnard, C., 12, 18
Barnes, L. B., 189, 203
Baron, R. A., 88, 91, 110, 113
Barrick, M. R., 26, 27, 35
Barsade, 28, 36
Basili, V. R., 180, 182
Bass, B. M., 18, 91, 112, 138, 203, 249, 250,
    251, 252, 259, 260, 265, 266, 267, 285
Becker, B. E., 175, 182
Becker, W. S., 72, 91, 92, 241
Bendick, M., 65, 66
Bennis, W. G., 99, 112
Berman, D. K., 140, 159
Beyer, J. M., 120, 124, 126, 128, 129, 130, 138

Blake, R. R., 194, 203, 248, 252, 265
Blanchard, K., 252, 266
Blauner, R., 169, 181
Boeker, W., 124, 138, 233, 245
Borman, W. C., 15, 18, 71, 91
Bouchard, T. J., 25, 35, 36
Boudreau, J. W., 52
Bowen, D. E., 173, 181
Boyatzis, R. E., 236, 245, 250, 266
Bretz, R. D., 52
Briggs, K. C., 26, 29, 30, 36
Brislin, R., 116, 117, 138
Brockner, J., 90, 91
Bullock, R. J., 171, 181
Burgeois, L. J., 201, 203
Burns, T. G., 13, 18, 144, 159
Bycio, P., 260, 265

Caligiuri, P. M., 27, 35
Cardy, R. L., 58, 66
Carroll, S. J., 87, 91
Cascio, W. F., 99, 110, 112
Castaneda, M. B., 53
Cattell, R. B., 23, 35
Chatman, J., 47, 53, 125, 128, 138
Chemers, M., 254, 255, 266
Child, J. C., 52, 120, 138
Christie, R., 28, 35
Clark, L. A., 27, 36
Cohen, M. D., 209, 220
Cohen, S. G., 103, 112
Cole, R. E., 117, 138

Colman, T. J., 276, 285
Conger, J. A., 237, 245
Cornelius, E. T., 250, 265
Cosier, R. A., 188, 202, 219, 221
Costa, P. T., 26, 35, 184, 185
Cowherd, D. M., 88, 91

Dalton, D. R., 157, 188, 202, 219, 221
Dansereau, F., 261, 265
Daughterty, T. W., 45, 53
Davis-Blake, A., 267
Dawis, R., 33, 36
Dearborn, D. C., 65, 66
Deluga, R. J., 260, 265
Dickson, W. J., 11, 18
Dienesch, R. M., 261, 265
Downton, J. V., 259, 265
Dreher, G. F., 53
Dunham, R., 49, 53
Dunn, W. S., 27, 35

Early, P. C., 44, 53, 87, 92
Ehrlich, S. B., 262, 266
Eisenhardt, K., 201, 203
England, G. W., 189, 202
Epstein, S., 23, 35
Erez, M., 87, 92
Erwin, P., 28, 35
Etzioni, A., 223, 224, 245
Evans, M. G., 253, 265

Farris, G., 174, 182
Feldman-Summers, S., 66
Felson, R. B., 63, 67
Fernandez, P., 66, 67
Ferraro, G., 116, 121, 138
Festinger, L., 43, 52
Fiedler, F. E., 253, 254, 255, 256, 265, 266, 267
Filley, A. C., 185, 194, 202, 257, 266
Fishbein, M., 41, 52
Fleishman, E. A., 248, 266
Fodor, E. M., 254, 266
Foldberg, J., 197, 203
Folger, R., 89, 92
French, J. R. P., 115, 117, 120, 121, 123, 138, 167, 227, 228, 245
Freud, S., 23, 35
Fried, Y., 174, 182

Frost, P. J., 261, 266
Funder, D., 23, 35

Gagliardi, P., 124, 125, 126, 138
Gannon, M. J., 115, 137
Garcia, J. E., 254, 267
Geis, F., 28, 35
George, J. M., 27, 28, 33, 35, 41, 52
Gerhart, B. A., 172, 181
Goldstein, H. W., 22, 36
Goleman, D., 33, 35
Gomez-Mejia, L. R., 171, 181, 246
Grabrenya, W., 117, 138
Graen, G., 261, 265, 266
Greenberg, J., 88, 89, 92
Greene, C. N., 31, 35
Greenlaugh, L., 191, 203
Griffin, R., 174, 182
Grube, J. E., 49, 53
Guzzo, R. A., 112, 174, 181

Hackett, R. D., 260, 265
Hackman, J. R., 76, 92, 169, 181
Hall, E. T., 119, 123, 138
Hall, J., 194, 203
Hall, M. R., 123, 138
Hall, R. H., 141, 159, 169, 181
Hall, R. V., 53, 113, 138, 246, 266, 267
Harke, D. D., 254, 266
Harkins, S., 110, 113
Hater, J. J., 260, 266
Hersey, P., 252, 266
Herzberg, F. A., 73, 75, 76, 92
Hickson, D. J., 185, 202, 231, 236, 245
Higgins, C. A., 260, 266
Hinings, C. R., 231, 236, 245
Hofstede, G., 108, 112, 115, 116, 118, 137, 226, 245
House, R. J., 76, 92, 228, 233, 234, 235, 245, 253, 257, 259, 266
Howell, J. M., 260, 261, 266
Huselid, M. A., 175, 182

Isabella, L. A., 278, 279, 280, 281, 285
Iverson, R., 28, 35

Jackofsky, E. F., 118, 138
Jackson, C. W., 65, 66

Jackson, S. E., 103, 112
Janis, I. L., 217, 221
Jarvenpaa, S. L., 111, 113, 179, 182
Jenne, R. D., 174, 181
Jensen, M. A., 112
Jermier, J., 262, 263, 266, 267
Jones, D., 15, 18, 184
Jones, G. R., 41, 52
Judge, T. A., 39, 43, 52
Jung, C. G., 29, 35

Kahneman, D., 219, 221
Kahwajy, J., 201, 203
Kanfer, R., 88, 92
Kanungo, R., 237, 245
Katz, D., 39, 52
Katzell, R. A., 174, 181
Katzenback, J. R., 96, 112
Kehoe, J. F., 58, 66
Keller, L. M., 25, 36
Kelly, H. H., 62, 67
Kerr, S., 262, 263, 266, 267
Kets de Vries, M. F. R., 131, 132, 133, 138
Kezsbom, D. S., 182
Kiesler, S. B., 66
Kilmann, R. H., 194, 203, 276, 278, 285
Kirkpatrick, S., 260, 261, 266
Kluckholn, F., 116, 137
Knoll, K., 113, 179, 182
Knowlton, W. A., 65, 67
Kohn, M. L., 45, 53
Konovsky, M., 89, 92
Krackhardt, D., 235, 245
Kulik, C. T., 63, 67

Landy, F. J., 72, 91, 92
Lane, F. B., 250, 265
Latane, B., 113, 138
Laurent, A., 120, 138
Lawler, E. E., 172, 181
Lawrence, P. R., 13, 18, 189, 203
Ledford, G. E., 181
Lee, T. W., 49, 53
Leidner, D. E., 113, 179, 182
Lemak, D. J., 174, 181
Lenn, D. J., 280, 285
Levine, D. I., 88, 91
Levinson, D., 46, 53

Lewin, K., 251, 266, 271, 272, 285
Liden, R. C., 58, 67, 245, 261, 265, 266
Likert, R., 13, 18
Lipparini, A., 156, 157, 159
Lippitt, R., 251, 266
Locke, E. A., 82, 87, 92, 181, 260, 261, 266
Loftus, E. F., 57, 67
Lorenzi, P., 110, 113
Lorenzoni, G., 156, 157, 159
Lorsch, J. W., 13, 18, 189, 203
Louis, M. R., 47, 53
Lubinski, D., 33, 36

Mahoney, T. A., 248, 267
Maier, N. R. F., 213, 214, 221
March, J. G., 12, 18, 208, 209, 210, 220
Marks, M. L., 174, 182
Martocchio, J. J., 65, 67
Maslow, A. H., 23, 36, 73, 74, 75
Mausner, B., 75, 92
May, K. E., 103, 112
Mayer, J. D., 33, 36
McClelland, D. A., 73, 79, 80, 92, 107, 112, 236, 245, 250, 266
McCrae, R. R., 26, 35
McGillicuddy, N. B., 197, 203
McGregor, D., 13, 18
McKenzie, S., 262, 267
McQuaid, S. J., 138
Meindl, J. R., 262, 266
Mero, N. P., 174, 181, 277, 285
Milgram, S., 227, 229, 245
Milkovich, G. T., 172, 181
Miller, D., 131, 132, 133, 138
Miner, J. B., 75, 92
Mintzberg, H., 16, 18, 208, 220
Mischel, W., 24, 36, 236, 245
Mitchell, T. R., 65, 67, 245, 257, 266
Moore, C., 21, 22, 147, 197, 203
Motowidlo, S. J., 15, 18, 71, 91
Mount, M. K., 26, 27, 35
Mouton, J. S., 194, 203, 252, 265
Mowday, R., 234, 245
Mumford, M. D., 248, 266
Murray, B., 172, 181
Murray, H. A., 23, 36
Myers, D. G., 219, 221
Myers, I. B., 26, 29, 30, 36

Nathan, B. R., 173, 181
Newman, J. M., 172, 181
Nordstrom, R., 110, 113

O'Brien, E. J., 23, 35
O'Neill, H. M., 238, 280, 285
O'Reilly, C. A., 125, 128, 138
Organ, D. W., 15, 18, 49, 53
Osipow, S. H., 45, 53
Ouchi, W., 118, 138
Overman, S., 101, 112

Parsons, C. K., 58, 67
Pascale, R. T., 275, 285
Perrow, C., 13, 18
Peters, L. H., 254, 266
Peters, T. J., 275, 285
Pfeffer, J., 124, 129, 138, 226, 230, 235, 238, 246, 248, 267
Podsakoff, P., 262, 267
Pondy, L. R., 185, 202
Powell, W., 156, 159
Presthus, R., 30, 36
Pruitt, D. G., 197, 203
Pulakos, E. D., 44, 53

Raven, B., 227, 228, 245
Reed, R., 174, 181
Reinganum, M. R., 248, 267
Roe, A., 45, 53
Roethlisberger, F. J., 11, 18
Rogers, C. R., 23, 36
Romanelli, E., 233, 246
Ronen, S., 119, 138
Ross, L. D., 44, 52, 61, 67
Rotter, J., 28, 36

Sackmann, S. A., 134, 138
Salovey, P., 33, 36
Schein, E. A., 47, 53, 224, 246, 277, 278, 285
Schmitt, N., 18, 44, 53, 91
Schneider, B., 22, 36, 123
Schooler, C., 45, 53
Seaman, C. B., 180, 182
Seigelman, M., 45, 53
Seltzer, J., 260, 267
Selznick, P., 12, 18
Senge, P. M., 211, 212, 221

Shaw, K., 82, 92
Shepard, H. S., 112
Shoop, T., 281, 285
Simon, H. A., 12, 18, 46, 53, 65, 66, 208, 220
Singh, J. V., 259, 266
Slocum, W. J., 118, 138
Smith, D. K., 9, 96, 112
Smith, M., 248, 267
Spector, P. E., 28, 36, 78, 92
Stalker, G. M., 13, 18, 144, 159
Staw, B. M., 28, 36, 44, 52, 53, 92, 138, 212, 221, 245, 246
Stogdill, R. M., 252, 253, 265, 267
Stone, E. F., 174, 181
Strodtbeck, F., 116, 137
Strube, M. J., 254, 267
Stulberg, J. B., 196, 203
Suttle, J. L., 76, 92

Taylor, A., 10, 197, 203
Thomas, A. B., 248, 267
Thomas, K. W., 185, 194, 202, 203
Thompson, J. D., 142, 150, 159, 165, 166, 168, 176, 181
Ting-Toomey, S., 123, 138
Tinto, V., 45, 53
Tjosvold, D., 189, 196, 202, 203
Tosi, H. L., 25, 36, 47, 48, 53, 87, 91, 144, 146, 147, 159, 171, 172, 181, 246, 262, 267
Tosi, L. A., 172, 181
Trerise, R. E., 189, 202
Trevino, L. K., 89, 91
Trice, H. M., 124, 126, 128, 129, 130, 138
Tubbs, M. E., 171, 181
Tuckman, B. W., 99, 112
Tushman, M. L., 233, 246
Tversky, A., 219, 221

Van Fleet, D. D., 110, 113
Van Maanen, J., 47, 53
Vaverek, K. A., 171, 181
Vecchio, R. P., 89, 92
Voss, H., 156, 159
Vroom, V. H., 84, 92, 215, 221, 253, 267

Waldman, D. A., 260, 265
Walsh, J. P., 65, 67
Wang, Y. J., 117, 138

Wanous, J. P., 47, 53
Waterman, R. H., 275, 285
Watson, D., 27, 36
Weber, M., 12, 18, 228, 246
Weiner, N., 248, 267
Weiss, H. M., 24, 36
Weissinger-Baylon, R., 210, 220
Welbourne, T. M., 171, 181
Welton, G. L., 197, 203
Wexley, K. N., 283, 285
White, M. C., 7, 248, 267
Whitely, W., 45, 53
Whitener, E. M., 65, 67
Whitney, K., 112

Whyte, F. W., 190, 200, 203
Whyte, G., 219, 221
Wiesenfeld, B., 90, 91
Williams, K., 110, 113
Wiseman, R. M., 171, 181
Woodruff, D., 171, 181

Yetton, P. W., 215, 221, 253, 267
Yukl, G. A., 235, 250, 267, 283, 285

Zahrly, J. H., 47, 171, 181
Zaleznick, A., 223, 246
Zuckerman, M., 63, 67

Subject Index

ability, 32, 33, 71, 166, 167, 180
  cognitive ability, 33
  emotional intelligence, 33
  perceptual ability, 33
  psychomotor ability, 33
absenteeism, 77, 239
Abu-Dhabi, 119
acceptance, 214, 215
achievement motive, 79, 250
achievement/power theory, 22, 26
achievement-oriented leadership, 258
acquisitions, 135, 270
action research, 282
actual behavior, 4
administrative model of decision making, 208
administrative theory, 10
affective commitment, 40, 49
affiliation need, 250
agreeableness, 26
alienation, 223
alliances, 242
ambiguity, 190, 242
American Psychological Association, 11
amended mindset, 278
anxiety, 27
arbitration, 197
Argentina, 119
Argyris, Chris, 13
articulation skills, 236
attitude cluster, 42
attitude surveys, 38

attitudes, 38, 39, 40, 41, 42, 44, 51, 52, 53, 266, 267
  intentions, 42
  overt behavior, 42
  work related attitudes, 44
attitudes, cognitive dimensions, 41
attitudes, psychological functions, 39
  express values, 39
  frame of reference, 39
  personal adjustment, 39
  protect our ego, 39; reconciling contradictions, 39
attraction-selection-attrition cycle, 22
attribution theory, 20, 60, 61, 210
  consensus, 62
  consistency, 62
  distinctiveness, 62
  privacy of the act, 62
  status, 62
attributional processes, 241
  Australia, 119
  Austria, 119
authority, 141, 146, 176, 225, 248
autocratic decision, 217
autocratic leadership, 251
automatic information processing, 63
autonomy, 78, 101, 169, 170
avoidant culture, 35

$B = f(P \times E)$, 4, 23
Bahrain, 119

bargaining, 197
Barnard, Chester, 12
basic organizational types, 145, 146
behavior shaping, 84
behavioral approaches to leadership, 250
    distribution of decision influence, 251
    Michigan studies, 252
    Ohio State studies, 252
behavioral theories of leadership, 250–3
Belgium, 119
beliefs, 41, 236
belonging needs, 73
benchmarking, 174
Big Five personality dimensions, 26
    agreeableness, 27
    conscientiousness, 27
    emotional stability, 26
    extroversion, 26; openness to experience, 27
blaming, 241
bounded rationality, 208
Brazil, 119, 121
British Petroleum, 127
bureaucracy, 12, 127
bureaucratic culture, 136

calculative involvement, 224
Canada, 117, 119, 226
categories, 5, 56, 63, 73, 74, 189, 261
centralization, 141
ceremony, 129
change, coping with, 278
    aftermath, 281
    amended mindset, 278
    event confirmation stage, 279
    pre-event stage, 279
    time frame, 280
    trigger events, 278
change, leverage points, 275
    culture, 277
    management, 277
    organization, 276
    setting, 276
    teams and team building, 278
change methods, 272
change, planned, 281
charisma, 260
charismatic power, 228, 229

child rearing practices, 45
Chile, 119
client relationships, 170
coalition building, 242
cognitive ability, 167
cognitive complexity, 34, 235
cognitive dissonance, 42, 51, 212
cognitive intelligence, see cognitive ability
cohesive groups, 217
cohesiveness, 97, 103, 105, 106, 217, 254
collaboration, 111, 179, 196
Columbia, 119, 127
combining tasks, 170
commitment, 223
commitment profile, 48
common sense, 4
communication, 111, 121, 179, 280
compartmentalization, 39
compensation practices, 169, 171
    gainsharing, 171
    Scanlon Plan, 171
    skill-based pay, 172
    team-based incentives, 172
competition, 106, 108
complex environment, 142
complexity, 141
compliance, 228
conflict, 5, 7, 8, 18, 22, 32, 34, 47, 80, 96, 100,
        102, 103, 116, 123, 130, 163, 176, 177,
        184, 185, 186, 187, 188, 189, 190, 191,
        192, 193, 194, 195, 196, 197, 198, 199,
        200, 201, 202, 220, 271, 278
    individual characteristics, 189
    organizational conditions, 190
    situational conditions, 190
conflict aftermath, 186
conflict, diagnosing, 191
    continuity of the interaction, 193
    interdependence, 192
    issue in question, 192
    leadership, 193
    perceived progress, 193
    size of the stakes, 192
    third parties, 193
conflict, optimal level, 188
conflict, organizational responses, 198
    change reward systems, 200

communications, 200
jurisdictional disputes, 199
policies, procedures and rules, 199
reallocate or add resources, 199
reduce ambiguities, 199
rotate personnel, 200
superordinate goals, 198
training, 200
conflict reaction style
accommodating, 194
arbitration, 197
avoiding, 194
bargaining, 197
collaborating, 196
competing, 195
compromising, 195
mediation, 197
principled negotiation, 198
conflict reduction rites, 130
conflict resolution, 186
conflict, views, 187
conformity, 213
confrontation, 196
confrontation techniques, 196
conscientiousness, 26
consequences, 5
consequences, reinforcement, *see* reinforcement
consequences
consideration, 252, 257
contextual performance, 14, 70, 71, 89, 109
contingency, 231
contingency theory of organization, 12
contingency theories of leadership, 248, 253
Fiedler's contingency model, 253
path-goal theory, 257
contingent rewards, 259
continuance commitment, 49
controlled information processing, 63
cooperation, 106, 108
coordination, 101
country clusters, 118
crafts, 175
crisis situation, 235
cross training, 171
cross-cultural differences, 107
cultural differences, 120
cultural identity, 125

cultural metaphors, 115
cultural stereotypes, 115
culture, national, 115, 227
organizational consequences, 119;
communications, 121; leadership style, 120;
managerial philosophy, 120; managerial style,
120; motivational strategies, 121
culture, organizational, 125, *see also* organizational
culture

decentralization, 141
decision control, 90
decision implementation, 212
decision making, 4, 12, 64, 99, 103, 105, 115,
134, 146 148, 163, 172, 188, 196, 199,
201, 205, 206, 207, 208, 209, 210, 211,
213, 214, 215, 217, 220, 242, 251, 261,
273, 274, 280
decision making process, 206, 212
decisions within decisions, 206
partial or temporary solutions, 206
small decisions accumulate, 206
decision quality, 207, 216
decision making, improving, 210
delegation, 8
quality, 6
decision making, models, 207
decision making, rational, 207
decision making, unilateral, 215
decisional dissonance, 43
degradation rites, 129
delegation, 8
Denmark, 119
departmentalization, 142, 149
departments, 149
dependence, 223
devil's advocate role, 219
directive leadership, 257, 258
disconfirmed expectations, 43
disorderly convergence, 210
disposition, 23
distribution of authority, 149
distributive justice, 87
diversity, 7, 65, 271
division of labor, 141, 146, 149, 150, 168
dominant coalition, 124, 125, 126, 130, 131,
134, 136, 233

downsizing, 270
dysfunctional tendencies, 212

effort-performance expectancy, 85
emotional intelligence, 33, 36, 167
emotional involvement, 239
emotional maturity, 250
emotional stability, 26, 27, 99
emotions, 211
employee-centered leadership, 253
engineering culture, 278
enhancement rites, 130
environment, 142
environmental change, 134, 144
environmental characteristics, 144
   stability, 144
   volatility, 144
environmental sectors, 142
   market environment, 143
   technological environment, 143
equity theory, 88
   inputs, 88
   outcomes, 88
   referents, 88
escalation of commitment, 212
esteem needs, 74
ethical performance, 5, 14, 70, 71
Europe, 121
executive culture, 278
existence needs, 74, 75
expectancy, 85
expectancy theory, 84, 178
expectations, 104
experienced responsibility, 78
expert power, 228, 229, 237
expressive meanings, 126
external threat, 105
extinction, 82
extroversion, 27, 29
extroverts, 29

feedback, 5, 78, 87, 113, 169, 170
feeling types, 29
Fiedler's contingency model, 253
   situational variables, 254
Finland, 119
flat organizations, 142
formal groups, 98

formal organization, 98, 149
formalization, 141
frame of reference, 39
France, 115, 117, 119, 120, 121, 123, 138, 167, 245
functional group, 98
functional organization, 151
fundamental attribution error, 61

garbage can model of decision making, 209
genetics and attitudes, 25
Germany, 12, 110, 115, 116, 117, 119, 120, 121, 123
globalization, 6, 270
goal difficulty, 87
goal setting, 198
goal setting theory, 87
good enough theory of promotion, 234
Greece, 119
group, 96
   interests and goals, 97
   opportunity for interaction, 97
   personal characteristics, 96
   potential to influence, 97
group composition, 102
group decision making, 213
   benefits, 213
   disadvantages, 213
group decisions, social influences, 217
   groupthink, 217
   polarization, 219
   riskyshift, 219
   social facilitation, 220
   social inhibition, 109, 220
group development, 99
   forming, 99
   norming, 100
   performing, 100
   storming, 99
group diversity, 103
group dynamics, 106
   competition, 106
   cooperation, 106
   social influences, 109
group effectiveness, optimum size, 102
group formation, 105
group maturity, 99

group performance environment, 102
group processes, 103
   development of norms, 103
group cohesiveness, 104
group size, 102
group socialization, 47
group success, 105
groups, types, 97
   formal groups, 98
   functional group, 98
   task groups, 98
   virtual teams, 99, 110; informal groups, 98
groupthink, 105, 188, 217, 219, 221
growth needs, 74, 75

halo effect, 59
Hawthorne effect, 11
Hawthorne experiments, 11
helping behaviors, 109
heredity, 25
Herzberg's two factor theory, 75
heterogeneous groups, 103
hierarchy of needs, 74
high involvement organization, 169
high LPC leader, 255
higher-order needs, 74
HIO, *see* high involvement organization
Hofstede model of culture, 115
hierarchical subcultures, 134
homogenous groups, 103
Hong Kong, 119
horizontal distribution of authority, 142
human relations perspective, 11
hygiene factors, 75

idea evaluation, 211
idea generation, 211
ideologies, 124, 126, 128
implementation, modes, 124, 130
impression management, 239
India, 119
indifferent, 31 32, 42, 48, 251, 262
individual differences, 107, 109
individualism-collectivism, 116, 117, 119
Indonesia, 119
induction rites, 129
industrial psychology, 11
Industrial Revolution, 9

influence, 5, 7, 12, 24, 44, 52, 80, 90, 97, 99,
   101, 102, 103, 105, 106, 108, 109, 115,
   128, 133, 148, 164, 189, 199, 206, 209,
   213, 215, 223, 225, 226, 227, 228, 229,
   230, 231, 234, 235, 236, 239, 242, 243,
   244, 248, 250, 251, 259, 260, 262, 277,
   280
influence agent, 223
   influence processes, 223
   legitimate authority, 225
   power, 226
influence, personal-based, acquiring and
   maintaining, 235
   charismatic power, 235
   expert power, 237
informal groups, 98
Information Age, 270
information technology, 270
in-group relationships, 261
inhibition, 80
Initiating structure, 252
instrumental meanings, 126
insufficient justification, 43
integration, 141
integration rites, 130
intensive work systems, 166
interaction, 179, 197, 238
interactional justice, 90
interdependence, 101
internal locus of control, 250
internal work motivation, 77
intrinsic motivation, 169, 176
intrinsic rewards, 109
intrinsically rewarding, 76
introverts, 26, 29
intuitive people, 29
invulnerability, illusion, 218
Iran, 119
Ireland, 119
Israel, 115, 117, 119
Italy, 115, 119, 157, 159, 226

Japan, 115, 116, 121, 123, 138, 285
job characteristics theory, 73, 169
job design approach, *see* job characteristics
   theory
job design programs, 169
job enrichment approach, 150

job redesign, 73, 169
job satisfaction, 25, 30, 41, 43, 47, 48, 51, 77, 89, 128, 168, 169, 174, 252, 258
judgment biases, 58
    first impressions, 58
    closure, 58
    consistency, 58
    halo, 59
    implicit personality theory, 59
    projection, 59
    stereotyping, 60
judgment types, 29
just-in-time inventory systems, 174

knowledge, 4, 9, 12, 16, 17, 46, 55, 78, 97, 120, 130, 144, 149, 164, 166, 167, 168, 171, 173, 175, 176, 177, 178, 179, 180, 213, 214, 227, 262, 272, 274, 277, 283
knowledge of results, 78
knowledge specialization, 168
knowledge workers, 164, 168, 175, 176, 177, 178, 179, 180

laissez-faire leadership, 251
language, 128, 278
Lawrence, Paul, 13, 18, 203
leader behavior, 254
Leader Behavior Description Questionnaire (LBDQ), 252
leader-member relations, 254
leader motive pattern, 80, 250
leader orientation, 254, 255
leadership, 193, 248
leadership theory, 248
    behavioral theories, 250–3
    contingency theories, 253–9
    process theories, 259–62
    substitutes for leadership, 262–5
    trait approaches, 249
    transformational leadership, 259–60
lean management structures, 8, 172, 191
least preferred co-worker (LPC) scale, 255
legitimate authority, 217, 223, 224, 225, 226, 227, 228, 229, 233, 234, 236, 244, 248, 255
level of interaction, 104
Likert, Rensis, 13
life satisfaction, 43

line, 191
locus of control, 26, 28, 29, 34, 36
    external locus of control, 28
    internal locus of control, 28
long- versus short-term patterns of thought, 118
long-linked work system, 166
Lorsch, Jay, 13, 18, 203
low LPC leader, 255
lower-order needs, 74

Machiavellianism, 26, 28, 36, 235
Malaysia, 119
management by exception, 259
management cultures, 277
management functions, 10
    March, James, 12
    Maslow, Abraham, 73
managerial work, 15
manifest conflict, 186
market-dominated mixed (MDM) organization, 148, 168
masculinity-femininity, 117, 119
Maslow, Abraham, 35, 73, 74, 75
matrix organization, 153
mature personality, 32
McGregor, Douglas, 13
McKinsey 7-S model, 274, 277, 281
MDM, see market-dominated mixed (MDM) organization
meaningfulness of work, 77
mechanistic organizations, 146, 147, 151, 168, 169, 262
mediating work system, 166
mediation, 197
mental models, 211, 269
mentoring, 282
mergers, 135, 270
Mexico, 119, 121
Microsoft, 124, 128
mixed organizations, 153, 176
modal organizational personality, 123, 131
modal personality, 116
mood, 27
    negative affectivity, 27
    positive affectivity, 27
morality, illusion, 218
motivating factors, 75

motivation, 72
  managerial meaning, 72
  psychological meaning, 72
motivation, content theories, 72–80
  Herzberg's two-factor theory, 73
  achievement-power theory, 73
  expectancy theory, 84
  job characteristics approach, 73
  need theory, 73
motivation, process theories, 80–91
  expectancy theory, 84–7
  goal setting theory, 87
  organizational justice theory, 87–90
  reinforcement theory, 80–4
motivators, 76
mutual usefulness of opposites, 30
Myers–Briggs dimensions, 29
  introversion–extroversion, 29
  perceptive-judgment, 29
  sensing-intuition, 29
  thinking-feeling, 29
myths, 4, 60, 124, 126, 128, 129, 205

national character, 116
natural work units, 170
nature–nurture argument, 25, 32
need, 73
need theories, 73
  ERG theory, 74
  Maslow's need theory, 73
needs analysis, organizational, 282
negative reinforcement, 81
network organizations, 156
networking, 243
neurotic cultures, 131
neurotic managers, 131
  compulsive managers, 133
  depressive personality, 132
  detached organizational personality, 133
  dramatic managers, 132
  suspicious managers, 132
neurotic organizations, 131
  bureaucratic culture, 133
  charismatic culture, 132
  depressive culture, 132
  paranoid culture, 132
  politicized culture, 133
neuroticism, 26, 27

new patterns of management, 13, 18
New Zealand, 119
noncompliance, 225
non-traditional selection, 173, 178
nonverbal communication, 236
norms, work group, 106
normative commitment, 49
normative model, 211
normative models of decision making, 207
norming, 103, 104
norms, 47
  peripheral norms, 47
  pivotal norms, 47
  work group, 104
Norway, 118, 119

occupational/task subcultures, 134
occupational levels, 117
Oman, 119
openness to experience, 26
operator culture, 277
organic organizations, 147, 168, 176, 262
organization theory, 12
organizational accommodation, 48
organizational behavior, 9, 10, 11, 12, 13, 17, 22,
    72, 115, 184, 202, 244
organizational change, 242, 271
organizational citizenship, 89
organizational commitment, 48, 239
organizational culture, 123, 124, 125, 126, 130,
    131, 135, 141, 149, 171, 172, 174, 226,
    273, 274
  changing, 136
  implementing, 135
  manifestations, 124
  multi-level model, 124
organizational design, 121, 149, 150
organizational development (OD), 281
  evaluation of organizational change programs,
    284
  organizational analysis, 282
organizational development methods, 282
  mentoring, 282
  team building, 283
  training, 283
  reinforcement of changes, 283
organizational entry, 47
organizational justice theories, 87

organizational personality orientation, 26, 30, 49
  indifferent, 30
organizational politics, 226, 238, 240
organizational structure, 3, 8, 13, 98, 121, 140,
  141, 150, 151, 172, 273
organizationalist, 30, 48, 226, 234
  professionals, 30
organizationally based influence, 229, 230
  access to key people, 229
  environmental changes and power, 233
  legitimate authority, 229
  perceived influence over the future, 229
  personal attributes, 233
  situational determinants, 230
organizations, 12, 141
organization systems, 142
outcome justice, 88
outcomes of influence, 228
  intended results, 228
  modification of relationships, 229
out-group subordinates, 261
overpayment inequity, 88

parental influence, 45
participation, 87, 173
participative decision making, 169, 215, 217
participative leadership, 251, 257
path–goal relationships, 178
path–goal theory, 257
perceived inequity, 88
perception, 34, 55, 58, 67
  ambiguity, 57
  characteristics of other people, 57
  contrast effects, 57
  intensity, 57
  presence of another person, 58
  selective perception, 55
  situational effects, 58
  size, 57
perceptual ability, 34, 167
perceptual biases, 58
perceptual blocks, 211
perceptual errors, 212
perceptual organization, 56
performance appraisal, 65
performance components, 70
performance potential, 167

personal adjustment, 39
performance-outcome expectancy, 85
performance-reward linkage, 86
personal-based influence, 229
  charismatic power, 230
  expert power, 230
personality, 4, 21, 22, 23, 24, 25, 26, 28, 29, 30,
  32, 34, 35, 36, 41, 44, 48, 49, 52, 60, 63,
  64, 66, 79, 91, 116, 123, 124, 131, 132,
  133, 135, 136, 176, 189, 237, 254, 263
personality, approaches, 26
  Big Five model, 26
  locus of control, 26
  Machiavellianism, 26
  Myers–Briggs, 26
  organizational personality orientations, 26
  positive and negative affectivity, 26
personality, bases, 25
  genetics, 25
  heredity, 25
  learning component, 25
  nature–nurture argument, 25; twin studies,
    25
person-organizational fit, 47
personalized power, 80, 235
Peru, 119
Philippines, 119
physiological needs, 73
polarization, 219, 220
policies, procedures, and rules, 199
political behavior, 238, 239, 241, 244
political orientation, 234
political tactics, 240
  blaming or attacking others, 241
  coalition building, 242
  control of information, 242
  impression management, 240
  networking, 243
pooled task interdependence, 150
Portugal, 119
position power, 255
positive affectivity, 26, 27, 28, 41
positive reinforcement, 81
positive-sum interdependence, 192
post-decisional dissonance, 212
power, 6, 7, 22, 26, 28, 33, 34, 41, 44, 73, 79,
  80, 89, 98, 104, 105, 115, 116, 117, 119,

120, 121, 123, 124, 125, 126, 128, 129, 132, 133, 134, 136, 141, 146, 163, 176, 189, 190, 195, 201, 223, 224, 225, 226, 227, 228, 229, 230, 231, 232, 233, 234, 235, 236, 237, 238, 239, 241, 242, 244, 248, 254, 256, 263
charismatic power, 228
coercive power, 227
expert power, 227
reward power, 227
power asymmetry, 224
power distance, 116, 117, 119, 121
power motive, 79
power needs, 79, 234, 236
power structure, 230, 273
Prato, 156
predispositions, 233
principled negotiation, 198
principles of management, 10
problem solving, 64
procedural justice, 87, 89
process control, 90
process theories, 72, 80
reinforcement theory, 80
process theories of leadership, 259
transformational leadership theory, 259
vertical dyad linkage theory, 261
product organization, 152
production-centered leadership, 253
productivity, 105
professional orientation, 176
professionals, 4, 27, 31, 36, 44, 46 47, 48, 49, 53, 60, 115, 120, 121, 128, 149, 179, 199, 255, 269, 281, 284
professions, 175
project, 154
project organization, 154
prosocial behavior, see contextual performance
proximity, 97, 180
psychological contract, 47, 216, 223, 224, 225, 226, 244, 263, 277
public boundary, 225
real boundary, 225
psychomotor ability, 34, 167
manual dexterity, 34
physical coordination, 34
strength, 34

punishment, 81

quality, 6, 214, 215
quality of work life, 77

ratebuster, 104
rationalization, 218
reciprocal task interdependence, 150
refreezing, 272
reinforcement consequences, 80
extinction, 82
negative reinforcement, 81
positive reinforcement, 81
punishment, 81
reinforcement of change, 272
reinforcement schedules, 82
continuous reinforcement schedule, 83
fixed-interval reinforcement schedule, 83
fixed-ratio reinforcement schedule, 83
variable-interval reinforcement schedule, 83
variable-ratio reinforcement schedule, 84
relatedness needs, 74, 75
relevant environment, 142, 156
renewal rites, 130
reputational capital, 244
resistance to change, 273
responsibility, 146, 169
reward power, 233
reward structure, 101
reward system, 277
riskyshift, 219
rites, 105, 126, 129, 130, 138, 173, 237
rites of passage, 129
role ambiguity, 177
role conflict, 177

safety needs, 73
satisfaction, 38
satisficing, 209
Scanlon Plan, 172
schemas, 56, 63
scientific management approach, 10, 150
selection, 11, 127
self-actualization, 74
self-appointed mind guards, 218
self-censorship, 218
self-confidence, 236, 250

self-deception, 211
self-directed teams, 169, 171, 173, 178
self-esteem, 28, 31, 64, 74, 176, 235, 255, 259
self-image, 59
self-serving behavior, 240
self-serving bias, 63, 241
sensing-oriented people, 29
separation rites, 129
sequential task interdependence, 150
service sectors, 6
Simon, Herbert, 12
simple environment, 142
Singapore, 119
situational context, 236
situational control, 254, 256
situational strength, 24
    strong situations, 24
    weak situations, 24
skill variety, 78, 170
skill-based pay, 173
skill-dominated work, 71, 167, 190
skills, 180, *see also* ability
small groups, 102
sociability, 24
social classes, 45, 117
social facilitation, 109, 220
social groups, 102
social influence, 219
social inhibition, 109, 220
social interdependence, 179
social loafing, 110
socialization, 25, 31, 44, 45, 46, 47, 48, 52, 53,
    111, 116, 123, 124, 126, 127, 128, 134,
    135, 137, 171, 173, 178, 179, 226, 263
    early socialization, 44
    organizational socialization, 46
    preliminary work socialization, 45
    occupational competence, 46
    occupational socialization, 46
    work socialization, 46
socialization strategies, 127, 173
socialized power orientation, 80
socioeconomic factors, 45
South Africa, 119
South Vietnam, 119
Spain, 119, 226
span of control, 142
spatial relationships, 179

specialization, 168
specific goals, 87, 101
stability/complexity dimension, 165
stable environment, 144
staff, 191
status distinctions, 128
stereotyping, 60, 218
strategic center, 157
strategic contingencies, 231
    coping with volatility, 231
    substitutability for activities, 232
    workflow centrality, 232
substitutes for leadership, 262–5
strategic contingency theory of organizational
    power, 230
strategic decisions, 149
strength of influence, 224
stress, 239
stress tolerance, 250
structured problems, 216
subcultures, organizational, 133
    culturally diverse subcultures, 134
    hierarchical subcultures, 134
    occupational/task subcultures, 134
subordinates' acceptance, 216
substitutes for leadership, 262
substitutes for leadership approaches, 178
sufficient justification, 43
superordinate goals, 198
supportive leadership, 257
suppression, 186
survey feedback, 282
Sweden, 116, 117, 118, 119
Switzerland, 119
symbols, 31, 88, 116, 124, 126, 129, 130, 131,
    134, 135, 226, 236, 260
symbols, 129

Taiwan, 117, 119
tall organizations, 142
tasks, 5
task and social behaviors, 252
task certainty, 258
task complexity, 108
task design, 101
task groups, 98
task identity, 78, 169
task interdependence, 106, 150

task involvement, 239
task knowledge, 262
task performance, 14, 70, 71
task significance, 78, 169
task specialists, 164, 168
task specialization, 168
task structure, 254
TDM, *see* technology-dominated mixed (TDM) organization.
team building, 278, 283
team effectiveness, 101
teams, 96, 278
technical occupations, 175
technological change, 274
technological revolution, 8
technology, 3, 4, 7, 8, 13, 14, 45, 71, 72, 111, 124, 125, 142, 143, 145, 146, 147, 158, 162, 163, 165, 166, 167, 168, 171, 175, 180, 181, 217, 262, 274
technology-dominated mixed (TDM) organization, 147
technology-dominated work, 167, 168, 180
telecommuting, 8, 110, 177
Thailand, 119
The Human Side of Enterprise, 13
Theory X, 13
thick screening, 173
thinking individuals, 29
time, 177
total quality management (TQM), 169
training, 102
training methods, 283
trait, 26
trait theories of leadership, 249
traits, 249
transactional leadership, 259
transformational leadership theory, 259–60
trigger events, 278
trust, 179, 243
Turkey, 115, 119
turnover, 77

twin studies, 25
type A/B personality, 22, 26

uncertainty, 144
uncertainty avoidance, 116, 119
underpayment inequity, 88
unfreezing, 272
uniformity, 219
unions, 6, 97
United Arab Emirates, 119
United Kingdom, 117, 119. 120
United States, 6, 7, 8, 11, 13, 18, 23, 53, 65, 66, 92, 96, 108, 112, 115, 116, 117, 119, 120, 125, 127, 128, 129, 130, 134, 135, 136, 137, 138, 151, 152, 157, 182, 203, 223, 226, 235, 236, 237, 270, 271
unity of command, 191

valence, 86
values, 41
VDL, *see* vertical dyad linkage theory
Venezuela, 119, 121
verbal ability, 33
vertical dyad linkage theory, 261
vertical loading, 170
virtual office, 270
virtual organization, 8, 156
virtual teams, 110, 111, 113, 177, 179, 182
    advantages and disadvantages, 110
    Improving Performance, 111
volatile environment, 144
Vroom–Yetton model, 215

Weber, Max, 12
work cycle, 168
work ethic, 7, 31
work values, 45, *see also* values
workflow immediacy, 232

zero-sum interdependence, 192

Lightning Source UK Ltd.
Milton Keynes UK
UKHW030537240420
362138UK00005B/11

9 781405 100748